SERVANT OF GOD

SERVANT OF GOD

GWEN CONIKER

God Leads
Faith & Trust Follow

NANCY E. MARTIN, M.B.A., MA THEOLOGY
JEROME F. CONIKER, EDITOR

Make the time

ENROUTE
5705 Rhodes Ave., St. Louis, MO, 63109
Contact us at contactus@enroutebooksandmedia.com

Paperback ISBN: 978-1-950108-16-9
E-book ISBN: 978-1-950108-17-6
LCCN: 2019908492

Printed in the United States of America
1 3 5 7 9 10 8 6 4 2

Table of Contents

Dedication

I would first and foremost like to dedicate this book to Our Lady who leads all to her Son, Jesus. Also, to Gwen and Jerry Coniker whose lives exemplified Holy Marital Love which is Free, Faithful, Fruitful, and Total. For their example to others of how to live an exemplary Catholic life encompassing one's vocation as husband, wife, mother, father while being faithful to the Catholic teachings of Jesus Christ.

Author's Comments

WORKING ON THIS "LABOR OF LOVE" has been both enriching and rewarding. I spent a lot of time with a person I consider to be a very holy and saintly man, Jerry Coniker; a man who devoted his entire life to the sole purpose of spreading that absolute Truth of God and trying to lead as many souls to Christ as humanly possible, so that they could achieve their heavenly home. In so doing, the Apostolate for Family Consecration, founded by Jerry and his wife, Gwen, produced and recorded thousands of videos which covered the authentic Catholic teachings as revealed by the divine sources of Sacred Scripture and Sacred Tradition, and taught in every given age over the last 2,000+ years by the Magisterium of the Church.

This book has been a few years in the making. As of this writing, Jerry's memory has been sealed forever due to a debilitating stroke he experienced the very day after we completed the final edits as it pertains to the factual statements within this book. This stroke severely impaired his speech and memory. How perfect God's timing always is!

When Jerry first asked me to write this book, he told me that he felt that it would be the impetus for transforming our culture, families, and civilization into one of life and love, even beyond its main goal of a biography of his beloved late wife and Servant of God, Gwen Coniker. Over time, because Gwen and Jerry were so 'one' with each other, it naturally morphed into a biography of both of them, with an emphasis on Gwen. The additional information on Jerry in my comments and comments from others about Jerry were without his knowledge. Only the historical facts of the Apostolate did Jerry know about and edit in order that it be factual.

This work also includes a historical account of the founding and growth of the Apostolate for Family Consecration, which produced over 30,000 videos of the top 500 teachers of the Church, in addition to the plethora of books and materials that the Apostolate provides and disseminates, the retreats and Family Fests they hold each year and other noble endeavors, all directed to leading families and souls to Christ and catechizing others in the fullness of the Catholic Faith.

In the early days of this project, Jerry would have his trusted IT assistant, Ben Leon, print off each chapter from Jerry's computer that I would email him so that Jerry could read it and make modifications as necessary to the factual details. As time progressed, Jerry's eyesight declined so much so that I would sit with him and dictate slowly each chapter. As I would read, he would interrupt mid-sentence where necessary to correct a particular statement and I would then make the appropriate adjustments.

We would work for hours on end together and then follow it up with going out to our favorite diner, *Home Run* in Kenosha, Wisconsin. It was our treasured 'thing' to do as we both enjoyed eating! It was a time for us to wind down, break bread together, and talk about other topics; a truly special time.

Home Run was like going back to the 1950s. It is an old-fashioned looking diner with very inexpensive food and so many items on the menu to choose from that I always had trouble deciding what to order. We became "regulars" there and the waitresses would see us coming with a smile on their faces. I assisted Jerry as he held his cane in one hand and his arm held onto my arm with the other ever so carefully. I assisted him through the door, for he was very feeble and had a hard time walking. Always gracious and kind, they would quickly rush to get us a booth as close to the door as possible,

Jerry would always order his favorite chocolate milkshake which would be presented in what looked like an old-fashioned, tall fountain glass. On one occasion, Jerry ordered *roasted* chicken with all the fixins, while I ordered the *broasted* chicken dinner with mashed potatoes and gravy. When the food arrived, Jerry began to experience buyer's remorse! "That looks really good," he said to me, admiring my meal. "What is that?"

I responded with, "It's the broasted chicken."

He retorted, "Well, what is it that I ordered?"

"You ordered the roasted chicken," I responded.

He then said, "Oh. Well, next time I'm going to get what you got!"

Of course, he declined my offer to give him some of my meal. And since they always served a lot of food, we both always had a take home box for food the next day!

Jerry, being the gentleman that he is, would always pay for the meal. In my attempts to protest and offer to pay sometimes, he would say, "Nonsense. It's the least I can do with all the work that you have done on this book." Then he would thank me once again, as he had done so many times, for all the work I did on this project of 'his.' And it was HIS project! I was only his instrument. I would respond in kind, "It is my honor and pleasure, Mr. Con-iker, to do this for you. I only hope that it meets your expectations and we are successful in getting it published." Jerry is indeed an officer and a gentleman; an officer in God's army fighting the good fight and battling for souls, and a gentleman *par excellence*!

SERVANT OF GOD

One time I was going through a particular heavy cross and he said to me, "Every time you start to think about that, simply say 'All For.'" (All For is short for: All for the Sacred Heart of Jesus, all through the Sorrowful and Immaculate Heart of Mary, all in union with St. Joseph.) Then later, as we parted ways after having dropped him off at his apartment and assisting him inside, he looked at me and said, "Remember, Nancy, All For!" His kindness and concern was quite touching.

And so here we are. My hope and prayer is that readers will be edified, enlightened, and moved to grow deeper in their faith and make any necessary changes in their lives which would lead them toward their heavenly home. But first, to lay the background, is a glimpse of the last six decades within the Church and Society.

This work was indeed a "Labor of Love." So sit back, grab your popcorn, and enjoy the show! All For!

Nancy E. Martin
February 22, 2018

Addendum to Author's Comments

EVENTS IN JERRY CONIKER'S LIFE took a turn which merits this addendum to the author's comments. On July 4, 2018 at 9:10 p.m. CST, Jerome Francis Coniker passed away peacefully in the middle of a family Fourth of July party at his daughter's, Maureen Skurski, home. He was surrounded by family members and friends, much love, and many prayers. He is survived by his twelve adult children, their spouses, seventy-five grandchildren, and numerous great-grandchildren and counting. It is interesting to note the time he died. It was right before the fireworks began in Kenosha, and exactly the same time that the finale of fireworks ended in Akron, Ohio, where I was at that moment (10:10 p.m. EST). So one could say that he certainly went out with a 'bang' both literally and figuratively, for he was also showered with the graces of the Sacraments and all grace that is possible with prayers and other means for him to die a very holy death. For Jerry is now part of the Church Triumphant; and that is cause for celebration! Yes, there will be some sadness for us, who are still part of the Church Militant, to be separated from him for a short time as we work out our own salvation in fear and trembling.

One of Jerry's favorite holidays was the Fourth of July! He kept asking his daughter, Maureen, "When is Fourth of July coming?" as though he had some premonition of the day of his birth into eternal life. He loved the party and the family togetherness that that day brings, for it was tradition for the family to get together and have a party that day.

Jerry felt called, along with his beloved wife, Gwen, to make a difference in the world. In founding the Apostolate of Family Consecration, he had the vision, the tenacity, the leadership, the perseverance [against all odds], and an unwavering trust in God that this is what he was supposed to do in carrying out its mission. He had also a passion for the salvation of souls. He believed that ALL are called to be saints; not just priests and religious. Mothers, fathers, families can all be holy by simply doing their daily duty according to one's state in life and offer everything up to God via his motto, "All For!" In following the inspirations of the Holy Spirit, Jerry positively affected thousands of lives and continues to do so through the catechetical teachings of prominent teachers of the faith that he produced.

Below are some of Jerry's comments throughout the years, taken from the Video produced by the Apostolate for Family Consecration and played at Jerry's funeral luncheon[1]:

> *I believe God is giving us an extra grace now in America to be used as an instrument of His mother, to sanctify the world; Totus Tuus, Totally Yours, Matera Ecclesia, Mother of the Church.*

> *What I found out in 1971 was that this was a spiritual battle; and it was not a political battle, and all my work in political work was for naught unless we had a basically a spiritual vanguard. So the Pope [St. John Paul II] said that the 21st century will be a century of religion, a great century of light, or not at all. There will be a great darkness and destruction. So why did we start the Apostolate? That's why. We started it because the family is under attack and we just knew if we couldn't get to parents and get them to love the Lord, know their faith, practice their faith in an intense way so that our kids can hang around their kids with the same values, our children would be in trouble.*

---

1   Luncheon Video Tribute by the AFC at Jerry's Funeral. n.d.

ADDENDUM TO AUTHOR'S COMMENTS

And if we are going to survive as a nation…we're going to have to get back to God. We're going to have to live a life of consecration, of total commitment to Jesus through Mary in union with St. Joseph.

On the grounds of the AFC is the John Paul II Holy Family Center, which is a place set apart for true formation of the spirit and the mind of Pope John Paul II.

For the first time in the history of the Church, we now have the tools to evangelize families and our parishes with literally the best teachers the Church has.

If we get back to God, that if we live a consecrated life, if we look to God as our source, He will take care of us [Jerry quoting John Paul II]. "And really, this is the mission of the Apostolate for Family Consecration, to systematically transform tens of thousands of neighborhoods into God-centered communities once again."

And you know that anyone who is successful at anything has to risk failure if he's going to be successful. If you're not willing to risk failure, you're never going to succeed at anything worthwhile. And if we put it all on the line, the reward will be unbelievable.

If we don't bring America back to a Marian spirituality, if we don't bring it back to a total conversion, there will be a dark age in the world that the world has never seen before. So a lot depends on America.

The Holy Father [St. John Paul II] and Mother Teresa [now St. Teresa of Calcutta] both thanked my wife, Gwen, for making this Apostolate possible, because they know if she wasn't backing me, I couldn't do what I'm doing. If she wasn't keeping harmony and unity in the home, and overcoming the problems of a husband who travels a lot and works late hours; if she wasn't making that sacrifice, I couldn't do it.

Jerry Coniker

SERVANT OF GOD

Many came to Jerry's funeral wake and mass held at Catholic Familyland in Bloomingdale, Ohio. Others wrote letters to the family who were not able to be there. These comments were supplied to me by the AFC.[2] Here are some of those comments:

The Apostolate for Family Consecration is a positive answer to a necessity. If you put on enough light, the darkness will disappear. When Jerry and Gwen came with 51 of their grandchildren [to Rome], John Paul II had plenty of time for them. We pray that God will bless the Apostolate for Family Consecration, bless Steubenville Diocese, and bless all who promote this Apostolate.

Francis Cardinal Arinze,
Prefect Emeritus, Congregation for Divine Worship
and the Discipline of the Sacraments

I am very confident that Jerry and Gwen Coniker, Apostles of the Holy Family to the families, are modern saints and will be raised to the glory of the altars one day. I consider it a big grace from God to have known them personally. May they intercede for us in heaven.

Msgr. Josefino S. Ramirez,
Archdiocese of Manila

He taught people the truths of our faith, unvarnished. He did not teach his opinion or the latest theological ideal coming down the pipe, but teaching them the core truths of our faith. Jerry wore his faith on his arm and he was never ashamed about his faith. He would never walk away from an argument about the faith, but he always did it in a gentle way, in a kind way. Thank you, Jerry, for being a witness to the faith in this world of ours which is often faithless. Thank you for being a beacon of light in a world that is often darkened. I firmly believe that he has gone home to the Lord

---

2   Ibid.

ADDENDUM TO AUTHOR'S COMMENTS

now. He has gone home to be with his beloved wife, Gwen, who was right there alongside him the whole time. His legacy is one of faith, and a witness to that faith. Well done, good and faithful servant.

Most Rev. Roger J. Foys

His work to build up and strengthen families, he rightly perceived that this was a great need. He seemed to be without fear. He was willing to take on any kind of risk, and that's the way things often went with Jerry. But he went ahead to promote what he thought God was asking him to do. This is the legacy that Jerry is leaving to the Church: the importance of the family, and how we need to do everything we can to build up family life.

Rev. Bernard Geiger, OFM Conv.,
Jerry's Spiritual Director

He not only developed the mottoes, he not only developed the theological approaches, he not only taught them, and he lived them.

Deacon Randall Redington,
Friends and volunteers of the AFC

We had a chance to connect on dozens and dozens of occasions. We filmed well over 100 hours of shows together. Personally, I do believe they [Gwen and Jerry Coniker] exemplified holiness as a married couple in a really unique, radical way. For American Catholicism, their life, their mission, their apostolate is truly a revelation of love and faith and family life. They were a saintly couple in raising kids to carry on their mission.[3]

Scott Hahn,
Biblical scholar, theologian and author

---

3   Pronenchen, Joseph. "National Catholic Register." *National Catholic Registe.* July 20, 2018. http://www.ncregister.com/daily-news/remembering-the-co-founder-of-the-apostolate-for-family-consecration (accessed 07 21, 2018).

SERVANT OF GOD

The ministry was founded at a time when there were not many lay-run ministries. At that time in the life of the Church, many of the activities were left to the priests and religious to carry out so he [Jerry] was walking in new territory, but I saw him with a conviction, with a vision, and a call from God to go forward no matter what the obstacles were. He captured some of the greatest teachers of the Church on video, and preserved that for generations to come. He was the head of our household, and he was the head of the Apostolate for Family Consecration. My mother was the heart. So that contribution of the head and the heart, and both of them giving forth their all, so the two of them are essential to the success of our family life and of the success of the Apostolate for Family Consecration.[4]

Theresa Schmitz,

Director, Executive VP, and COO of the AFC,

and 11th child of Gwen and Jerry Coniker

He ended up selling his business and taking a big risk and moving to Fatima, Portugal, with his family, thinking he was going to start a business and separate his family from the secular world of the United States. But ultimately, it meant for him to be in prayer at the Basilica, and then eventually within two years, he was then back in the United States with a direction of the bishop there [in Fatima] saying, "Take the message of Fatima back to America." And so, that's what he did! He started the Apostolate for Family Consecration in 1975. He had no problem risking everything with the potential of losing everything for God.[5]

Alan Zimmerer,

Director, President and CEO of the AFC since 2012

---

4   Luncheon Video Tribute by the AFC at Jerry's Funeral. n.d.
5   Ibid.

ADDENDUM TO AUTHOR'S COMMENTS

It is not by accident that he was born on the Feast of All Souls (November 2nd), nor that he died on Independence Day. His life was a perpetual giving of self for 'all souls,' including and beyond his immediate family to aspire them to build a personal relationship with God through this Family Apostolate. His independence from this earth is recognition of the purpose of our existence, focused on a life beyond here and now. Faith and hope with his passing offer us the opportunity to experience a realization that our time on this earth is only temporary and we need to have a greater, more permanent goal for our future too.[6]

John and Debbie Kukula,
AFC Disciple Members

In honor of FREEDOM, he went home on his beloved country's day of Independence. He was a 'freedom fighter' in every sense of the word. His zeal for souls has forged the way for many to find spiritual freedom from the bondage and enslavement of the world's values. He was radically counter-cultural, teaching us all to swim upstream against the current of our times. He fought courageously for the protection of families. And now he, along with Gwen, are receiving their heavenly reward. Now they [Gwen and Jerry] will become canonized saints together as husband and wife. They are truly the heroic model of a married couple that our world needs desperately at this very moment in time.[7]

Skip and Fanny LeFever,
AFC Disciple Members

I have met spiritual people in the past, but I have never met a man who had come from business and left a brilliant career to dedicate himself solely to follow the path of the Holy Spirit in his life. To say something about Jerry, it wouldn't be fair to say anything without mentioning Gwen as

---

6   Ibid.
7   Ibid.

well. Together, they brought balance, talent, and grace to everything they touched at the Apostolate.[8]

Robert Snyder,
Director of AFC, Disciple Life Member since 1995

Here's a guy that had no formal theological training and yet was reading the great saints, and created essentially his own 40-day consecration.[9]

Joseph Menkaus,
Director of AFC, Disciple Life Member since 2001,
parent of eight children

Without his faith and his unswerving fidelity to the truth, many of us, and many souls would never have come to know the beauty of our Catholic faith and the road to salvation.[10]

Carolyn Stegmann,
AFC Catholic Corp member since 1987

Jerry never ceased praying, even in his most physically weak condition. Even after suffering a severe stroke while already suffering from Parkinson's disease, he composed this beautiful prayer while at in-home hospice at his daughter Maureen's home on December 17, 2017.

Heavenly Father, Please ask St. Joseph and the Holy Family to hold my hand and guide me home when it is Your will. Thank You for the life You allowed me to live with my dear wife, Gwen, our beautiful family, and the Apostolate for Family Consecration. Thank You for all the wonderful times and memories we had together. Bless all families that come to You in prayer and please grant their requests, especially please watch over all

---

8   Ibid.
9   Ibid.
10 Ibid.

ADDENDUM TO AUTHOR'S COMMENTS

*my children and their families. In union with St. Joseph, I ask this in
Jesus' name, Amen.*

Jerry was laid to rest at the Apostolate for Family Consecration on July
12th in Bloomingdale, Ohio, in the crypt of St. John Vianney Chapel, next to his
beloved wife and Servant of God Gwen Coniker. Jerry and Gwen: May you rest
in peace, and enjoy the Beatific Vision. Amen.

Nancy E. Martin
August 3, 2018

Foreword

Having faced many challenges (the loss of a sister through suicide, financial woes, near-death experiences, heartaches of married life and motherhood, and persecution, to name a few), the life of my mother, Gwen Coniker, affectionately known as Mama C, was anything but a bed of roses, but she lived her life finding the roses among the thorns and made her life out of them.

What one will discover through the journey of Gwen's life is that doing God's will isn't always easy (to accept), but it is the easiest thing to do. And it is where true peace and joy are found, even amidst great sacrifice, uncertainty and suffering. Gwen trusted and followed God—even when she fell, she'd get right back up and resume her focus. God gave the peace and joy, and Gwen thrived on it—she was a beacon of love, peace, and joy because it flowed from her belief, love, and trust in God.

My mother taught me through her witness that surrendering to God's ways and placing complete trust in him and living in the grace of the present moment was the best and only option. May she intercede for all who read this story, to give them hope in life and the conviction to know that holiness is simple and attainable for all of us if we ourselves just believe, love, and trust in God.

I recall hearing stories surrounding my birth. Born in 1975, the same year my parents founded a ministry, I came forth from a womb that had already provided a temporary home for my ten older siblings. My mother was facing a very complicated pregnancy, and as the pregnancy progressed, her doctor became more concerned that she would not survive the birth. With each passing doctor's visit my mom was encouraged to seriously consider terminating the pregnancy—terminating me—as it was not fair to the other ten children that she could die to give birth to me.

My mother, however, never once contemplated aborting me (neither would she have for any one of her other children); instead, her response to the doctor was that God would take care of us, and she set out to write a letter to her family to be read two days before I was to be born through a high-risk C-section.

The letter was a personal reflection on each one of her children's births. She drew her children into the love story of how they came into this world and how she prepared her heart, home, and family for the new addition that each one of us was to the family. She set the stage for love and acceptance no matter the outcome. This is how she dealt with matters. By turning everything into love, she made it real, simple, and true. That's love, and, in the end, that's all we need.

As I ponder this, something I have frequently done over the past decade, I am overcome by her love. I have begun to see her love for me (and all those she loved) was the personal love of Jesus. She did not want me to feel abandoned or rejected by the family if she were to die while giving birth to me. So, instead of fighting for her life, she fought for mine in a very beautiful way. I am so grateful to her for her love and the love of Christ, which I have encountered through her. I am thankful for the gift of life and the desire I have to use my life to be love and to give love to those who are abandoned or rejected.

I can only imagine the glory of her reward for laying down her life for her husband, her children, and all the families that benefit from the ministry she founded with my father. Thy Kingdom come. Thy will be done. On earth, as it is in Heaven.

Theresa (Coniker) Schmitz, daughter of Jerry and Gwen Coniker

Preface

A Glimpse of the Church and
Society over the Last Six Decades

IN THE MID 1950s when Jerry and Gwen were both High School students, there started what would be a monumental shift in the Church and in society at large. Living during the next five to six decades would be challenging but also prove their heroic virtue. While many in society would conform to the world and the world's new morality, or lack thereof, Gwen and Jerry would stay the course and be a light in the darkness. The divorce rate in the 1950s was less than 5 percent then. The changes starting to occur in the Church and in society were driven by political, social, economic, and technological factors. The Second Vatican Council, aka Vatican II (October 1962 and December 1965), is right around the corner. Although the Council itself was good, producing sixteen beautiful documents, the fallout was mass confusion, or rather, an opportunity for some to capitalize on various aspects which could be spun to one's advantage and push for things that the Council never advocated.

What resulted in the coming years was, in fact, a watering down of the faith. No longer was the Majesty of the Faith: the true, the good, and the beautiful, being taught. Meat, potatoes, and vegetables were exchanged for junk food. Most nuns dumped their habits and donned street clothes. They abandoned their teaching posts of imparting the faith to children in the schools to obtain more worthwhile jobs such as sales jobs at used car dealerships or other some such positions. The laity then took over this noble effort, who themselves did not know the faith. It was the blind leading the blind, so to speak. The tabernacle, in which our Lord is present: Body, Blood, Soul, and Divinity, was relegated to the side or 'out of the way.' Women's ordination was all the rage. Liturgical music went from music fit for a king to more contemporary music incorporating guitars and drums. Mass attendees started exchanging their Sunday best for jeans and T-shirts, if they attended at all. The overall reverence of the Holy Sacrifice of the Mass for our King was diminished.

Concurrently, there started an infiltration by homosexual priests and clerics within the Church, an undercurrent of the homosexual lobby taking a powerful stronghold which will exert its control and ideology for years to come and in the formation of seminarians in seminaries across the country, and manifest itself much later in the homosexual priest abuse crisis amongst other egregious things. And this is just for starters. Things get far worse as the decades progress, as shall be witnessed. Many priests, bishops, and cardinals, out of cowardice or because they were part of the problem itself pushing an agenda, chose to remain silent in the midst of scandal after scandal occurring inside and outside of the Church. Homosexual pedophile and pederast priest abusers were shuffled to other parishes when discovered instead of dealt with appropriately, other victims or people paid off in exchange for their silence. No longer did they preach about the sinfulness of politically incorrect truthful yet tough topics as contraception, abortion, cohabitation, homosexual *acts*, or about the existence and reality of Hell for that matter and on and on. So-called Catholics-in-name-only politicians would be pushing pro-abortion legislation and be out front and center expressing their positive views about contraception, abortion, gay rights and the like while receiving communion on Sundays. Yet these scandals continued unabated and without reprisal by the clerics in the Church, save those few courageous clerics who were then later reprimanded by their superiors, or received vitriolic backlash from lay people who would demand they be transferred or laicized.

Today, as of this writing [2017], the Church has been decimated as well as society in a tsunami-like fashion. Few Catholics go to church anymore and those that do either do not know the teachings of the Church or have dissented from them, making up their own beliefs or picking and choosing what they like as if they were in the cafeteria line picking food choices, yet still identifying as Catholic. Then there are the "*Chreasters*": Those who bless the church with their presence as Mass only on Christmas and Easter, mostly out of a ritualistic habit or to please mom or dad and not because they really want to be there or believe in such anachronistic beliefs.

CONTRACEPTION AND THE CONTRACEPTIVE MENTALITY

The 1960s and 1970s brought in the hippie era and free love, the idea of having sexual relations according to choice, without being restricted to marriage or commitment. No fault divorce appeared on the scene and a 'contraceptive mentality' was gaining traction, an attitude which leads to erroneous belief structures, ignoring long-term consequences for short-term pleasures. Society was pushing toward a culture where sex would be free of consequences; that is to say, the consequence of pregnancy. Children are beginning to be viewed as burdens instead of joys, and pregnancy was a problem to be avoided at all costs, or better yet a disease in which one needed to be inoculated. Margaret Sanger (1879-1966), founder of the American Birth Control League in 1916, was instrumental in this effort. The American Birth Control League later came to be known as Planned Parenthood Federation of America, which would become the most powerful abortion provider in America and even stretch its influence abroad, enjoying yearly funding in the millions from the Federal and State governments as well as private enterprises. PPFA underwrote the initial research for the birth control 'Pill,' the research and development of which was driven by Sanger. The Pill was approved by the FDA in 1957 for severe menstrual disorders, not as a contraceptive. It would be 1960 which would usher in the full force the Pill for contraceptive use and its pernicious effects on society. 1965 brought about the landmark U.S. Supreme Court case of *Griswold v. Planned Parenthood of Connecticut* which allowed for married couples to use contraception, rolling back previous state and local laws outlawing it and overthrowing the federal Comstock Law established in 1873 which banned the sale and distribution of contraception. Thus we now have the 'contraceptive mentality' which will be ubiquitous and spread its errors throughout society in the coming years, leading to conjugal infidelity, lowering morality, and objectifying women as Pope Paul VI predicted so accurately in *Humanae Vitae*, and even far exceeding those predictions.

This contraceptive mentality will mutate like run-away cancer cells that thrive in the face of chemotherapy and radiation treatments. The permutations and devastating effects on the Church and society are staggering! Some effects which have ensued include abortion, cohabitation, increased divorce, homosexual rights, so-called same-sex unions then same-sex marriage (an oxymoron if there ever was one), and much more, institutionalizing the very things which St. Paul warned Christians against. Adding to societal ills are also two landmark U.S. Supreme Court cases, one in 1962 of *Engel v. Vitale* declaring school-sponsored prayers unconstitutional, and one the following year, *Abington School District v. Schempp* prohibiting Bible readings in public schools. Both served to essentially "kick God out of the public schools," and certainly did not help the moral and spiritual health of children, our future generation. God is relegated to the sidelines, not necessary to be part of one's school day, essentially sending our children into the day's battle without their weapon of prayer.

How is man made in the image of God? By the fruitfulness of the love between man and woman which springs forth into a third life. This exchange of intimate, conjugal, love between man and woman, which is total, free, fruitful, faithful and indissoluble, images the Blessed Trinity. It is this expression of love which permits man precisely deep within his body to become a sincere gift of self and to find fulfillment. Hence, God has willed that sex is sacred and holy *only* when directed toward its intended purpose as established and designed by Him as being *both* for the permanent and conjugal *unity* of the *husband and wife in marriage*, becoming a joyful affirmation of true love between them and mutual support, and for the *procreation* and education of children, the fruit of their married love. These two essential elements, the life-giving (procreative) and the love-giving (unitive) aspects, are inseparable. Sex outside of marriage between one man and one woman is gravely sinful as is anything that removes one of these procreative or unitive components from the marital act.

But what if Satan could pervert God's plan for authentic love and marriage by removing either one of these two essential components or both, and in so doing, undermine the family, marriage, and life all at the same time…a trifecta effect, if you will? Remember that our Lord's first recorded miracle took place at a wedding feast at the request of His mother even though His time had not yet come. Jesus also elevated marriage to a sacrament. So naturally, Satan wants to undermine this. Remove the procreative aspect and let love, or rather 'feelings' dominate and be the only reason for engaging in sex, or remove the unitive aspect of the couple coming together for reproducing the next generation by relegating that function to a laboratory whereby only capturing one's gametes is necessary for reproducing. In fact, why not attack both ends of the spectrum? Then that would cover all bases related to marriage, family, and reproduction.

The 1970s brought about the infamous U.S. Supreme Court case in 1973, *Roe v. Wade* and its companion case, *Doe v. Bolton*, whereby Roe allowed for abortion up to the third trimester before restrictions were imposed by the state. Doe then extended the right to abortion on demand all nine months up until birth. This ruling not only killed more than 60 million lives to date and counting in the United States alone, but devastated the lives of many of the mothers and fathers in its wake. Radical feminism was also on the rise in the 70s, which began with the Equal Rights Amendment. Women were leaving their homes in droves to enter the workforce, leaving their children to be cared for by outside help, another risk to children. And as G.K. Chesterton so correctly and cleverly stated, "Feminism is mixed up with a muddled idea that women are so-called 'free' when they serve their employers but yet slaves when they help their husbands [and children]." Women with careers started postponing marriage and having children later so cohabitation then became the new norm in the 80s and 90s. Cohabitation, formally shunned within society, became acceptable, all part of the contraceptive mentality expanding its tentacles. Cohabitation is not even scorned at today, even by the parents of the cohabiters. It's just expected as the prior stage to marriage, if marriage even occurs. When sex is separated from the commitment of marriage, sexuality is demeaned and is robbed of its profound human expression. And sin does not cease to be sin because it becomes fashionable, endorsed, approved, tolerated, accepted, and most especially becomes the so-called "law of the land."

Society is progressing deeper toward the god of lust, the god of 'feelings,' the god of relativism and the like. In 1976, then Cardinal Karol Wojtyla (later to be known as Pope John Paul II), in a speech to the American Bishops and printed in the November 9, 1978 issue of *The Wall Street Journal*, had this to say: "We are now standing in the face of the greatest historical confrontation humanity has gone through. I do not think that wide circles of the American society or wide circles of the Christian community realize this fully. We are now facing the 'final' confrontation between the Church and the Anti-Church, of the gospel and the anti-gospel. This confrontation lies in the plan of Divine Providence." He clearly saw the spiritual battle being waged between God and Satan and played out in society and the Church which was leaving millions of souls' lives in the balance.

As mentioned, each and every marriage act must remain through itself open to the transmission of life. Contraception deliberately impedes the procreative dimension of sexual intercourse, and in so doing, affects also the unitive aspect as well. *Contra*-ception, by its very definition, means "*against*"; against conception, against life. It's an inversion of the true meaning of love. It is *contra*-love. In a word, it's a lie. It changes the act from one of self-giving to one of self-serving and thereby alters its value. When sexuality is separated from openness to life, sexual 'love' is no longer an expression of love. All that is left is the sexual association without the full value of the personal relationship. Nothing could be more incompatible with love. The spouses are not a total and sincere gift of self to each other because they have withheld their fecundity; rendered themselves sterile, if you will, by intention and design with a free choice of the will. Their "*I do*" to each other becomes "*I do with exceptions*," that exception being an openness to new life. By withholding a part of themselves, the procreative nature of the act is radically violated, serving to divide the spouses and be contrary to love. When the contraception fails, no longer do we need "shotgun" weddings due to an un-wed pregnancy. There is then recourse to the ultimate contraception, called abortion on demand, with a trip down to the local abortion mill as the fail-safe cure. The irony is that women demanding to do what they want with their own bodies under the guise of 'freedom' are actually enslaving themselves and harming themselves in many ways in the process: The Pill is a class-one carcinogen, "A known and probable cancer-causing agent to humans," according to the World Health Organization. The effects of the Pill on women's health is enormous, leading to breast cancer, irritability, weight gain, depression, and decreased libido. And who can deny the post-abortive harm to women physically, psychologically, emotionally, spiritually, mentally, not to mention the 60+ million missing children who would now be contributing to society in many ways, not the least of which is the economic contributions via GNP and social security?

Pope John Paul II's correctly coined term that we live in 'a culture of death' is quite apropos. In his encyclical, *Evangelium Vitae*, he states: "*Contraception and abortion are often closely connected, as fruits of the same tree... The life which could result from a sexual encounter thus becomes an enemy to be avoided at all costs, and abortion becomes the only possible decisive response to failed contraception.*" He goes on to state that the "culture of death" is a *"mentality which carries the concept of subjectivity to an extreme"* and a *"notion of freedom which exalts the isolated individual in an absolute way."* The US Supreme Court confirmed this in Casey v. Planned Parenthood in 1992: "*In some critical respects abortion is of the same character as the decision to use contraception...People have...made choices...in reliance on the availability of abortion in the event that contraception should fail.*" [Please refer to Appendix D on *Evangelium Vitae*.]

IN VITRO FERTILIZATION

The other side of the coin is In Vitro Fertilization (hereafter IVF) and some other reproductive technologies. IVF is a procedure whereby numerous oocytes or eggs are removed from a woman's ovaries through ovarian hyper stimulation and combined with sperm (collected by masturbation, and itself gravely sinful) in a Petri dish where fertilization takes place. The resulting embryos are then cultured for about forty hours and then a process known as embryo transfer (ET) takes place in which numerous embryos are transferred into the uterus of a woman in hopes that at least one survives and results in a pregnancy. Just as contraception deliberately impedes the procreative aspect of the marital act, IVF deliberately impedes the unitive dimension of marital act, where mother and father are nowhere to be found and conception occurs in a laboratory. They are two sides of the same coin and both destroy life. IVF has left a wake of destruction of life lost in its path, and in so doing, violating the dignity of the human person.

At the outset, it can't be overemphasized the plight of couples who are unable to have children. But while illicit forms of reproductive technologies might resolve one problem, they create many others. Although compassion should always be shown with those dealing with infertility, compassion never means condoning, giving moral acceptance to, or even participating in those acts that are by their nature intrinsically evil and contrary to Natural Law.

God has willed that humans be "begotten" not "made" within the natural sexual act of intercourse between husband and wife only. A child is not something owed one, but a *gift*, and a supreme gift at that. *Donum Vitae* by the Congregation for the Doctrine of Faith states this: "*Marriage does not confer upon the spouses the 'right' to have a child, but only the right to perform those natural acts which are per se ordered to procreation.*" [See Appendix D, *Donum Vitae*]. The marital act cannot be reduced to mere biology. Rather, it goes well beyond physicality. As Pope John Paul II attests in *Theology of the Body*, the act of conjugal one-flesh union is meant to speak the "language of the body" of total self-giving love and spousal union similar to Trinitarian love, that love that Father and the Son have for each other which springs forth and proceeds the Holy Spirit. It is an intimate moment between husband, wife, and God that is so rich in meaning. God is one and three and self-giving and fruitful all at the same time. Marriage mirrors, if you will, this inner life of the Trinity. The husband and wife are two, yet one in the one-flesh union which begets a third when a child proceeds from their love. Marriage is triune in nature. To exclude either the unitive aspect or the procreative aspect is to falsify this language of the body. In addition, because we are physical *and* spiritual, as we are not merely bodies but we are united totally as embodied spirits in the image of God, human persons have intrinsic dignity and should be treated in a way befitting this dignity both at their conception, gestation, birth and throughout the whole of their lives, and be guaranteed the inviolability of the right to life from the first moment of conception.

That said, July of 1978 ushered in the first human being, Louise Joy Brown from England, who was born after being conceived via In Vitro Fertilization (IVF). IVF since then has become widely prevalent as a form of assisted reproduction. Ironically, in an effort to desperately "get a baby," couples are killing numerous lives in the process, often without realizing it. It's abortion on steroids. How so, do you ask? This procedure demands that a good number of embryos be fertilized in a Petri dish outside the womb, hoping that one or two will survive transfer to the body and successfully implant in the womb, others being destroyed in the process as is clearly envisaged and commonplace. When too many embryos successfully implant, resulting in multiple pregnancies, then "fetal reduction" occurs which is none other than a euphemism for abortion, killing some of the fetuses so the others have a better chance for survival. A system of eugenics or "quality control" takes place like in a production assembly line whereby the 'defective' or those deemed to be inferior embryos or fetuses are destroyed. If that is not bad enough, leftover embryos are "frozen" for years in nitrogen liquid in a procedure known as cryopreservation. Many thousands of souls are "on ice" as of this writing, souls in a state of "limbo" between the precipice of life and death, trapped, if you will, in this state until freed by being "un-thawed" and transferred to someone's womb if even successful, experimented upon (itself intrinsically evil), or destroyed as though the human being was useless waste.

Any attack on the human person is an attack on God Himself. We have lost the sense of sin and the dignity of the human person which has led to atrocities of innocent human life. These embryos are human persons, both body and spirit, with immortal souls. There are more lives lost in the utilization of these reproductive technologies than gained. The proportion of evil far outweighs the good. It is ironic to note that man, in his quest to be free from annoying and 'oppressive' moral laws so he can seek his own desires, ends up becoming the oppressor himself of the weak and defenseless.

Let's Mix It Up a Bit: The Plot Thickens – Introducing Donated Gametes and Surrogacy

Will the *real* mother please stand up? In an age whereby the precious name of *mother* has become so skewed and convoluted to mean anything from: biological mother, genetic mother, legal mother, intended mother, surrogate mother, gestational mother, foster mother, and adoptive mother, it makes for quite an interesting experience when the priest at Mass asks all the "mothers" to stand up in church on Mother's Day so he can give them a blessing and acknowledge their wonderful work as *mother*.

Now enter surrogacy. Surrogacy is an arrangement whereby a woman participates in a contractual agreement, typically with a fee, to have an embryo implanted into her uterus using IVF, thereby becoming impregnated, and to carry to term that child upon which she surrenders him or her to the party who sought her services. The child may or may not be genetically linked to the surrogate mother. IVF and surrogacy further aggravates the situation by placing newly conceived embryo(s) back into the womb of one who is *not* the mother. For nine months, that is the home of the child (or children). Food, nourishment, and blood is exchanged between 'mother' and child, but the mother is not his mother but a 'false' mother. The child learns the smells and voice of his *mother*. Upon birth, it is natural for the child to nurse at the breast of that mother. But the child is ripped away from the substitute mother and placed in the arms of a stranger, even though that stranger may be the biological mother. What further confusion and violence done to the child who goes into the arms of parents not genetically linked in anyway, both mother and father. And all this says nothing about the bonding effects on the surrogate mother herself who runs the risk of not wanting to give up the child upon birth.

Surrogacy has been portrayed by the media as a Godsend, helping that poor 'sympathetic' couple who are unable to bear children naturally, and who ought to have the 'right' to a child while portraying the surrogate woman as altruistic, engaging in heroic charity in helping them achieve their goal of parenthood, thereby fulfilling their great and otherwise unquenchable desire. However, the reality is quite different. Surrogates, especially poor women in more poor countries such as India and Thailand have been exploited, as surrogacy has become a big money-making commercial business. Surrogates have also been solicited by wealthy women for convenience, so they don't have to endure the suffering of labor or ruin their figure. It objectifies women to be egg farms, baby-making machines, womb renters, and gestational carriers, all sub-human descriptions for one who is supposedly being 'altruistic' or exhibiting 'heroic charity' as they are described.

The use of surrogates and IVF does not end with the nicely packaged sympathetic situations of infertile married couples using their own gametes to impregnate the surrogate. No, it extends well beyond that. To make matters worse, introducing 'donated' gametes opens up a plethora of problems and confusion to children conceived and gestated in this manner. Gametes are the reproductive components such as eggs and sperm. Sperm is procured via masturbation, itself a sinful act. Children are 'bred' to then be placed in the homes of homosexual couples or single persons (either homosexual or heterosexual), thereby intentionally depriving that child of a father or a mother, both which are necessary to the full flourishing and rearing of that child. God saw fit to have life be the fruit of husband *and* wife, not one or the other or a redundancy of two moms or two dads, because it is this kind of family that is best suited for the rearing and education of children. Both father and mother bring unique and necessary gifts to the family and to the education and rearing of children. The most psychologically well adjusted, healthiest, and happiest are those with a father and mother. Voluminous social science research proves this. It is bad enough when a child loses a parent due to death, the suffering that comes about; or the child who is adopted into a home who is not his biological parents. Adopted children yearn to know their biological parents, to connect with them, to know them. There is a void every time the topic of genealogy comes up. Utilizing donor sperm and/or eggs further blurs familial bonds and kinship, actually removing them entirely. It brings about and manifests a rupture between genetic parenthood, gestational parenthood, and responsibility for upbringing. There is a huge identity crisis today with these children born to surrogates who are the product of IVF because we as human persons have a need to know our genealogy, who our parents are, where we have come from, what is our nationality, and so forth. The Old Testament is replete with examples of how genealogy and bloodlines were very important for them to connect with their kin.

But is this really a loving thing to do to a child? Nothing could be more incompatible with love. What is love? Love sacrifices oneself for the good of the other. These technologies invert this and sacrifice the nascent human life for oneself. Love does not seek its own interests but that of the other, in this case, the child. The child's interest is not even considered. Love rejoices in the truth, the truth of God's moral laws, not the contravening of them. Love endures all things, even the suffering that proceeds from lost dreams and desires not fulfilled and unites that suffering to Christ's, and it becomes redemptive and powerful.

Self-centeredness supersedes self-giving. Man creates in his mind the illusion that he has the power to create and destroy life at will. He is his own God with his own decrees and relativistic and subjective moral code. When things don't go according to plan, resentment ensues and lawsuits fill the courts. Pride hath overtaketh man. The real infertility is what could be called the *spiritual infertility* which emanates by utilizing these medical technologies, which is fruit-*less* and leaves the souls of those who participate devoid of spiritual life. What does it profit a man (or a woman) to gain a child at the high cost of doing violence to the very child so desperately sought after and forfeit his (or her) own spiritual fertility in the process? The anecdote: humility and submitting to the loving natural moral law of God.

Not only is there the blurring of family lines but there is also huge ramifications for the legal system in grappling with situations gone wrong when employing these high tech reproductive marvels. There are countless court cases which have issued forth for things gone wrong. Couples contracting the services of a surrogate have been known to demand she abort upon finding out that the child has a medical issue, even minor, against the wishes of the surrogate, thus ending up in court as to which party has more authority to decide the fate of the child at hand. A baby is the object of a legal battle for numerous so-called 'parents' vying for custody: The homosexual biological father and his partner, the biological mother who donated her egg, a surrogate or gestational mother, and the current foster parents. When the moral law is broken, one ends up with numerous and more serious other problems which are created, some foreseen but typically unforeseen. And this is just for starters.

Deuteronomy 30:19 reads, *"I have set before you life and death, the blessing and the curse. Choose life, then, that you and your descendants may live,"* could not be any more relevant for our times as many of our descendants have already perished. Isaiah 5:20 reads, *"Woe to those who call evil good and good evil."* When we invert evil practices for good, we no longer know that we don't know what is good for we think what is evil is really good. This is a dangerous precipice both for the individual and for society as a whole. We are living in such times. These times especially are pernicious. Why? Because technology has given us the capability to kill more people systematically and efficiently in a more hidden way and on a larger scale. Things a generation or two ago which were considered morally repugnant and unthinkable are not only accepted today but demanded as so-called 'rights.' The infertility issue we should really be focused on and seeking a remedy for is the 'spiritual infertility' of our life-*less* souls which results when we utilize surrogacy and these illicit reproductive technologies.

MORE PROBLEMS ON THE HORIZON

It is no surprise that abuses occur when utilizing these technologies because when we reduce human life to mere biology or treat the human person as a physical product, instead of the embodied spirit in which he or she is, we then become depraved and devoid of any moral compass and lack responsibility toward the human persons involved. Then anything goes, as it were.

The 1980s and 1990s heralded an all-out assault by homosexual activists to change attitudes and behaviors about homosexual acts by focusing not on the act but on the homosexual person, using 'discrimination' as their catchphrase. Sexual sin is no longer viewed as sinful. Political Correctness is in full swing where reality and sin are denied so as to not offend the sensibilities of others, as truth is offensive.

Human acts, which proceed from the will with knowledge of the end, are either good or evil. Human acts are good insofar as they are rightly ordered to God. Homosexual *acts*, or sodomy, are never and can never be rightly ordered to God but rather, are diametrically opposed to God and His order for human sexuality and procreation and are contrary to Natural Law. It is quite obvious and self-evident that two males' or two females' sexual parts don't fit together, nor are they capable of procreating. It cannot be emphasized enough that the homosexual person is not condemned for having the inclination to such acts but it is the *act* itself which is being deemed objectively sinful as revealed by God and passed down through the Church and taught throughout history. Each and every human being is precious in the eyes of God and has worth and dignity immeasurable regardless of his or her sexual attraction toward persons of the same sex.

With divorce commonplace and marriage already severed from its unitive and procreative purposes, with marriage being based solely on 'love,' which really only means 'feelings,' logically then what is to stop homosexuals for arguing first for homosexual unions and rights, and then marriage? That is to say, if marriage is merely based on two people loving each other and that is it, then two men or two women could love each other and it would be discriminatory to not allow them also the opportunity to marry and have benefits. And this is exactly what happened. Judicial activism and verbal gymnastics by the U.S. Supreme Court issued forth on June 26, 2015 in *Obergefell vs. Hodges* Supreme Court Decision when five of the nine Supreme Court Justices 'found' in the Constitution the right to Gay Marriage. It's funny how this was suddenly discovered in the Constitution after over 200 years. To have a right to do a thing is not at all the same as to be right in doing it.

Homosexual 'marriage' is the law of the land. But again, if marriage is merely based on people loving each other and that is it, why limit it to two adults or even two people at all? The Pandora's box is now wide open, allowing for incestual marriages, polygamy, even marriage of three or more persons. Lawsuits fill the courts if bakers, photographers, or wedding banquet halls refuse their services for a same-sex wedding. People are losing their jobs for merely expressing their God-given right to believe that marriage is to be between only one man and one woman. As an aside, it is not the *person* to whom one objects to providing products, be it a cake or photography services. It is the specific *product* they object to, by using their God-given talents, to making a 'wedding' cake AND the specific *event* (a gay 'marriage' which is a sinful event) for which they are asked to provide the product. Naturally, Christian bakers have no issue selling any other kind of baked goods to homosexuals or homosexual couples such as birthday cakes, cupcakes, etc. any more than they would not object to selling baked goods to divorced persons.

The Health and Human Services Mandate (aka ObamaCare) has deemed everyone pay for contraception and abortifacients, barring very rare exceptions, essentially violating the consciences and religious freedom of many, including Priests for Life, whose sole purpose is to fight against abortion and abortion causing contraception.

The cancer which spreads its tentacles from the homosexual arena branches out to gender confusion, gender ideology, and transgenderism. We are abandoning our Creator's design for gender identity. Genesis 1:27 states, "So God created humankind in his image, in the image of God he created them; male and female he created them." It does not say, "male and female I have created them but if they think otherwise, well, go ahead with that choice then." The consequences have been, and will continue to be, tragic for individuals, families, and society at large. Science is negated in favor of feelings which reign supreme. No longer is one a male or female due to objective and scientifically proven biology whereby every cell in the male body has an X and a Y chromosome, and every cell in a female body has two X chromosomes. One's gender is subjective and merely based on how one 'feels' or identifies. If one is biologically a woman but thinks she is really a man, then in fact, by today's mentality she is a man, regardless what those pesky scientists say, not to mention what has been known since the beginning of time or more importantly, what God has pronounced. And if one then identifies as a man, then therefore "*he*" can use the male bathrooms, locker rooms, changing rooms, etc. The State of Massachusetts has deemed that taxpayers must pay for the sex change of an inmate because they believe that a sex change operation is a medically necessary right. Then there was Bruce Jenner, the once very masculine Olympian who transgendered into Kaitlin Jenner and was hailed by the media as a hero.

Verbal engineering has been exercised to obscure the reality of what is really happening, to legitimize, normalize, affirm, and construe what is *ipso facto* morally insidious as "entitlements" and "rights" demanded upon society by select individuals. Everything is "relativistic" and inevitably leads to "practical materialism which breeds individualism, utilitarianism and hedonism," as Pope John Paul II attests in *Evangelium Vitae*. It's a perverse idea of freedom. Vatican II's document, *Gaudium et Spes*, declares "When God is forgotten, the creature itself grows unintelligible." So we now live in a hedonistic, utilitarian, relativistic, secular humanistic, progressive, narcissistic, materialistic culture. This "Dictatorship of Relativism" as Pope Benedict XVI so aptly expressed, is where each individual makes up his or her own subjective truth about morality, what is right, what is wrong, what is sinful and what is not. There is also what the author of this book would say is a "dictatorship of feelings." If one "feels" offended, then the offender must cease speaking and apologize profusely, never mind whether what the offender said is the objective truth or not. Additionally, love is now just about mere feelings, which are capricious in and of themselves, and since marriage has been reduced to whether a person "loves" another, then leading that argument to its logical conclusion, any human can marry another human if they "love" each other; or an animal, or their child for that matter. So it is no wonder that same-sex "marriage" is the law of the land. And it opens the door wide open to polygamy, incest and the like because marriage, again, has been reduced to being how one "feels" about another. And if one is in love with the married man at work and he loves her, well, hey, they love each other so all is good. The sin of adultery is so anachronistic anyway, as if sin can at some point cease to be sin since we, as humans, have "evolved." Another example, feelings about oneself reign supreme over what is objectively real, obvious, and visible such as one's objective biological gender of maleness or femaleness. So one who is really a male, but "feels" as though he is really a female, demands and is given the right to use the female bathroom because he feels uncomfortable using the male restroom. And his feelings about his "gender" trump the majority of objectively female persons who feel that they are, in fact, female and desire to use the female restrooms so as to have privacy from males. And society, laws, and policies cater to this illusion, or delusion, as I would say, while simultaneously denying the "feelings" of the majority and even offending the sensibilities of the majority, but alas their feelings do not matter.

When God is marginalized, minimized, and excluded, we lose our way. The more we move away from God, the less we are able to discern and adhere to proper moral behavior. Man attempts to become God, as it were, continuing the great sin of pride first committed by Eve in the very beginning. We've lost sight of the real Trinity and substituted it for a false trinity: me, myself, and I. People reach the point of rejecting one another in order to make certain that their own subjective "rights" prevail, which to them is freedom, albeit erroneous. And it is repeated with so much pertinacity, disregarding doctrine and objective moral norms as antiquated, creeds that are enslaving and oppressive. Yet, *de facto*, it is heretical creeds which are dead and brings death, and it is objective moral norms which are reasonable and live long enough to be considered antiquated.

Society has become so accepting of sexual immorality, that is to say, sexual sin. The problem is that it is not even recognized anymore for what it always has been and still is and will always be: Sin. Art, like morality, consists of drawing the line somewhere. When the line is not drawn, there is no art, and certainly also, there is no morality. God is indeed merciful. However, here is the catch: God's mercy never confirms us in sin nor tells us to continue in sin. Rather, He calls us to recognize an act as sinful first and foremost and then to turn away from it.

PREFACE

Mercy, just like forgiveness in the confessional, demands of one to recognize the sin and have a firm resolve to turn away from it in order to receive the grace of the sacrament. Just like the woman caught in adultery. Jesus never confirmed her in her sexual sin. "Jesus straightened up and said to her, 'Woman, where are they? Has no one condemned you?' She said, 'No one, sir.' And Jesus said, 'Neither do I condemn you. Go your way, and from now on do not sin again.'" (John 8:11-12) Similarly, Jesus will always forgive but one must turn from sin and obey his commands to at least attempt to not commit the sin again. In order to do this, one must believe and acknowledge the act to be a sin.

But what if one cannot even see sin for what it is? That is, one has denied that the given human act is no longer a sin and firmly believes that because, after all he says, "I love so and so and God is such a loving God and my intentions are good because I 'feel' love for this person so surely God understands. And besides, we are not young adults anymore. We are older now and have come of age." Today, unfortunately, as it pertains to sexual sins, many do not believe they are sins at all, as though society has somehow evolved and God changed the rules of the game. Are we really believing God's mercy is some sort of guilt-free, tolerant (of sin that is), sin-approving behavior because we have denied the act is sinful and/ or because we don't want to offend the sensibilities of someone else's sinful act for fear of being called judgmental? Let us not be deceived. For God has revealed His truth of what acts are sinful. These truths are written on every human heart, located in Sacred Scripture, clarified by Sacred Tradition and constantly proposed and taught by the Magisterium of the Church throughout the ages. And if that is still not enough proof for the reader, the Blessed Mother herself in the Church-approved private revelation to the Fatima children in 1917 said, "More souls go to Hell due to sins against purity than any other sin." Hans Christian Andersen's children's fairy tale story *The Emperor's New Clothes* is such a profound story and lesson for our times. In this story, those in society were coerced to deny reality and what was obvious out of fear of retribution or being thought of as a fool. Yet a child who is innocent and cares nothing about status or perception speaks the obvious: "The Emperor has no clothes on!" while the surrounding adults are aghast in horror. "…and a little child shall **lead** them." (Isaiah 11:6)

The inimical effects of all this have been catastrophic. Since the widespread acceptance and use of contraception with the onset of the sexual revolution since the 1960s, the following ills have issued forth while others have skyrocketed: contraception, abortion, pre-marital sex, cohabitation, adultery, objectification of women, abuse, single parent families, divorce (now 60 percent), surrogacy, IVF, wife and child abuse, increased depression and drug and alcohol addiction, suicides, assisted suicide, euthanasia, violence, crime, homosexual activity, homosexual unions, homosexual so-called "marriage," and now, gender ideology, gender confusion and transgenderism.

Satan has indeed most likely exceeded even his wildest dreams of perverting God's plan for authentic love, marriage, family, and life for His children along with their authentic happiness.

This is the culture that Gwen and Jerry lived in as the years progressed. Do many people these days even consider life after their time on earth, or rather, the state of their eternal and immortal souls? Many live only for today or for this life with little regard to the hereafter. Or they have an erroneous idea of God's mercy. Not for Gwen and Jerry. The thoughts of the state of their souls were constantly on their minds, not only the state of their souls but the souls of many others as well. We saw as their lives progress together how they felt a need to do something to warn the masses as the culture progressively gets worse. Moreover, living their commitment to the marriage vow religiously and faithfully in a cesspool of gunk of a culture demonstrates their heroic virtue and what an awesome example their married lives are for today's society and beyond. Their marriage and love shown to each other is certainly one for others to emulate.

Prologue

JERRY, AS THOUGH IN A DAZE, kept walking around the house in circles. He was fidgety and not certain where he was going or what he was going to do; this, the day following the death of his beloved wife, Gwen. Gwen was always the only girl for him. There will never again be another woman in Jerry's life. Yesterday, today, and always forever, Gwen will be Jerry's beloved lover and spouse and Jerry would be Gwen's. This beautiful, mutual, symbiotic reciprocal self-giving love is a rarity in our day and age. Even today, many years after her death, Jerry still wears his wedding ring.

It was clear that Jerry was lost without Gwen. She always took care of the meals and household matters. Although Jerry did help Gwen with simple household tasks while she was ill, he suddenly found himself wondering how he was going to pick up the pieces and cook his own meals and other practical matters.

Jerry was a very pensive man and a man of purpose. In reflecting on Gwen's death, he pondered quite extensively over the spiritual aspect of her death, convinced that his 'Love' was now experiencing the Beatific Vision in heavenly bliss. Both he and Gwen were convinced that the joy is not only worth the sacrifice, but even greater than the sacrifice...so strong was their faith, and a faith rare in our day. But for now, although Gwen has gone to her heavenly reward, Jerry is still on his journey and part of the Church Militant.

SERVANT OF GOD

Jerry's method of processing and coping with grief is to bury himself in his work. Dealing with Gwen's death was no different. Now, he was always a man of laborious endeavors. However, even more would he become so following difficult times in his life, namely his initial separation from Gwen after high school and now his current permanent separation from her, through her passing on to her heavenly abode. In the days and months following Gwen's death, Jerry did just this. He buried himself in the work of the Apostolate.

Jerry temporarily moved his office to, and slept in, the room where Gwen lay ill. This room was the living room of their home. He had previously set up the family room with a brick fireplace, large enough for gatherings for their growing, extended Coniker family, as well as the Men and Women's Catholic Corps members. It would be used for family functions for years to come, and would be the room in which Gwen would eventually pass away. It would also be known to be called the Fatima House.

He also continued to sleep in that same room for months after her death. Moreover, he set up that living room like a memorial museum. Pictures of Gwen and the family, and picture albums as well as various artifacts filled the room, covering every square inch. One could spend an entire day looking through everything.

Jerry would always make his bed, even while traveling, in this manner: He would place Gwen's nightgown, folded up, at the foot of his bed. On his pillow he would place Gwen's rosary that she used and held in her hand in the casket during her wake. There also on his pillow, he would place three or four pictures of Gwen. In the beginning, however, his neatly made bed would be covered with her pictures. He would take these pictures everywhere he traveled. Sometimes, he would switch out some pictures for others. In addition, he would have pictures of her on the steering wheel of his car or on the passenger seat while driving. He would keep up this ritual of placing Gwen's pictures, rosary, and folded-up nightgown the rest of his days; so great was his love of her.

Interestingly, Jerry showed little emotion outwardly or visibly, yet his heart ran very deep with feelings and care and compassion for others. Rarely would anyone ever see him shed tears. However, there were times when his emotions would, in fact, shine through. One such example was during one particular Christmas season; Jerry came home very excited with a big teddy bear for his children as though he were a child himself, and an album called *Fenwick* which was a Christmas music album that he couldn't wait to play for the family. He gathered his children and pulled out all the Christmas decorations, and together, they decorated the Christmas tree and the house while listening to that album as they prepared for Christmas. He was right there with them as excited as they were to be preparing for the coming of our Lord. To this day, that music drums up memories of that event in the Coniker children, eliciting warm and fond emotions.

Jerry's emotions did visibly betray his normal comportment at the funeral Mass of his wife Gwen at the playing of the Ave Maria. He could be seen by his daughter Kathy, wiping a tear or two emanating from his eyes and flowing down his cheeks. Rare was it that the children saw their father choke up. For Sheri, another daughter, her memory was only one other time in 1999 at a healing retreat that the family attended by Fr. John Hampsch, cfm, where she saw her father choke up and trying mightily to hold back his tears.

It has been said that behind a great man is a great woman. This is certainly the case here. For Jerry is a great man for having followed the inspirations of the Holy Spirit in order to found the Apostolate for Family Consecration and creating a plethora of Catechetical materials, so as to lead as many souls to Christ as possible. Gwen is a great woman as well for supporting and assisting her husband every step of the way in such a monumental and holy endeavor. Both love the Church and love God and tried to do His will as best they could.

It was the two of them who made the Apostolate. Gwen's role was different than Jerry's role.... just like Jesus' role was different than Mary's role...and Joseph's role was different than Mary's role, yet all important to God's work. For even as the body is one and yet has many members, and all the members of the body, though they are many, are one body, so also is Christ... For the body is not one member, but many... If the foot says, "Because I am not a hand, I am not a part of the body," it is not for this reason any less a part of the body. And if the ear says, "Because I am not an eye, I am not a part of the body," it is not for this reason any the less a part of the body. If the whole body were an eye, where would the hearing be? If the whole body were an ear, where would the sense of smell be?... And the eye cannot say to the hand, "I have no need of you"; or again the head to the feet, "I have no need of you."... And if one member suffers, all the members suffer with it; if one member is honored, all the members rejoice with it. (1 Corinthians 12: 12, 14-17, 21, 26)

Gwen and Jerry lived for others. Jerry always provided for the family while Gwen paid attention to every detail when it came to the home, food, cooking, getting birthday gifts, Christmas gifts for family members, and so forth. As a matter of fact, after her passing, it was found that she had a back room filled with future gifts for her children and grandchildren for their birthdays and Christmas.

Our crosses, no matter what they are, present opportunities to grow in holiness and grow closer to Our Lord and His heavenly mother. We can even transform our own crosses, no matter how painful they may be, into power to conquer evil and into occasions of holiness and even joy.

In our turbulent modern world, Gwen taught us how to live, how to die gracefully, how to make a house into a home, how to be compassionate, how to be hospitable, how to be a loving mother and grandmother, and how to be a faithful, loyal, loving, devoted wife. She took the marriage vow seriously; unto death do us part. Her life exemplified the vocation of marriage. She also treasured life in the womb as well as the gift of her living children.

GWEN'S CAUSE

After the Fifth Anniversary of her death, June 15, 2002, the Most Rev. R. Daniel Conlon, Bishop of Steubenville, opened the Cause for the Beatification and Canonization of Gwen Cecilia Coniker. She became a Servant of God on September 9, 2007. Bishop Conlon saw that Gwen had her priorities straight and her family came first. One example that demonstrated this was when they were in

PROLOGUE

Rome in 1988 for the Marian Year, and Jerry had a binder with a signed copy of two thirds of all of the Bishops in the United States for the Marian Year Program to present to Pope John Paul II; however, because there was a limited amount of time with the Pope, Gwen stepped in front of Jerry so as to present her children to the Pope first, which was her priority, instead of putting the Apostolate first, even if it meant that Jerry would run out of time to present the binder to him. As it was, there was enough time for both the presentation of the family and presenting the binder to the Pope.

In 2007 also, the Cause for 'Venerable' of Gwen Coniker was opened, again by his Excellency, Bishop R. Daniel Conlon. Please see Appendix A for a "Prayer for the Servant of God, Gwen Cecilia Coniker, & Family Unity" for her veneration and beatification to come to fruition. There are less than one hundred people in the United States who are currently Servants of God. Of these, Gwen is one of only three who was a wife and mother; the other two being Cora Evans and Dorothy Day.

Chapter 1

The Beginning

THE YEAR WAS 1939. Into the world was born Guenevere Cecilia Billings, or Gwen as she would come to be called, on September 27th in Chicago, Illinois. Her father, George Henry Billings, was of Irish descent, and her mother, Rose Katherine (née Polito) Billings, was Italian. Gwen was the youngest of the Billings' three daughters; the other two daughters, Georgia Rose and Geraldine, were nine and eleven years older than Gwen, respectively.

The Billings family lived on the north side of Chicago where folks took pride in the upkeep of their homes in their neighborhood and streets were lined with trees. Also living with them was Gwen's grandfather, Joe, and her Uncle Joe. Gwen was showered with affection and love. She had a happy and peaceful childhood.

Dad had a milk route and would occasionally take Gwen with him. This delighted her greatly! Mom worked for a blueprint firm as an office manager. They went on vacations most every summer and loved to celebrate happy occasions, especially St. Patrick's Day! On that day, Dad, being the Irishman that he was, would color the milk green! Gwen's childhood was a simple yet happy one, and one shared also by her best friend, Duke, the family German shepherd.[1]

Gwen's parents instilled the faith in their children. They attended Mass

---

1   Lappin, Fr. Peter, *Challenge and Change Volume One: The Foundation* (Bloomingdale, OH: Apostolate for Family Consecration, 1999), 16-17.

regularly, participated in May processions, prayed novenas, and so forth. Gwen also attended St. Matthias Catholic grade school.

As a testament to Gwen's love for her parents and how grateful she was for her wonderful upbringing and beautiful family life, she writes to her mother in a letter dated March 1, 1971:

> *You see I was raised in the faith by two very good parents. How thankful I am today for all your hard working years in order to educate your girls.*
>
> *In the article you sent me on Marguerite Piazza, she too valued her girls a good education, sense of well-being and being loved. So you see, you have done the same for your girls and you are the wonderful Mother everyone wants and would hope to have. Now I want nothing more than to have you back here [from Florida]. However, I want to tell you how I feel.*
>
> *So Gene [Rose's second husband after her first husband died] is a quiet man. He has many qualities and faults. We all do. You must help him and he helps you in order to obtain peace and happiness. Never think of money – that's material and it means nothing, in this world or the next. We don't need money to get to heaven. We need graces. So I would like to see you both come back and complete your life with a true devotion to Our Lovely Lady who does love both of you.*
>
> *Please think about what I've said and say prayers, many prayers; the Rosary, Holy Mass and Communion. This I assure you will carry you through all the days of your life.*
>
> *All my love, Gwen*

Gwen also had a very close relationship with her older sister, Georgia, as depicted in the following birthday letter:

> *Dearest Sister, Georgia,*
>
> *You mean so much to me. A sister has a special place in the heart that*

nothing can ever change. We've both changed a lot through the years and so have things around us, but the one thing that hasn't changed is the special bond between us that keeps us close to each other no matter where we are.

Happy Birthday! With Love, Gwen

Meanwhile, a year earlier, in 1938, Jerome Francis Coniker was born on November 2nd in Chicago, Illinois. Jerry, as he is known, was the youngest of three children by John Coniker and Margaret Cecilia Coniker (née Cummings). Jerry's older siblings were Mary Ann, age three, and William (Bill), age eight, at the time.

The Coniker family lived for a time in Chicago before moving to Skokie, IL. John Coniker, known to be very generous with his money, was also a fun-loving man who greatly valued his family and religion. He had a deep devotion to the Sacred Heart of Jesus and regularly prayed the rosary. Margaret Coniker, his wife and an attractive brown-haired woman with blue eyes, was well-educated. She was brought up with proper manners and taught how to be a lady. She was somewhat aloof in her demeanor, yet strong and resourceful with a courageous spirit.[2] She set a strong example for them by saying three complete rosaries a day, although she never imposed that on them. They just observed her and learned from her example.[3]

Financial difficulties plagued the Coniker family when John Coniker lost a lot of his income. This happened when his partner confiscated all of the gas money and left town, and at the same time, the Depression caused the economy to tank. John then lost the gas station he owned in Chicago. In those days, you couldn't file for bankruptcy. This, coupled with a heart attack that he suffered, led to the family losing their home as well. John tried to take whatever odd jobs he could find in order to support the family. Times were indeed precarious for the family as both jobs and housing were scarce. They were forced to move of-

2   *Challenge and Change*, 2-3.
3   Ibid, 8.

ten from apartment to apartment and each time, conditions worsened. Poverty in today's standards is akin to living in a Hyatt Regency hotel compared to the rat-infested living conditions they endured. Poor nutrition also led to Jerry contracting rickets.

At school, Jerry was subjected to a series of humiliations by Sr. 'Not so Nice' when she assumed that Jerry's low grades were attributed to a stubborn character. On the day he was to receive his First Holy Communion, she let him know that he did not pass to the next grade.

Jerry and Mary Ann were forced to move to two separate boarding schools, in La Grange, Illinois. The separation caused great sadness for everyone, both parents and children alike. The parents would visit them every Sunday which brought great joy to both Jerry and Mary Ann. As an aside, Jerry and Mary Ann had a close relationship and loved to go boating together on the lake or pray at the Grotto of Our Lady.

Trouble appeared again at the boarding school where Mary Ann was living when Sr. 'Uncharitable' told Mary Ann that she needed to leave since her parents could not pay for her tuition. What followed from this young child was a strong rebuke to that Sister in front of the whole assembly present in the dining hall, elucidating exactly how she thought of such conduct which, in her words, was very unbecoming of a religious order of nuns. Sr. 'Uncharitable' then sent for Mary Ann's mother immediately, telling her that she must come and get her daughter at that very moment.

The stress experienced by Jerry's father was starting to take its toll on him. His heart was weak from his previous heart attack, coupled with financial difficulties. Then, on July 23, 1950, John Coniker was found slouched over on his face in the chair by Jerry and his mother after Sunday Mass holding a rosary in his hand kneeling. He died later that day. If there ever was a way to go, it would be in the midst of praying to Our Lady while covered by her protective mantle.

Troubles for the Conikers continued unabated. That Christmas, in 1950, Mary Ann, Bill, and their mother scrimped and saved to buy the family new clothes, a very joyful time for all indeed. However, a fire erupted in the apartment the morning after

Christmas. Jerry first noticed smoke emerging from the closet which housed their new clothes. He ran to Bill for help. Bill then closed the doors and ran to the landlord's apartment. When the landlord mistakenly opened the closet door, a backdraft spewed. This engulfed the entire three-story apartment complex within minutes.

Mom was at work at the time. The three Coniker children: Bill, Mary Ann, and Jerry, along with the landlord, barely escaped. All their worldly possessions were lost. They had no insurance. However, in the midst of this calamitous situation, a grace-filled moment manifested itself when the strength of Jerry's mother took hold of her, and she accepted all as the will of God, resigning herself as she prayed, "Jesus, Mary, Joseph, help us!"[4] It is no wonder with such resignation of his mother that Jerry, a witness to such horrific events, was endowed with such a resolve and strength of character from his mother's beautiful example. If Sr. 'Not so Nice' thought Jerry a stubborn individual, then stubbornness will become his strength as time went on, for stubbornness can also be perceived as a strong resolve to not go with the crowd, to stand one's ground on strong, moral, and ethical principles. This trait, as well as witnessing the hard work ethic of his parents and older brother to support the family in times of trouble, surely contributed to Jerry's strong work ethic, as will be demonstrated by his typical long work hours later in life. God was purifying his faithful instrument, Jerry, with the fire of Divine Love by way of crosses and trials in order to prepare him for the great work He had in store him later.

Due to these setbacks, the Conikers were finally forced to move in with Margaret's mother and brother in Park Ridge, Illinois, an upscale suburb northwest of Chicago. Such a last resort option was exceedingly difficult for Margaret to do, due to ill treatment she experienced from these family members in the past and the pent-up jealousies they had of her. Once there, they reverted to their old ways of treatment toward her. This angered the Coniker children to such a degree that they packed their bags and left, but not without first expressing their indignation toward them and letting them know that in no uncertain terms were they going to treat their mother in such an offensive manner.

---

4   Ibid, 7-8.

THE BEGINNING

Back to Chicago they ventured. Jerry was only eleven and Mary Ann fourteen years of age when they settled at Our Lady of Lourdes Parish and accompanying grade school, while brother Bill entered Quigley Minor Seminary in Chicago to study for the priesthood. He too suffered an unpleasant experience and left, again over money, no less. What is it, Bill thought, about the Church that they seem more concerned over money matters than saving souls?

In 1953, when Gwen was thirteen years old, tragedy struck the Billings family. Geraldine, Gwen's oldest sister, suffering from liver cancer and post-partum depression, committed suicide. At the same time, Gwen's other sister, Georgia Rose, had just given birth to a baby girl just two days earlier on Thanksgiving Day. Within the span of roughly forty-eight hours, birth and death paid a visit to Gwen.[5] The birth of her niece, and later her nephew, however, seemed to captivate her and marked a pivotal point whereby she fell in love with babies and the love of life. She even quipped one day, "I'm going to have a dozen babies when I grow up."

---

5   Ibid, 18.

Chapter 2

High School

GWEN AND JERRY MET in High School at St. Gregory's when they were both about fifteen years old. When Jerry spotted Gwen in a sophomore class, it was as though it was love at first sight. He thought to himself, "I'm going to marry that girl!" Not so for Gwen. Jerry would make funny noises at Gwen to get her attention. Gwen mused to herself, "He must really think he's witty!" Jerry would make fun of her make-up, telling her she looked like an Indian squaw, adding some Indian "pow wow" noises and gestures! Gwen found him to be a nuisance at first, even if she found him good-looking. She decided to ignore him. Well, Jerry was not going to let that happen, being the persistent person that he was! However, she soon gave in to his persistence to go on a date with him.[1] Within a short period of time, Gwen discovered within Jerry a charming, conscientious, serious-natured, very disciplined, and well-organized young man who quickly grew on her. Jerry attended Gwen's Sweet Sixteen Party on September 27, 1955. After that, they started to date regularly.

"Jerry was a man of purpose," said his sister, Mary Ann. Others claimed he could be somewhat feisty. He was driven and when he set his sights on something, he pursued it fervently until his goal was achieved. It was that way with the business that he started later in life, his work for saving souls, and it was that

1   Ibid, 19.

way when he pursued Gwen. For her part, Gwen was quite the opposite. She was laid-back and had a way about her that made others feel relaxed around her. She had a calm and patient demeanor and was happy and cheerful. "It took a lot to upset Gwen," Mary Ann Presberg, Gwen's sister-in-law would say of her. "If it happened, you knew she meant business. She was also very beautiful." Both came from families where the faith was instilled in them from a very young age. Jerry's faith kept him out of serious trouble despite occasionally getting into fights initiated by others.

Gwen helped her mother at home and also babysat her sisters' children. In high school, she landed a job where her sister worked, at "Z" Frank Chevrolet, working for August Mauge. Mr. Mauge, and his wife Frances, would end up being a significant relationship in the life of Jerry and Gwen. They loved Gwen like a daughter. They too were devout Catholics.

There was a teacher, Sr. Colleta, who took notice of Jerry and discovered in him some rare leadership qualities. She began to mentor him. It was as though Jerry's father was looking over him from above; something in which Jerry firmly believed. One day, she was speaking to Jerry's mother and said to her, "Your boy has some rare qualities, and I am going to see to it that he develops them." These qualities were the gifts of organization and strong leadership skills. Indeed, time would prove Sr. Colleta spot on! At the same time, Sr. Colleta also noticed that Jerry suffered from a learning disability in reading, which by today's terms is dyslexia. Hence, she saw to it that he was given special help to overcome this. The kindness that this Sister showed toward Jerry was a turning point for him.

Another important event in Jerry's life was when his mother, in her wisdom and foresight, took Jerry to the most prestigious law firm in Chicago. It was called Sidley, Austin, Burgess, and Smith. She took him there in order to teach him "how to speak and act properly," as she explained to him while en route there. She had reviewed the list of firms in the *Lawyers Guide* first before deciding upon this particular one. She intentionally picked the best law firm in Chicago. She managed to somehow get an interview with Mr. Burgess, the senior partner and the most important person in the firm. He was moved by Margaret's attitude and sincerity, as well as the glowing account of her son's gifts, despite the fact that Jerry was only fifteen years of age. Mr. Burgess, who normally did not get involved in personnel, introduced them to William Jansen, the general office manager. They both decided to give Jerry a shot at the mail room and hired him at thirty-five cents an hour. Jerry, at first, was not too thrilled about the idea, as he already had a job that he liked which paid much more money at eighty-five cents an hour. But his mother reassured him, saying, "This is the kind of environment you should be living in. Here you will pick up good manners and you will be associating with the best people." The striking thing about this experience is the lesson it taught Jerry: His mother sought out *the* most important law office in the Chicago Loop, and within that law office, asked to see the head honcho. "When you want anything done, always go to the top," she would say. He would remember that lesson and use it to his advantage many times later in life.

Jerry went to Mass every day and would spend additional time in adoration. At school, he went every day with Gwen and made friends with the celebrant, Fr. John May. While downtown at the law firm, he attended the Franciscan church of St. Peter's. Incidentally, Fr. John May and Jerry would continue their friendship throughout the years. Fr. May later would become Archbishop of St. Louis and, at some point, contracted brain cancer. He offered up his sufferings and his life for what would then be the Apostolate for Family Consecration that Jerry and Gwen would found in 1975.

Jerry's confidence began to increase while working at the law firm as people there began to depend on him for other tasks outside the mail room. One such task he was given was to organize the firm's legal forms, as they were very disorganized and causing a lot of time wasted trying to find the correct one. Jerry noticed the inefficiency and asked Mr. Jensen, the office manager, if he would be allowed to try to put order into the disorder of the various legal forms. This task was right up Jerry's alley and Sr. Colleta would surely have agreed. This event would prove to be extremely profitable for Jerry later on.

After assessing and analyzing the situation, and although challenging, Jerry developed an index and coding system which both streamlined and expedited the time it took to find the correct form. The lawyers were thrilled! It was a huge success! Jerry's reputation for organizing escalated by leaps and bounds! Because of this, Bill Jensen, the office manager, provided Jerry with a large private office and another opportunity to utilize his organizational expertise by putting in order the firm's vast legal library. This effort took Jerry several years to accomplish. He later would develop a universal, retainable communications system. It was a codification system which would enable a person in a jiffy to find the information he or she needed. He would, in time, offer this system on a commercial basis.

COURTSHIP OF GWEN AND JERRY

Jerry and Gwen loved to go dancing, sometimes going twice a week. They would attend a sock hop at St. Gertrude's Parish gym or a dance at the local high school. Jerry occasionally would take Gwen to the "Aragon" ballroom, which goes back to the 1920s, and was the most elegant dance hall in the city. The Arragon would have different bands brought in. Chevy Chase in Wheeling, Illinois, was another dance hall which included dinner and a show. They were both excellent dancers, and they danced and danced and danced! And when they danced, Gwen would anticipate Jerry's steps. It's as though Gwen was anticipating Jerry's steps ever since!

The two of them would go to the Bellarmine Hotel along the North Shore of Chicago, which had one of the nicest lounges with a piano player. It was a beautiful atmosphere. They would also go to other places such as the Drake Hotel, an upscale hotel, where Nat King Cole was singing at the time. They really enjoyed his beautiful voice. They looked older than their age so they were able to order a drink. They would order one each and nurse that same drink all evening. They had a great social life.

They would walk along beautiful gardens, enjoying the beauty, the ambiance, and the company of each other. At school, they would attend Mass together in the mornings before school began. They were on the same page in terms of the faith. They were seen together often at school and ate lunch together. On Sundays, they would sometimes go for a Sunday drive in the country with Jerry's mother or down Sheridan Road near the shores of Lake Michigan or into Niles and Northbrook, looking at houses. Jerry even taught Gwen how to drive a car!

Jerry was beginning to be 'one of the family.' Both the families' parents really liked each other. He was invited to family celebrations. They attended the Good Friday services at Jerry's Parish of Our Lady of Lourdes, and the Midnight Mass at Christmas. It was quite apparent how important the faith and receiving the sacraments were to this young couple.

Jerry and Gwen were elected King and Queen of the senior Prom, a testament to the respect accorded them from their classmates. Unfortunately, however, because Gwen skipped a choir concert, she was prohibited from wearing the crown. Therefore, another couple was chosen.

Sister Anna Marie, the principal, took notice of the very close relationship of Gwen and Jerry at school and became concerned. She informed Gwen's mother about the situation, as well as the priest counselor. The priest exhorted Jerry and Gwen to break up, to give the relationship time to see if the love was really true. Fr. 'Concerned' did not think it wise to not date other people. He felt it would be healthy for them to explore other relationships. So upon graduation, June 6, 1957, Jerry and Gwen, did indeed break up.

Gwen was devastated. She became depressed and lost her appetite. It caused her great suffering. It was a trial for both of them to be apart. During their time apart, Gwen contracted shingles. One month went by, then two, and three, then a year. With each passing day, Gwen grieved more and became more certain that Jerry didn't care for her anymore.

Jerry became engrossed in his work at the law firm and attended De Paul University night school in Chicago. He had been introduced to the workings of the legal and business district. He discovered that men highly sought after were actually approachable, which increased his confidence in interacting with them.

Jerry continued the sacramental life as he always had. He continued to attend Mass daily at St. Peter's and made yearly retreats. He especially liked retreats alone at the Redemptorist Villa Redeemer Retreat House in Glenview with Father Peter Sattler as retreat master.

HIGH SCHOOL

Meanwhile, time went on and fifteen months had gone by, during which there was no communication between Gwen and Jerry. Gwen's boss, August Mauge and his wife, Frances, feeling Gwen's pain over Jerry, suggested that she do a fifty-four-day rosary novena to pray for God's will to be known pertaining to Jerry. The first twenty-seven days would be in petition for her intention, and the next twenty-seven days would be in thanksgiving for the favor received. Gwen thought it a great idea and started the novena immediately. Her intention was that she would see Jerry again.

"GWEN WILL BE GOOD FOR YOU!"

In June of 1958, Jerry's mother suffered a stroke. She fell into a coma for thirty days. Gwen heard the news and went to visit her. When she went, Jerry happened to be there. It was the first time they had seen each other in over a year. They talked much. Gwen left. Still, nothing happened. However, Gwen kept up her rosaries.

One evening, Jerry's mother woke from her coma and demonstrated a remarkable lucidity of mind. It was as though God allowed her this grace, so that she could put her affairs in order and say goodbye to her children. She told them where the papers could be found. She also had final words to say to each of her three children. To Jerry, this is what she had to say, "Take care of Mary Ann. She will need you." She later sat up in bed and exhorted Jerry as if giving him a command and looking straight into his eyes said to him, "You marry Gwen. She will be good for you." Throughout the night, Jerry kept whispering to her, "Offer up your sufferings to the Lord, for He loves you so much." She then went back into her coma and died a week and a half later, on August 19, 1958, with Jerry alone at her side.

Gwen heard the news and attended both the wake and the funeral. She felt a great deal of pain for Jerry's loss. After the funeral, time went on yet again, and Gwen continued to pray the rosary. It would be almost three months later on a cold November evening, when Gwen would come home from work and her father said, "You got a phone call from Jerry. He will call back at 10 p.m." She was ecstatic and praised God! She was so excited! Jerry did indeed call back. When Gwen answered the phone and heard the sound of his voice, her heart started pounding! He asked her out on a date! When she hung up the phone, she could hardly contain herself! She had thought she had lost him forever.

They dated frequently after that. It was the happiest time in her life up to that point. Less than three months later, on Valentine's Day, February 14, 1959, Jerry Coniker, age twenty, proposed to Gwen Billings, at the tender age of nineteen.

When it was asked of Jerry as to what his thoughts were and if he missed Gwen during that eighteen-month absence from her, he had this to say, "I missed her but I was so involved and busy with starting my company. I got lost in my work. I did go out with two of Gwen's girlfriends from St. Gregory during that time but it did not go anywhere. I didn't really know any other girl. Gwen was my one and only girl."

"What traits attracted you to Gwen," he was asked? "Gwen was my best friend. Our children today even saw it in our marriage. I was very relaxed around her. We were two different personalities and totally opposite. I'm rather radical and a driver. Gwen was very laid-back. But you couldn't push Gwen around. If you pushed her and got her riled, you went too far. Everybody knew that. But she would get her way. She never yelled. She made a commitment to herself never to yell. Her mother always yelled. That was one of her goals in life."

Gwen's words as she reflects back and describes the sacred union with Jerry in a talk she gave in 1996:

GOD ANSWERED MY PRAYERS

Deciding a vocation was easy for me, as I loved babies and children, so once I found Mr. Right, whom I wanted to spend my life with – for keeps – all went well only because I searched and prayed for God's will. I understood peace and happiness come from knowing who God is and what He expects of me.

HIGH SCHOOL

I knew at 18 years of age that I didn't know everything, but believed in God and in prayer. And you will see how my prayers got answered, unknown to me, and what God's plans were for my life (it was very plain as the years progressed).

I discovered this very charming, good-looking, conscientious, serious natured, very disciplined and well-organized young man, sitting across from me in our school homeroom back in 1955.

Well, as time went by, and after taking the good counsel from the priest at our school, we graduated from high school in 1957 and parted ways, with the idea we would see each other occasionally.

Well, one month passed, then two, now I was beginning to wonder, I was swelling in anxiety, full of sadness that I lost the man of my dreams. Still in hope for that special phone call, one year passed. As my hope was running out a very dear friend who knew of my disappointment gave me a little booklet called the 54-day Rosary Novena, which consisted of 27 days of prayer in petition and 27 days of prayer in thanksgiving.

Now fifteen months had gone by when I heard of the death of Jerry's mother. I knew her and had great love and respect for her, and was greatly saddened by this news. My mother and I went to her funeral Mass and, of course, I saw Mr. Right, but only had a brief greeting.

Needless to say, this was a very tender, sorrowful time to see him. He, at the young age of 19, had just lost his mother, whom he loved and admired so much [compounded by the sadness that he had already lost his father when he was eleven]. I cherished that moment of seeing him and we parted ways again.

After praying this most powerful Rosary Novena, three more months passed and since my prayer petition said; "May we meet again, dear Lord, only if it is your will," and because this never happened, I thought, it's all over for me. I'm done, cooked, that's it; he is not interested in me.

Never give up, never become discouraged or think God does not answer prayers. We know God is very attentive to all of our needs, wants and desires, but in His time and according to His ways.

To finish this story, I came home from work one cold November evening. By this time 18 months had passed since Jerry and I went our separate ways, when I walked into the house and my dad said, "You got a phone call from Jerry." Well, I was ecstatic, so full of joy, my thoughts flew into praise to God. Thank you, God. I'm so excited, Mr. Right called. God answered my prayers. He must have plans for our life.

In a little less than a year's time, the wedding bells were ringing on August 15, 1959, the feast of the Assumption of Mary, Mother of God and our Mother.

Chapter 3

Early Years of Marriage

ON SATURDAY, AUGUST 15, 1959, the Feast of the Assumption, Gwen and Jerry stood at the altar of St. Matthias' Church in Chicago and pledged their love and lives to each other until death do them part with their simple but profound vow of "I do." Following the Sacrament of Marriage, they immediately went to the altar of Our Lady and entrusted their marriage to her. It would be a defining moment for them in which supernatural grace was poured out upon them and they were given the power to help them sustain their lifelong love. This will be demonstrated throughout the trials of their married lives together. Many years later, in 1990, Gwen, in a letter to Jerry, would re-count that day with these words:

> ...my wonderful spouse, Jerry, remember the day we united our lives in the Sacrament of Love on the feast of the Assumption of Mary, August 15, 1959? We stood at her feet and prayed, asking her to watch over us and guide us in marriage. We gave our lives to Jesus through Mary and she has always been with us in good times and bad. It's been Our Lady that has shown us the way in all our joys and sorrows.

Jerry and Gwen honeymooned in Wisconsin, first at Lake Delevan and then the Wisconsin Dells. They drove there in their 1953 Ford which actually broke down within walking distance of their new home, a two-bedroom apartment on the top floor of the Billings' house. The apartment was re-painted and filled with second-hand furniture provided by Gwen's parents and friends so as to be a suitable dwelling place for the new couple to start their life together.

It was not long after their marriage, several months, in fact, when Gwen became pregnant. To Gwen, though, it seemed like forever! She was starting to become concerned as to whether she would ever be able to get pregnant! Once Gwen did get pregnant, however, other fearful thoughts entered her mind as expressed in her own words:

> *Will I be able to be a parent? Will I know how to care for this baby and those to come? Will I know how to raise them? What will God expect of me? All too many fears crept into my thoughts.*

GWEN AND JERRY'S WEDDING DAY! AUGUST 15, 1959

EARLY YEARS OF MARRIAGE

As time went on, Gwen had many more children. She often referred to her family as 'one of her greatest treasures.' She loved her vocation of motherhood and she looked to the Blessed Mother as her primo role model and example as to how to be a great mother.

While at a Christmas party with relatives, current events were being discussed. Some of these discussions included such topics as the spread of Communism throughout the world, the threat of big government, the possibility of sex education being taught in the schools with no values, and abortion. Abortion would not become legal until 1973 in a landmark U.S. Supreme Court case of *Roe v. Wade*. Already, however, in 1959, it was making its push into society. They all concurred that should the push for these continue without fighting back, a scourge would befall America and transform the very fabric of society. These issues were interconnected and morality was being tested.

It was so disturbing that Jerry had a hard time really believing what he was hearing. He wanted evidence and so challenged his conversationalists to provide him such. Uncle Bob piped up, "Jerry, drop by my house sometime," he said, "and I'll give you plenty of proof."[1]

Jerry did in fact go to Uncle Bob's house, and he did in fact provide Jerry with enough evidence to elicit in him a zealous anger akin to the anger Jesus felt, when he overturned the tables in the temple, accusing the people of making a mockery out of His Father's house.

At the prompting of Uncle Bob to read the book, *Masters of Deceit*, by J. Edgar Hoover, Jerry did read it and was more than convinced of a diabolical influence to destroy America and corrupt the morality of its citizens. Hence, Jerry went to work. There were certain organizations that were spearheading these efforts. The F.B.I. had infiltrated these groups only to discover their true intentions, which were disguised to the public as noble and innocuous endeavors. Jerry was both very patriotic and a man of faith and morals. To him, it would be inexcusable not to take action. It would go against everything he believed in should he fail to act.

So Jerry energetically began to organize groups of like-minded people who

---

1   Ibid, 31.

would be willing to join him in this effort to oppose abortion and valueless sex education in the schools. He held meetings where he could find space, be it in his apartment or even in the basement of the Billings' home. Night after night, these meetings were held. Sometimes multiple meetings would be held and Jerry would have to travel to other places to be at these meetings. He would be up very late at night only to rise and be at Mass at 4:30 am. He fortunately, did not need much sleep. His hard work ethic that he learned so early in life kicked into high gear.

Jerry also could survive on very little food. It was as though eating was an inconvenience to him which took up valuable time which he could be putting to better use. "When it came to eating," Gwen would say, "Jerry was easy to please, and his meals simple to fix. He wished he didn't have to eat. He'd rather skip it. It took up too much time. If it weren't for the peanut butter and jelly, cold roast beef, cottage cheese and peaches, he would have withered away! Hubby always ate on the run; a sandwich in one hand, wheel of the car or telephone in the other and rushing to get to his next appointment. He even had a car phone in the sixties, long before they would become commonplace. That was Jerry. His favorite bedtime snack was graham crackers or fruit or both or sometimes popcorn. Breakfast was important, a must, but toast and cereal did the trick and off he went for a new day."[2] Gwen was always looking after Jerry's needs. As his wife, she made sure that she kept the home going so Jerry could focus on his work, be it his business or his ministerial pursuits.

During this time, Gwen gave birth to their first child on June 22, 1960. A bundle of joy greeted Jerry and Gwen as a baby girl, Maureen Therese, and entered the world seven weeks early and weighing only four pounds. Maureen was kept in the incubator in the hospital until she gained enough weight. As is typical of first time mothers and most especially since Maureen was premature, Gwen kept that little fragile babe next to her day and night to ensure that she kept breathing. Gwen soon learned that babies are tougher than she originally thought.

Gwen's parents were equally delighted at their new granddaughter and

2   Ibid, 32-33.

assisted in taking care of her as well. Gwen thought to herself that every child can have more than one father and mother.

Meanwhile, Jerry had left the law firm and began his first job as a salesman for an office supply company. Essentially, he had to 'cold call' their clients in order to drum up sales, either via phone or in person. In approaching his first client, The Liquid Carbonic Company, Jerry drove around for an hour before gaining enough courage to enter the building. Once he took this first step, though, he made the sale rather easily, much to his surprise! This gave him great confidence to venture forth with zeal. He went the extra mile with his clients which earned him a positive reputation.

Over time, he built up his clientele. In companies with large sales forces, he noticed the inefficiencies and redundancies of record keeping, and the chaos and confusion of the process to just get information easily and quickly. One company, in particular, used over three hundred manuals to oversee their operations. A client like World Book Encyclopedia, with over a hundred thousand salesmen, used special binders and portfolios. Jerry thought about his days at the law firm whereby he brought order from chaos and organized legal forms and the library for the firm. "Why couldn't I do something similar?" he thought. On May 13, 1961, Feast day of Our Lady of Fatima, at the tender age of twenty-three, Jerry founded Coniker Enterprises, which would create, sell, and distribute his customized products and system, including the Control Master-Time Management System. His company would assist other companies to prioritize and organize their information and to provide a standardized sales control system for all salesmen. Later, the company name would change to Coniker Systems, Inc.

Jerry became a very successful businessman. He based his principles and philosophy of success largely on the teachings of Earl Nightingale's *The Strangest Secret*, and Napoleon Hill's *Think and Grow Rich*. He would listen to their records over and over again. Their teachings instilled in him the confidence to be able to be successful at whatever he put his mind to. Part of their philosophy was to maintain a positive attitude and control negative thoughts. "When I went out on my own," Jerry recollected, "I learned that fear paralyzes an individual and literally puts into motion a chain reaction that upsets the body chemistry and affects health. Going on my own at such a young age right at the time when we were beginning a family with our baby, Maureen, and only three hundred dollars in the bank, was not easy. The Nightingale materials helped me to set both long and short-term goals and to discipline myself. I learned that constancy was vital if one was to succeed. That means never to give up no matter how impossible the task."[3] It was an integral part of Jerry's 4C's formula of confidence, conscience, charity, and constancy that he later perfected in his organization of the Apostolate for Family Consecration.

These early lessons learned by Jerry would greatly aid him later in the spiritual life: Discipline to stay the course and develop a regular and consistent prayer life, a positive attitude re-directed to a positive trust in God, taking risks in business to taking risks for God or rather, trusting in God in order to accomplish His will and working to saving souls.

Jerry would, of course, seek only the top executives of corporations, a lesson he learned early from his mother, "When you want anything done always go to the top," she would say. Jerry reflected back on that day his mother brought him to the top law office in Chicago to meet the most important person in that firm. Some of Jerry's clients included Walgreens, Kraft Foods, Culligan, Baxter Laboratories, Wilson Sporting Goods, and IBM Midwest Data Processing Division.

"I learned to pay attention to developing clients," Jerry recounted, "researching them and methodically calling on them until I finally broke through. Kraft Foods was a very large client of ours with some fifty thousand employees. We did over two hundred thousand dollars of business with them in a year, which was a lot of money in the sixties. But it took me several years to crack Kraft Foods, because they were so loyal to their suppliers and such a large, multi-faceted organization. In one deal, I sold one hundred thousand custom easel three-ring binders to Kraft. I became a 'system bug!'" Jerry dropped out of De Paul University to spend his time on his business.[4]

---

3   Ibid, 45.
4   Ibid, 25.

EARLY YEARS OF MARRIAGE

Jerry and Gwen's family was growing! On January 16, 1962, they were blessed with a second daughter, Kathy Lynne! She had dark hair and eyes and was just delightful! Gwen would describe her as "wiggly and healthy!" On July 8, 1963, their third child, another daughter, was born! Laurie Ann would be her name! This was the "tons of fun" baby that Gwen would describe her as! On September 14, 1964, their fourth child, another daughter, Margaret Rose, was born. Now with four children, Gwen was happier than ever! Motherhood just seemed to fit her well, as though she was born for it! She said, "Motherhood kept me busy and I loved every minute of it. Dressing the girls alike was never a chore." She also made look-alike dresses for them!

The children were showered with love. Jerry and Gwen would drive to the country on some weekends, admiring the big houses, dreaming of perhaps owning one someday. They would stop to eat and enjoy their growing family.

The family would move around as their family grew; from a three-bedroom apartment in Niles to a three-bedroom ranch in Highland Park, and later to Deerfield where they bought their first house.

On February 18, 1966, Gwen's father died, having suffered a brain tumor. Eight days later, Gwen gave birth again to another daughter, their fifth, Sharon Marie on February 26, 1966. Five young children and Jerry was rarely home. His business kept him quite busy, as well as his ministry of fighting against the sex education that was being taught in the schools at the time.

As Jerry's business became stabilized and he built up his clientele to a good level, Jerry was able to devote more of his time to the "Movement to Restore Decency Committee," as he called it. He worked at this ministry from 1959 to 1971 some sixty to eighty hours a week. No wonder he had no time to eat or sleep! He would give speeches, nourish his relationships with members, and recruit more members. This experience only served to enhance his talent for organization. God would use this experience as a stepping stone to build on his organizational talent later in life.

With five daughters, Gwen's hands were full and quite busy at home. She loved being a wife and mother. It was her vocation and she knew it. However,

Jerry was rarely home. Mary Ann, Jerry's sister, was asked years later if it bothered Gwen that Jerry was never home. She responded emphatically, "Divorce was never part of her vocabulary. Gwen was always figuring out how she could work with Jerry and the situation at hand, such as Jerry being away a lot, and how she could be there for him." And Gwen demonstrated both her love and fidelity to Jerry in the simple meals she made for Jerry that he could take on the run as he whisked away to his next meeting. For the other family members, however, Gwen would always prepare an elaborate dinner.

As for Jerry, he was thrilled to have a large family. His job was stable and there was enough money to provide for his family. Jerry's goal was never to become rich. As long as his family had a good home, good food, good clothing, and the children had good schooling, Jerry was content. On the weekends, he would take them somewhere such as on a picnic or to the zoo or the park and so forth. Gwen tended to the home and did not concern herself with Jerry's business or ministry. Jerry gave her the entire paycheck and Gwen managed the bills and the house, so he did not have to worry about it.

Five children in about five years were exhausting for Gwen. But Gwen truly loved babies. Still, Gwen prayed to God for some space before they were blessed with more children. Jerry was also sleeping very little. He could go from Monday morning to 9 p.m. Tuesday with no sleep at all! It's surprising he never ended up with mononucleosis!

There was, in fact, a breather but not too much! On February 19, 1968, their first son was born! Their sixth child was named Michael John. "Finally a boy! Now they can stop having children," said some friends exhorting them. However, God would have other plans.

At this time also, the Conikers added to their family a German Shepherd named Rex. The children soon took a liking to him, most especially Kathy, who was six, as they found him to be a gentle animal despite his size. They also bought their first home! It was a four-bedroom house in Deerfield, Illinois. Finally, they had a dishwasher! The balcony overlooked a beautiful weeping willow tree. The patio was also a nice addition.

EARLY YEARS OF MARRIAGE

However, as nice as this was, the neighbors were not too friendly. The Conikers had six children and the neighbors mostly had the typical two. When Rex would break loose, it would cause quite a ruckus with the neighbors who would call the police instead of trying to resolve it with the Conikers. The police would then reprimand the Conikers. Within two years, the Conikers would move to a different neighborhood in Deerfield to a colonial house nestled among tall oak trees. This home had five bedrooms which was a good thing because on August 3, 1970, their second son, Robert Anthony, was born, the Conikers' seventh child.

Jerry's company had grown to forty employees. Every night, Jerry would continue to meet with the Movement to Restore Decency Committee ministry, giving lectures and meeting with people. He would need to travel across the state sometimes and would continue at this hectic pace until 1971.

One time, Jerry was invited to speak to the seminarians of an Episcopal seminary. In that meeting, he was enlightened to a new morality called 'situation ethics.' Situation ethics holds that an act in and of itself is not good or bad, but it becomes so depending on the values it serves and seeks to realize. It is a subjective moral methodology unlike the objective moral methodology in which the Magisterium of the Church has taught for centuries. Situation ethics is a false ethics which serves to justify intrinsically evil acts such as abortion and contraception.

Based on Thomistic theory, a morally good act requires the goodness of the three moral determinates or fonts of morality, which comprise the moral object chosen or objective act, the intention of the person committing the act, and the circumstances surrounding the act; who, what, where, when, how, and by what means. All three must be good for an act to be good. If any one of these determinates fails, then the act itself is not ordered to God, and thereby evil.

Juxtapose 'situation ethics' with the Church's Magisterial teaching of authentic morality of human acts in the case of abortion, for instance. Situation ethics would justify abortion by holding that the act of killing the child is not good per se but then evaluates the intention of the mother for doing so, the innocence of the victim, and/or the circumstances surrounding the situation. It's a subjective approach where there are no rules, no values; only material and nonmaterial things which happen to be valued by a person with a rule of thumb, as it were, to guide one in assessing each concrete situation at hand in making moral choices. So in the case of abortion, the mother might justify it as good, since her circumstances are such that she is a teenager who is unable to support herself, much less a child. She reasons that it is in the best interest of the child to not be brought into the world to a mother who is not able to properly care for the child. Moreover, if the child has a major or minor abnormality, is deformed in anyway, the norm of 'love' is used to justify the mother's decision to abort because, "it would be unfair for the child...no child would want to live with such suffering. It is a decision out of love to abort this child." So the intention and/or the circumstances alone or together are used to arrive at the goodness of the moral goodness of an act.

However, the Church teaches that all three of the moral determinates must be good for the act to be good, not just one of them. Abortion, which is the moral object, is intentional and premeditated murder of an unborn child in the womb of its mother, by the mother with the help of a doctor while giving that doctor her consent. The moral object chosen, ending an innocent life, is deemed bad. Therefore, no amount of good intentions or bad circumstances can make good an act whereby the moral object itself is bad. It contravenes God's laws and is diametrically opposed to love and against human dignity. It says 'no' to God's plan for the life of that child. God is the only One with the authority to take life; He Who is the Author of life.

So here is Jerry at this meeting and faced with this new-fangled morality, much to his shock and dismay. "How can this be," he thought?

On another occasion years later, he was invited to speak to some young women at a girls' camp, ages seventeen to nineteen. It was a camp which attracted well-educated women and was rather strict in the sense of no drinking or smoking allowed. Jerry began to teach them the purpose of Christian marriage and family morals. They began to yell and scream at him, using rather crass and vulgar language, and even hurling insults. This shocked both Jerry and even the counselor, especially at such a well-respected type of camp. It was apparent that these women were already indoctrinated into the culture of death mentality and the left-winged feminist movement. This type of feminist mentality held the belief that being a stay-at-home mother was oppressive. Women needed to delay childbirth and prioritize their careers. So instead of being what they considered a slave to their homes, they entered the workforce in droves so they could be a slave to their bosses instead. "We didn't have the Catechism of the Church like we do today," said Jerry, recounting the incident. "It was post-Vatican II and we were basically told we were going against the Church with our orthodox beliefs. Liberalism had infiltrated the Church and society on a grand scale," he said.

It came to pass that in the section of Deerfield where the Conikers were then living, the local school board announced that it was going to introduce sex education into the schools, including the lower grades. Well, one can only imagine the disappointment this was to Jerry, to say the least. He went into action, gathering his troops and organizing an offense. From mailers, going door to door gathering signatures, to radio promotions as though he were running for public office, Jerry worked tirelessly to stop this insidious proposal. By this time, 1971, he had begun and assisted in beginning twenty-five chapters in Lake County, Illinois to restore decency. He was very confident going into the vote despite sex education becoming a hot issue. He had amassed signed petitions of half the people in his school district. At the meeting, there was utter pandemonium while the opposition shouted and screamed. He was dumbfounded when the board unanimously voted to introduce sex education into the schools. "How could this happen?" Jerry thought to himself rather perplexed. "What about all those signatures which we gathered?"

Jerry did not give up hope but then went to Plan B. He figured he and his allies would campaign for people on his side of the argument to be elected to the school board to reverse this horrid proposal. His efforts ultimately failed, however. It was a bitter pill to swallow for him. The culture of death began to spread all over the country with a contraceptive and abortive mentality. He would ponder and meditate as to why this happened and what he could do to reverse this trend.

It was now 1971, and Gwen, in a letter to her mother March 1, 1971, spoke of her experience of marriage after eleven years with her chosen one, Jerry:

SERVANT OF GOD

*On our wedding day we didn't have the love for one another that we have today. Love is something that grows with each day, through joys and sorrows, thru successes and failures, ups and downs. But you learn to perfect these experiences with each other. The vow promised is **until death do we part.***

It is through life's bumpy ride of the crosses and joys of life in which we come to love our spouse more and more, much like we become closer to our Lord Jesus through the same means.

Chapter 4

First Trial: The Accident and Ensuing Move

In January of 1971, Gwen and Jerry were introduced to Total Consecration to Jesus through Mary according to the St. Louis Marie Grignion de Montfort charism by their friends John and Nonie Hand. They were invited to attend a meeting at the Hands' home in Glenview, Illinois where they would listen to tapes on the Consecration. Jerry and Gwen already had a strong devotion to the Blessed Mother but Jerry had another motive for accepting John's invitation. He had hoped that he could draw John back into the political battle for which he had left.

The tapes were composed by a Servite Father by the name of Fr. James Mary Keane. This priest also had composed the Novena to the Sorrowful Mother, a most popular novena post World War II. Along with Jerry and Gwen at these meetings, there were some ten others there as well. The Hands' presented a homey and inviting environment and served refreshments.

The Conikers were actually pleasantly surprised! Despite their devotion to the Blessed Mother, this time, truths were presented unlike those of what they had heard before and in a very moving and quite convincing manner. They decided to give full attention and study to the book, *True Devotion to Mary*, by St. Louis de Montfort. The more they delved into its mysteries, the more they were convinced that there was a direct message for them personally.

SERVANT OF GOD

As winter progressed, so did their newfound study of the profound writings of St. Louise. But it was one cold winter day, February 4, 1971, that would live on in the Conikers' lives forever. It had snowed during the night, leaving the roads slippery. It was customary for Jerry to drive his four oldest children to school on bad snow days–six, seven, eight, and nine years old. The three youngest children were still at home. Today, however, Jerry felt the weight of a backlog of work and wanted to catch up, so he asked Gwen if she would drive the children to school that day. Gwen complied, as was her custom and all piled into the station wagon.

Gwen was driving down a two-lane country road frequented during the early morning hours with folks driving their children to school or themselves to work. As she was driving, the car suddenly hit a patch of ice. She swerved and veered into the other lane. She attempted to gain control of the car and turn it back into her lane but was unable to do so. The station wagon crashed head-on into a Volkswagen coming in the opposite direction with a seventy-mile-an-hour impact. Both cars, doing about thirty-five miles per hour each, crumpled up like paper.

Miraculously for Gwen, she and her children survived. In a state of shock, she immediately checked on her children. Only one was hurt, Laurie, who had a minor scratch on her forehead when her head hit the dashboard. Not so, however, for the woman in the Volkswagen. Gwen ran to the other car to check on the driver and any occupants. There was only the driver in that car; a woman in her late forties and mother of three. She and her husband were Christian Scientists and did not believe in doctors or modern medication. Gwen found her crushed between the seat and the dashboard and bleeding profusely. Gwen became frantic and immediately sought help from the passing cars. None of the cars stopped. She then decided to run to a nearby home. Upon ringing the doorbell, there was no answer. She went on to the next house. A woman answered the door. Gwen, still in a state of shock, told the woman that there was a serious accident. She asked to use her phone to call her husband and the police. The police soon arrived, followed shortly by an ambulance. It took some time to free the woman from the wreckage. When Jerry arrived, he drove them all to the hospital for observation. Laurie was treated for her minor wound.

The effect of the accident would linger on for Gwen and the children. Reflecting back on that day, they all marveled that they escaped rather unscathed, at least physically. They attributed their protection to the fact that they were praying the rosary together at the time.

As for the woman in the other car, she was in critical condition. The Conikers kept a vigil of prayer for her life and her recovery. Two days later, Gwen would receive a dreaded phone call from the hospital informing her that the woman had passed away. She was devastated. Thoughts ran through her head. What would those poor children do? That could have been me. Then what would have happened to my children? For months, these thoughts kept haunting Gwen. She came to realize that her life and those of her husband and children were at the mercy of God. In an instant, Gwen thought, "God could very much radically change my life." This was very disturbing for her to ponder. Yet, as is God's ways, He would turn tragedy into something good and use it for the betterment of His children.

Up until then, Gwen had been caught up in the hustle bustle of daily life. Her daily duty consumed her life: washing, cooking, taking care of the home and children. For Jerry, it was his job and his efforts to restore decency in the schools and neighborhoods. Had all the focus on daily life blinded them to the truth that God was in charge? That is to say, the truth that all that mattered was to serve God and to belong to Him completely and unreservedly? These are the thoughts that went through Gwen's mind. However, it is true that doing one's daily duty *is* the will of God. Yet to Gwen, she still felt that something was missing from her life. It was that trust in God; trust in Him completely and in Divine providence. Hence, she decided to place her entire life in His hands by re-arranging her priorities. Before, her priorities were family, country, and then God. Now, they would be God first, then family, then country.

Jerry comforted his wife during this period of shock. He was very concerned about her emotional well-being. In an effort to calm her, he kept playing her favorite tape, the "Ave Maria." He also experienced pangs of guilt. "If only

I had done what I was supposed to do," he kept telling himself. "If only I had driven the children to school, none of this would have happened." This was a very trying period for both of them. "The only peace that came to us during this difficult period was from the Blessed Mother," Jerry reflected years later. He continued, "Gwen couldn't get over the accident. She felt so bad for that mother, that family. It was an accident. There was no harm intended. Still, a mother died. I don't think a Volkswagen 'Bug' stood a chance against a station wagon." Asked if Gwen ever met the family, Jerry, reflecting back, recounted, "Gwen met the woman's husband, father of three, only once because the lawyer did not let Gwen talk to anyone or let anyone talk to her. It was a troubling experience for Gwen. The case was ultimately thrown out."

During this period, Jerry and Gwen continued with their meetings at the Hands' house with study and prayer about Total Consecration. They also kept weekly devotions to Our Lady of Fatima, even hosting the Pilgrim Virgin statue in their home and making the Enthronement to the Sacred Heart of Jesus. After hosting the Pilgrim Virgin statue, they adopted the daily rosary. They decided that they, too, would start the thirty-three days of preparation and prayer for total consecration prescribed by St. Louis de Montfort, which they began on February 20, 1971. On April 28, 1971, the Feast of St. Louis de Montfort, Gwen and Jerry Coniker made their formal Act of Total Consecration to Jesus through Mary. The next goal was to get their children to do the same. Gwen would reflect on her consecration experience to others in her writings:

> It was a giving soul who invited Jerry and me to learn about Total Con-
> secration..... After six weeks, Jerry and I made a Total Consecration
> to Jesus through Mary on the feast day of St. Louis de Montfort, April
> 28, 1971. Life has not been the same ever since. Our priorities in life
> changed. God became the center. He became first in everything we did.
> Without Him, we were nothing. He's the boss, Our Creator, Redeemer,
> and Savior. God is in charge of our lives, so why not cooperate with Him
> and go to His mother? Uniting your will with Jesus's and Mary's brings

peace of heart. Now, peace of heart does not mean you're going to live on easy street. No way! You will be sent crosses, trials, disappointments…but nothing will come that you won't be given the grace to bear.

Here's what happened…. Right away a catastrophe, a cross, hit our life. I hit a head-on collision early one morning, taking the children to school. The cars were totaled and the woman driver of the car was killed. Our four daughters and I were not injured. But this traumatic accident affected our entire family. Where could I turn? I felt terrible knowing some mother of a family was killed. I could only think it was my fault. How could I face her family? So I turned to the Blessed Mother and I was comforted. The prayers and support from family and friends helped too, but if I didn't have an attachment to the Blessed Mother, I know I wouldn't have made it.

After our consecration and catastrophe, a series of events took place in our family life that brought great joy. We invited the Pilgrim Virgin statue into our home and set her in a place of honor for one week, and we adopted the family rosary. At the end of the week, when the Ambassadors of Mary came to pick up the Pilgrim Virgin, we had the Enthronement of the Sacred Heart of Jesus in our home. Jesus had a place of honor in our home, and He became the center of our life. Devotion to Mary and the Fatima message was most important to us and it drew us to Jesus in a deeper way.

In a letter dated March 1, 1971, Gwen would tell her mother all about the Consecration, how she came to learn about it, what it entailed, and her experiences of it. So in this letter, after Gwen's initial affectionate greetings to her mother and happenings of her children and their recent flu experience, Gwen continues:

…. You did beat me to the punch [mother] because once I told you of my mishap [accident], you would be uneasy. I had planned to call you to see if you were doing good…. The Blessed Mother is taking care of things….

SERVANT OF GOD

Let me tell you the most wonderful experience Jerry and I had [about the Consecration].... It was a wonderful experience. I learned so much on the Blessed Virgin Mary and how we can consecrate our lives to her. Mary, Queen of the Universe is the guiding star to Jesus. Nothing happens without her. So by making the Act of Consecration you give her your full will willingly. In other words, you become a 'slave' of Mary. Since she is the Queen of the Universe everything and everyone is hers anyway. So therefore, this study took me approximately fifteen hours so you can just imagine how long I could be writing.

To sum it up Mother, I would like to send you the book, <u>True Devotion to Mary</u> by St. Louis de Montfort. If you just read the book now and when you come back we could go to a forum together. I know you will gain a lot more love for Our Lady and will in return receive many graces. I know how I feel each day – so light and bright, good inside as well as outside. The peace of mind and heart.

So we do have a lot to look forward to while we are here in this life. But the real life is Life Everlasting with God and His Mother in heaven.

Also this forum [weekly Consecration meetings] has brought me into spiritual reading. My oh my! Where have I been that I haven't discovered this a long time ago? Every chance I can find, it seems I'm reading. When you think of it, Mother, you are truly lucky on how you received the gift of Faith as this is a gift from God.

You have taken the vow of Matrimony. This is one of seven sacraments from which much grace can be obtained. Now this isn't just words. This is very serious and important. I can only speak of my experience through the last eleven years with my chosen one, Jerry.

FIRST TRIAL

PORTUGAL

During one of the meetings at the Hands' house, the Hands expressed their desire to move to Portugal. It was actually more than just a desire at that point as they had taken steps to contact family members there and had already made up their minds to go and live there. When asked as to why they were taking such a radical step, the Hands told them that they believed that atheism was gaining a stronghold in the United States and the immorality of the country was in great decline. They did not want to raise their children in such an environment. They recounted the promise of Our Lady to always preserve the Dogma of the Faith in Portugal and it was a very Catholic country. They would raise their children there in the faith. Once they were older and had a solid Catholic foundation in the faith, they would return to the United States and work at converting their native land. It was then that they invited the Conikers to come with them.

Well, this thought, at first, seemed ridiculous to them. However, after their Consecration, they started to see things with a different set of lenses. They pondered what the Hands had said. For Gwen, the recent accident had a huge effect on her. She immersed herself in the thirty-three days of preparation for the Consecration and her spiritual life began to take on a whole new meaning for her. Had it not been for the Consecration and resorting to prayer during this most tragic experience of the car accident, in order to overcome her grief, she would have been torn apart. For her, Portugal afforded the opportunity to immerse herself in Mary, Our Lady of Fatima, by being on a spiritual retreat, if you will. So the accident was an impetus to go to Portugal. "Until the accident happened, I don't think I could get Gwen to leave the country," Jerry reflects years later.

For Jerry, however, things were a bit more complicated. They already had seven children and Gwen was pregnant with their eighth! They also had a home and Jerry had his own business. Moreover, Jerry was very involved in leading the effort in the organization to restore decency. This was definitely something that required careful prayer, pondering, and discernment.

Gwen expresses her thoughts and feelings about this whole concept of moving to Portugal in her writings:

The idea or thought of living in Fatima, Portugal, was talked about with the Hands and we thought they were crazy. I said, 'You mean you want to leave this country, your home, relatives and friends and move to Fatima? That's giving up everything!' But after several visits with our friends, the Hands, about their idea of moving to Fatima, they invited us to join them. Well, that was out of the question! We were expecting our eighth child and we had just purchased a large home. Jer had his own company and he was coordinating 25 evangelization teams in Lake County, Illinois, for the campaign to stop abortion and keep sex education out of our schools. After much prayer and many novenas, we asked the Blessed Mother for some signs. The thought of Fatima, the love and concern we had for the Fatima message became so alive in our hearts and some signs were beginning to appear. We decided to move there on September 8, 1971, Our Blessed Mother's birthday!

Like the garden, if you prepare the soil, plant, water and weed, it causes growth. So, too, our soul if it's prepared, enriched and nourished through prayer, consecration and knowledge, God causes growth. We are all 'God's co-workers.' In St. Paul's First Letter to the Corinthians, he was urging the Corinthians not to be divided but to be united in the same mind and in the same purpose. (1 Cor. 3:6-9)

Over time, Jerry's outlook began to change. Was God trying to tell him something? His self-assured attitude and relying only on his own efforts were thus far very successful in his business. But why is it that his efforts to restore decency, a spiritual battle, had so little success? Could it be that the tactics he used in the business world were not going to be effective in a spiritual setting? The spiritual realm is much deeper, much more ominous. The forces are much more powerful, and therefore, require skills and strength far greater than any mere human would have. This battle is evil, against the forces of Satan. In the business of saving souls, Satan is not going to play by the rules. He is going to pull out all the weapons in his pernicious arsenal to defeat his earthly opponent. Unless, of course, if that earthly opponent brought in reinforcements far more powerful than himself; spiritual forces; heavenly forces.

At these meetings at the Hands' house, Jerry was hearing for the first time how to go about fighting these evil forces. The more he studied the writings of St. Louis de Montfort, the more he understood that he was being introduced to a new strategy for carrying on the struggle. He finally became convinced of this and began to ponder seriously the Hands' invitation to go with them to Portugal.

Still, there remained the practical obstacles standing in their way before the Conikers could consider such a magnanimous move. They would need to sell a home. What would become of Jerry's business? And also, what about the organization to restore decency? Who would take the lead on that? However, the thought of raising their children in a God-centered country was appealing to Jerry and Gwen. The more they pondered it, the more the idea was not as ridiculous as once thought. So accordingly, they began a discernment period.

They decided to ask for a sign from heaven. But what kind of sign? If they asked for one sign, it could easily be misinterpreted. So they decided to ask for several. Well, since there are several obstacles preventing them from moving, why not ask for all three of their obstacles to be removed? That's it! Then there needed to be a time frame. So they prayed that if it was God's will that they move to Portugal then all three obstacles in their way be removed by the end of June. As it was currently the end of April, two months seemed like a reasonable time limit. Surely if all three of these obstacles were removed, that would certainly be a strong argument that it is God's will that they uproot their large family and go, for these were very difficult obstacles to overcome. Never underestimate the power of God!

THE MIRACLE

One night, Jerry and Gwen were unable to make it to the Consecration meeting. So John Hand later brought the tape recorder over to their house. As he approached the house, he was blinded by the lights surrounding their home which was at a dead-end street. John thought to himself, "They must have installed some new floodlights." When he arrived, he asked Jerry, "When did you get those lights installed outside? They're blinding!"

"What do you mean?" Jerry asked, confused, "We just have the usual one hundred-watt light bulbs."

John responded, "Well, when I got out of the car and walked toward the house, they were blinding me." They both then went outside and John could no longer see the lights. John was convinced it was a miracle.

"Sell all that you own and distribute the money to the poor, and you will have treasure in heaven; then come, follow me." (LK 18:22) The Conikers started their efforts to sell their house. It was a large one and there was a similar house very near them which had been up for sale for over a year and had not yet sold. The real estate market, at the time, was poor. As if this is not enough of a challenge, they also insisted that no "For Sale" sign should be placed near the house in an effort not to disturb the neighbors. The Blessed Mother and St. Joseph would just have to sell the house without the sign, they reasoned.

Then there was the organization to restore decency. It had grown to over four hundred people and Jerry was the leader. He just couldn't abandon them without leadership. He would not only face hostility by both friends and enemies but more importantly, without proper leadership, what would become of this noble effort? Could he find a suitable leader in time? Would that person be willing to take on this important responsibility of opposing sex education and abortion?

Finally, there was Jerry's business. Even if he could find a buyer, how would the new owners be able to get along without at least a year's training? It was not yet that lucrative of a business even though it had the potential. But it was enough for Jerry, at the time being, to support his family in a comfortable manner. The business also allowed Jerry to be his own boss and it allowed him time to tend to the organization.

These obstacles sure seemed insurmountable, especially with only two short months to overcome them. "There was a lot of prayer going on," Jerry's sister, Mary Ann who was a Supernumerary member of Opus Dei, would say, reflecting back. She continued, "It was not Gwen's personality to leave family and home and sell everything to follow Jesus. The accident brought Gwen to give everything up. Jerry provided well. They never needed anything material. The children dressed well. They had a nice five-bedroom home. Going to Portugal would be a huge contradiction to their marriage. Gwen had to give up everything: home, country, family, and friends."

In addition to these seemingly insurmountable obstacles, there was pressure from family and friends to get them to change their minds. Jerry's brother, Bill, sought to dissuade Jerry from 'making such a drastic move.' "You have seven children and are on the way to having your eighth! Yet you are thinking of uprooting yourselves and taking off for a godforsaken country like Portugal?" objected Bill.[1] The whole concept was beyond his comprehension.

Friends of Gwen pressured her as well, even suggesting divorcing Jerry. But Gwen would have none of it. They all thought the Conikers were crazy! Gwen's mother had just moved from Florida at the pleading of Gwen so that she could be a grandmother to her children. Upon hearing the news, she was very angry and frustrated. She wondered why on earth they were moving to a place like Portugal. "Where is Portugal, anyway, and why there?" she questioned Gwen. Even the children needed to get a map to find out where it was. For the five younger children, the whole idea of moving to Portugal was one of great adventure!

Then there was Rex, the family German Shepherd. Although he was Kathy's dog, the whole family loved him. Kathy was eight years old at the time. It was hard for Kathy and all of family to see Rex drive away with someone else. Even the children experienced crosses amidst the excitement of the move.

Jerry reflecting back on their reactions is as follows: "If I'd said that we were going to Portugal for our health, people would have said, 'Fine!' If I'd said we were going to Portugal for pleasure, they would also have said, 'Fine!' If we had even said we were going for business reasons, they would have still said, 'Fine!'

---

1   Ibid, 51.

But when we told them that we were going to Portugal because we believed that it was what God wanted us to do, they said, 'You're crazy!'"[2] One by one, much to their amazement and surprise, the obstacles started to melt away. For Gwen and Jerry, God had made known His will clear enough. Only God's hand could be in the removal of all these obstacles as will be now elucidated.

Their home sold very quickly despite little advertising. The contract for the sale of their home was submitted on May 13, 1971, the feast of Our Lady of Fatima! Soon after, out of nowhere came a very capable and energetic young man from amongst the members of the Movement to Restore Decency Committee who volunteered to take over the organization. The only thing that remained was the sale of the company. This took a bit longer.

Days became weeks and still no sign of a buyer. Close to the end of June, Jerry received a phone call from the president of a company in which they were closely associated. Jerry had told him that he would not be able to see him until after the Fourth of July holiday. However, the man insisted, "No, come see me Tuesday July First." Jerry went to see him, and on that very day, he sold Coniker Systems to Flick-Reedy Corporation! Just in the nick of time! "We agreed," Jerry said, "that the company would honor all of Coniker Systems obligations, including the employment of forty people and the maintenance of the systems that I had installed for Baxter Laboratories, Walgreen's, Wilson Sporting Goods, DeSoto, Chemical Coatings, Culligan, Kraft Foods, Illinois Bell Telephone, and others." These were the clients who yielded consistent revenues. Jerry continued, "my Company would have been worth a small fortune with the contracts, clients, patents, and exclusive systems that we owned."[3]

"Being a preferred supplier for word-processing supplies was a great plus. An entirely new industry was starting to blossom, one that IBM pioneered with their MagCard Automatic typewriter, which promoted Word Processing Systems. But since I was unwilling to stay for a year to arrange a smooth transition and train personnel, I was forced to sell the company for only twenty thousand

---

2   Ibid, 51.
3   Ibid, 49.

dollars. It was, in fact, a substantial loss considering the value of good-will and the systems value." In reality, Flick-Reedy Corporation wanted to use Jerry's clients to sell their computer systems to.

Still, for Jerry, it was enough money to cover his debts, transportation of his family and furniture to Portugal. Jerry was making $40,000 a year before he sold the company; but, after the sale, his salary would be twenty thousand dollars a year that he would need to support his family in Portugal, because the cost of living was much lower there. Miraculously, his salary was renewed annually, because the Chairmen of the board of Baxter Laboratories told Flick-Reedy people that they probably wouldn't do business if Jerry was no longer associated with them. He figured that once in Portugal, he would simply start a new business that would support his family for the duration of their stay. Our Lord gave Jerry just enough for his current needs and no more.

The whole family now set about preparing for the big journey! They needed to tackle the very practical aspects of the move such as shipping furniture and appliances in advance, so that they would arrive about the same time that the family would arrive and not have to wait too long for them. They set a departure date of September 7, 1971. That way, they would arrive in Portugal on September 8th, the Feast of the Birth of Mary. Meanwhile, Gwen was getting more pregnant by the day! By September, she would be a whopping eight months pregnant! Imagine trying to relocate a family of nine with seven young children including a baby and a couple of toddlers to another country. Even getting on the plane would be an exhausting feat for a pregnant mother with little ones, and all the belongings that they are taking with them!

As their home sold and they needed to move out, an interim place was necessary until their departure in roughly three months. So Jerry went in search of a suitable place for his family. He found a small summer cottage for rent along the shores of Powers Lake, Wisconsin.

Jerry recalls that special peaceful summer on Powers Lake. "While there, we had a beautiful statue of Our Lady of the Immaculate Conception in concrete that we placed in the back yard with a blue floodlight on it. Every night, when I would come home from work, I would turn on the light and play three records of spiritual hymns. It was a consoling experience seeing Our Lady bathed in blue in a completely dark area near Powers Lake. I was also starting to slow down from the extremely active life I had been accustomed to leading. That same statue would later stand in the front yard of our home in Portugal."[4]

Maureen, the oldest and eleven at the time, recalls the wonderful memories of that summer home and being by the lake. She would help her mother with the little ones. She too, like her mother, loved babies! Maureen recounts, "We would pray the family rosary in the evenings. We didn't always want to do it, of course. It helped that our parents had some beautiful pictures of the various mysteries that we would look at to help us meditate upon. Today, I am glad that Mom and Dad gave us our faith and instilled in us the importance of prayer, and especially the family rosary."[5]

The Conikers were moving with two other families: The Hands who had two teenagers and a twenty-year-old mentally handicapped son, and the Morans with their four young children. They were also in correspondence with the Drakes who lived in Lisbon, who were relatives of the Hands. They prepared a place for them upon their arrival.

Mary Ann Presberg, Jerry's sister, who had twelve of her own children, went to the airport to see them off with her children. She recalls that time, "It was quite a scene. Everyone was crying. Their cousins didn't want them to go." The Presberg children were close to the Coniker children, having lived close to each other in Deerfield, and would frequently get together often for family dinners, birthdays, holidays, and so forth. Mary Ann continues, "Gwen and Jerry felt that moving to Portugal was where they belonged. The Church in America was in turmoil. They left with the idea that they would not be back and that it would be very good for the children. So as you can see, it was quite an emotional day for all of us.

---

4 Ibid, 52.
5 Ibid, 53.

Chapter 5

Life in Portugal

THE CONIKERS TOUCHED DOWN in Lisbon, Portugal, and went to the hotel that the Drakes had secured for them. While the Drakes had described the hotel as 'a nice place,' it was in fact far from nice according to the opinion of the others who described it to be akin to a fourth-class hotel, which was also located in a questionable part of the city.

It took time getting used to life in Portugal and their customs. They experienced many inconveniences from their initial living conditions, to missed meals due to not being aware of the time the meals were served throughout the country, to trying to live day by day not understanding the language, and getting along in the practicalities of life. It was hard to realize one couldn't even get a sandwich in a city like Lisbon if it were not the meal time.

Kathy Coniker recalls, "I remember when we first landed in Portugal. I found it very strange hearing the people babbling on in Portuguese. The people drove like maniacs. The hotel where we stayed did not have bathrooms in the rooms. Rather, they were down the hall. The cleaning woman could not understand us when we told her that we needed soap. So we tried to show her by acting out washing ourselves. It was quite an ordeal!"

Kathy continued, "I remember looking out the window of our hotel room and seeing a man carrying a table on his back while pulling a little wagon. I kept watching him. He stopped and set up a shoe-repair stand. I couldn't believe it! I also saw women carrying things on their heads. It was a very different experience for me than what I was used to."

After a brief time, the three families moved out of the hotel and into a large home on a hill that the Hands rented in a little town called São Pedro. São Pedro was roughly twenty miles east of Lisbon. There were twenty people total living in that house with only one bed and no furniture. Since Gwen was expecting baby number eight very soon, she slept in the bed while all the others slept on the floor.

The village of São Pedro was one of the many villages along the Atlantic coast in a hilly area. It was populated with wealthy Portuguese folks as well as Americans who had business dealings at the capital. The people there were friendly. Fisherman made their living by providing a fresh supply of seafood to the inhabitants, while vacationers basked in the sun on the beach.

Although the winters were mild, heat was still necessary. Butane-gas heaters were used since they had no central heating. The electric heaters often blew up the transformers outside when connected. As far as shopping for groceries, small stores were in abundance. For Gwen, it took some time before she actually understood exactly how much money she was spending on groceries.

The men went exploring around the area, being careful to note the street signs so that they could find their way back home. They did manage to meet a waiter in a restaurant who spoke some English. He proved to be quite an asset to them in numerous ways plus helping them translate.

Maureen reflects on her experiences, "It was a difficult adjustment for everyone. On the day we arrived, I remember Dad taking us for a ride with some man who was showing us where we were to go to school, which was a school for American students. It was held in a garage! We were not interested at all. We were moaning and complaining that we were tired and hungry for some good American food. We finally found this little restaurant where someone spoke English. Only one thing on the menu sounded good; fried eggs, steak, and French fries. It soon became our favorite."

Over time, the cramped living conditions motivated Jerry to seek a place where they would have their own space to live. Jerry found a three-story duplex house that had private front and back yards, bearing hedges and shrubs with beautiful pink flowers. He rented it for ninety dollars per month. The home was situated about half-way down a hill while the Hands lived at the top of the hill. Living on the side of the hill gave visibility to the sea, and it assisted them in getting their Volkswagen bus started by rolling it down this hill.

It was after this that the Conikers' furniture arrived from the States; three truckloads full! But the rented house already had plenty of furniture. When the caretaker of the house, the sister of the owner, saw all that furniture, she got very anxious. "If you try to get all that furniture into the rooms," she complained, "you'll ruin my brother's house!" Jerry used his persuasive powers to convince her that he not only would not ruin the house but he would put everything right.

Before the men were allowed to unload any of the furniture, Jerry went through each room and assigned code numbers to the spot where each piece of furniture was to go and then he codified each item as it came off the truck. Jerry's genius for organization paid off! All the furniture fit into the house without causing any damage to the landlord's existing furniture!

The Sears electric appliances were next. They needed to be hooked up. Jerry was assured by Sears that the appliances would operate normally in Portugal. This would remain to be seen. They meticulously followed the instructions for each machine. The washer and dryer were the most important items. After all, they were a family of nine, soon to be ten. All that laundry! However, after connecting the plugs, the machines both blew up! What an inconvenience, for Gwen especially, as she was the one who did most of the washing. Fortunately, Jerry was able to get the washer working but not the dryer. Spare parts would need to be ordered from the States. In the meantime, Jerry rigged up a clothesline using knotted cords, coat hangers, and pulleys that hoisted the clothes up and down their three-story stairway! It was quite a conversation piece to their Portuguese friends but it worked!

One of the Coniker children describes daily life and living conditions in Portugal: "We were all excited when our parents found a house which had a small pool in the back yard. When the trucks came with the furniture that our parents had shipped from the States, the landlady kept rattling on and on in Portuguese, but we could not understand. She just could not believe all those things were ours. We had even brought a stove and a refrigerator. The Portuguese appliances were doll-size! One thing we did not bring was a dishwasher." One wonders how the Portuguese people managed at all without all the appliances that the Americans used and took for granted.

"We used a room on the third floor as a little chapel where we would often pray. Dad used this space a lot. Family prayers and the rosary were prayed in the living room since the chapel was too small for everyone to fit. Dad would have us pray the whole rosary. Sometimes on long journeys, like when we drove to Fatima, we would pray all fifteen mysteries of the rosary!"

The house had three floors. Maureen, Kathy, and Laurie stayed on the third floor. On that floor were also Jerry's office, the chapel, and the bathroom. The yard was divided into four parts by tall bushes–the marble patio, the pool, the swings, and the garden. The statue of the Immaculate Conception, which was at the Conikers previous home in Powers Lake, was placed in the front yard. A blue light shone on it at night.

Gwen expresses her experiences of Portugal in a September 12, 1971 letter to her mother and sister, Georgia:

> *What an experience already! We are in for a big adjustment. We may or may not survive it. We would like a place of our own. There is a shortage of homes so we will have to hunt. No such thing as a realtor here. You find homes by talking and asking people.*
>
> *The food is different of course. Menus are in Portuguese so it is a hit or miss. Fruit is plentiful and sold on every street it seems. Peaches, grapes, bananas, pears, melons, inexpensive and delicious. The food is very reasonable but you have to know what to order. The U.S. dollar exchange was great so it wasn't at all expensive.*

LIFE IN PORTUGAL

All cars are VW or Fiats. No such thing as stop signs, just beep and go – policemen control traffic in busy sections. Churches are huge and many of them three on one block. Masses are every hour. Our Lady of Fatima Statues are everywhere.

Women dress very modestly here, colorful and fashionable people look much like Italians. They seem to be polite, thoughtful and happy.

Waiting in line for the washroom, the people must like or respect Americans, they offer you first. At the park, waiting for the children to ride the horse or swing, they offer you a turn. One boy about 10 years or so offered to give Robert a turn on a swing. A lady in the store took time to explain the money system to me. The people at the bank too were wanting to be helpful – he traced down a doctor for me and set up an appointment – and then took us to her office so I would know how to find it when my appointment came up.[Gwen was due in three weeks.]

This whole country is filled with parks, flowers, fountains, really pretty. It is also very clean. There is swimming all along the ocean–waves very scenic and thrilling. I guess swimming season goes through November and starts again in April.

We send our love and prayers to you.

Jerry and Gwen

p.s. All the homes here are addressed by a phrase.
Ours is: "House of the Good Morning Sun."

In Portugal, Maureen and Kathy took turns every other day to stay home, get the boys dressed, and make breakfast. This consisted either of oatmeal or cream-of-wheat with toast, fruit and Dad's famous hot lemon-peel water. Some days they had eggs. Maureen would get the little boys: Mike, Robert and Joe, into their pajamas every night. Kathy was in charge of doing all the dishes by hand every night. Laurie helped with the laundry. The family went to 7:00 a.m. Mass every day. To start the Volkswagen bus, they had to push it down the street and up the little hill so it could roll down.

The children did not attend the school held in the garage for very long. Soon, they were enrolled in a Portuguese school run the by Salesian Sisters. Maureen struggled with the language. Maureen recalls, "I hated the school. Our classmates made fun of us on a regular basis. *Americanas*, the kids would call us. One reason was because we had to wear long skirts. School hours were long, from 9 a.m. to 5 p.m., not what we were used to. There was a two-hour lunch which seemed to me to be the longest part of the day. I remember being so bored I would sometimes write to my cousin back home, whom I dearly missed. Or sometimes Kathy and I would take the bus home and Mom would have a good lunch ready for us. This made it a treat to go home during lunch."

"One of us would stay home to make breakfast for the family," Maureen continued. "I was now twelve years old and starting into the rebellious stage. At that time short skirts were in style, but Mom and Dad had a seamstress make our skirts go below the knee. I was furious and cried for a couple of weeks. But Dad did not give in. Then I remember giving him a hard time about going to daily Mass. I was always in trouble for sassing and spent a lot of time in my room."

The Conikers were enriched by many varied experiences. Life in Portugal was filled with constant annoyances and inconveniences. The Portuguese people simply did not do things the way they were done in the States. One needed to be humble and accept this. People there could not be pushed to do things quicker, even with money as a motivator. "It doesn't matter," was their constant response. The language barrier also presented its own set of challenges. Some of the children picked up the language while others struggled. Gwen and Jerry would use tapes and dictionaries to assist them in learning the language. Still, Jerry would take along Laurie as his 'interpreter' when he needed one!

Then there were the shopping experiences! One cannot buy in bulk in Portugal. With such a large family, the Conikers were used to buying in bulk. But there, items were sold only in ones or twos. This made things a bit challenging. Gwen went to the butcher to order some rabbit. Much to her surprise, the butcher took a rabbit out of the cage, snapped its neck, skinned it and handed it to her, head, eyes, the whole shebang! If that wasn't shocking enough, when she went to buy a turkey for Thanksgiving from a farmer, he picked a fat one from the flock, and, while his partner held it by the legs, he chopped off its head and, with the blood gushing from its neck, handed the whole bleeding mess to Gwen, who was shocked and speechless.

Once they settled into daily life, it became for them like a two-year retreat. It was a time for slowing down, enjoying family, praying, and visiting Fatima monthly. For Jerry, it was a complete opposite lifestyle that he was used to living in the States. In the States, he would hustle and bustle, rushing about to one meeting or another between the demands of his company and the organization. He would get little sleep, smoked like a chimney, and eat on the run. But now, in Portugal, in peaceful surroundings and quiet, Jerry could sit back and think and pray. Amazingly, he also quit smoking cold turkey and never smoked another cigarette again! Jerry wondered how he had led such a hectic lifestyle. There was plenty of time now to spend with his children. They were happy to have their Dad around a lot more. They would sit and talk, go on walks, picnics, or go visit some of the interesting historic places in the area. While the children were at school, Jerry would go off to pray, sometimes nine to ten hours. He would attend Mass daily and read a plethora of spiritual books. He had a strong devotion to St. Joseph whom he prayed would provide for his temporal needs and family. Our Blessed Lady was forming Jerry in the spiritual life and for his future mission. It was there in Portugal, and in his quiet reflection and prayer time, that the Apostolate of Family Consecration was conceived, later to be born in America.

As Gwen was already eight months pregnant upon arriving in Portugal, it would not be long until the little one would arrive, so Jerry solicited the names of the best doctors in Lisbon. Lisbon would be the place they would go for Gwen to give birth. Surely their medical care would be more sanitary than what Jerry had witnessed in a hospital in the village of São Pedro. In the hospital at São Pedro, Jerry watched as a nurse gave an injection to a patient, only to use the same needle to give an injection to another patient after holding the needle over a gas flame. That must have been her idea of adequate sterilization. "The truth was," says Jerry, "that medical care in Portugal was so bad that only God could have preserved us from any serious illness or injury. I believe that as Americans our resistance was so low I doubt if we could have survived Portuguese hospitals."

Jerry settled on a female doctor who came highly recommended. As Jerry is a man of mission and purpose, he stressed to the doctor the need for her to be available and present at Gwen's delivery. He requested multiple contact phone numbers. Amazingly, she gave him at least twelve phone numbers! Jerry, always the planner, also made several practice runs, to ascertain the time it took and the best route to take to drive from São Pedro to the hospital in Lisbon, a distance of twenty miles. Gwen had a tendency to wait until the last minute to leave for the hospital.

On the morning of October 28, 1971, Gwen told Jerry that she felt that the time had come to go to the hospital. While the Hands watched the other children, Jerry ran Gwen to the hospital. She clutched her green scapular of Our Lady as she went through her labor pains. They sped along.

As they entered the hospital, Jerry tried to communicate to the nurses the fact that Gwen delivers very quickly. They didn't believe him. Gwen started to deliver the baby and everybody panicked. The nurses put the gas mask on Gwen but did not connect it to the tank. It was utter mayhem! The doctor rushed in, however, in her haste, she got her hand caught in her coat and was not able to deliver the baby. Jerry stood right next to Gwen's bed as the nurse delivered little Joseph Vincent! Of all of Gwen's pregnancies, this one was the fastest, the easiest, and totally natural with no pain reliever!

About two weeks later, the Conikers had dear friends, Frank and Mary Fran Flick, visit from the United States. What a treat that was for everyone! The Flicks also were devout Catholics. They were first in Lisbon where Frank bought a case each of peanut butter and grape jelly for the Conikers. Grape jelly was hard to find since most of their grapes went to make wine. Hence, the Coniker children were so excited to receive such a rare find and thought it a gift from heaven!

On November 10, 1971, the Conikers and the Flicks went by car to Fatima for the first time, which was about sixty miles north of São Pedro. To both Gwen and Jerry, who both had such a strong devotion to Our Lady, especially to Our Lady of Fatima, this was a dream come true. Jerry experienced some of the deepest emotions of his life. As he climbed the steps to the Shrine, he felt as though he would do anything for Our Lady even unto death if necessary. He was moved to tears by this experience.

After visiting the Basilica, they went to the tombs of the two Fatima children, now Sts. Jacinta and Francisco, to whom Our Lady appeared to in 1917. Their cousin, Sr. Lucia and the third Fatima seer to whom Our Lady appeared and spoke, was still living and a religious sister at the time. Sr. Lucia Santos is now a Servant of God, and steps are being taken for her cause to progress toward Beatification. They also visited the *Cova da Iria*, the place where Our Lady appeared, in which a chapel now marks the spot, and knelt and prayed before her statue. The entire family loved the Fatima experience. The Conikers would afterward make monthly pilgrimages to Fatima.

Gwen and newborn son,
Joseph Vincent,
October, 28, 1971 in Portugal.

"What was embedded in my mind," says Jerry, "was that Our Blessed Mother at Fatima had told the children every time she appeared to them, 'Say the rosary every day for the end of the war because only I can obtain it.' She spoke about the future, about Russia and the spreading of Communist error throughout the world, and about her ultimate triumph." Gwen expresses her life in Portugal to her mother in some excerpts from letters dated April 3rd, April 6th, and May 8th 1972:

SERVANT OF GOD

We are at this very moment enjoying our [duplex] house [only $95 per month]. I can remember living on Berwyn in my bedroom without central heating and having a wardrobe – that is not how it is here. No closets and no central heating. People here have learned to do without and don't care for heaters.

It is beautiful. The waves are huge and cold but the children love it. All are here [at the beach] except Joseph who is home napping while Maria [a woman that befriended the family the first week they arrived] is cleaning house. Even our pup, Butterscotch, is here. The beach is very clean and the kids are making castles in the sand. This is really lovely. The tide is moving closer and I can write until I'm washed out.

Mom, you should come. You would love it. You are perfectly free to come – no job, good health. Put all your troubles and worries in a box and get a flight here.

Boy! These waves are breathtaking! This is quite a vacation spot. We happen to be living amidst all the beauty in Europe. My only big wish is – for my whole family to come here and live. I miss you all. Georgia, Don & kids, Maryanne and family. This is my suffering.

We have just finished Easter vacation with the children. They had two weeks off, and it was great as every day Jerry, the kids and I have worked, prayed, and played together. Holy Thursday was bright, sunny and warm. While I stayed home with Robert who had a little fever, Joseph, Jerry, and Mike and the girls attended services at 5:00 p.m. at St. Anthony's Church. Good Friday we started our day with the Stations of the Cross in the church. After lunch we took the three older girls to downtown Lisbon to see 'The Greatest Story Ever Told' – the life and death of Jesus. What a beautiful movie in one of the grand theatres in Lisbon. It was in English.

Easter Sunday after Mass, the Hand and Moran families and us went to a restaurant high in the mountains surrounded by beautiful gardens and excellent food. After dinner, we walked through the garden and the children played games on the lawn. We returned home about 6:00 p.m. for our outdoor Easter egg hunt. Peggy won—she found the most eggs. We ended our glorious day with the Rosary to our dear Blessed Mother. I could feel the sorrow she had over the death of her Son when I was looking at my three sons. Having sons is wonderful. They are different than girls and at this point are easier to care for than girls. Maureen is becoming quite particular and grumpy. I see she is reaching her teens. Hope I can obtain more patience with her. Laurie is happy and carefree, always singing and full of laughter. Kathy in the middle – quiet but smart. Peggy and Sheri are still sweet little girls. Big Mike my pride and joy. Mike sure is a good boy, very tranquil and loving in nature. Little Robert a real terror and clown in the family. Robert has grown since you've seen him, he was a baby when we came and you remember how strong willed he was and his famous screaming. He has improved but is so different than Michael. He is a real clown and loves to show off. Joseph seems easy natured but too little to tell how he'll be.

Easter Tuesday I took the three older girls to see 'The Ten Commandments' – a spectacular movie. It lasted 4 hours and the girls sat tight in their seats as the Bible that we have been reading came alive. The great life Moses and his people had with God.

By the way, we enjoyed the chocolate chips immensely. We had a baking party – and since we went through Lent without cakes, cookies, and candy, the chips were a big hit. Thank you Mother from all of us.

Both Sheri and Peggy have received their First Holy Communion. The Mass was in the school chapel and the sisters sang. They sounded like angels – it was so pretty to the ear. They prepared two kneelers in white puffy satin and net with tiny green ferns here and there. Sheri and Peg were all in white with veils and looked like two little angels (wish they were).

We decided to double the First Communion as we prepared them togeth-

97

er and Sheri leads the Rosary with the rest of the girls. To complete this happy event, we had a dinner party at 4:00 p.m. with the Hand and Moran families and ourselves, we were a group of 21. I baked ham, bean casserole, two fruit molds, banana nut bread, deviled eggs, carrot sticks, Nonie baked au gratin potatoes, tossed salad, apple slices, and Geri baked cinnamon cake. Everything tasted so good. It was a lot of work, as the dressing for the salad was homemade, apple slices, banana bread, as you can't seem to buy prepared foods here. When you cook it is from scratch, sure getting a lot of use out of my cookbook.

The 13th of the month of May through October marks the anniversary date of the apparitions to the three children. Some 60,000-75,000 people go to Fatima for the grand procession, and the ceremony starts at midnight with outdoor Mass in the Cova da Iria and through the day. We are planning to take four girls, leave Friday morning and return Sunday.

This is a beautiful life for us as Jerry's only concern is for God and us. How nice it is for me to have him here to help raise all these children. When I think back, I did it all by myself, as his business took much of his time; and then, his political activities were hectic and once in a while he was with us.

Parenting is not only feeding, clothing, and sheltering the family – it is teaching them their religion and how to live it. This is a terribly big task. The unity between home, school, and Church is most important. We have many traditions here like I had as a young girl.

We could see this loss coming through the schools throughout the U.S. Not everyone is aware of the breakdown of this unity but to us it was prominent. There are more private schools throughout the states opening, in order to preserve the rights of the parents, so there may be a number of sound good living Catholics as God Almighty had intended for His creatures.

LIFE IN PORTUGAL

Portugal is not perfect, but as of today they are in unity, and their belief in family is treasured. Within the last two years immoral magazines etc. have shown up. But now there is strict control of the drug problem. You see when anyone is caught there is punishment – they are very strict. The schools aren't concerned with this. It is hard to explain in writing but we have our rights to do what we think as parents. I experienced this in Deerfield schools. It's not the parents, it's the teachers. There is a school board of seven parents that have the say. When we wanted to talk to them they couldn't be bothered. When election came, three independent candidates ran and we saw the crooked politics they played. This was our experience but we have since learned that this is happening all over. The time is here for parents to wake up and accept their responsibility.

The move has been somewhat difficult for me but I have the assurance of God on my side, and we don't do a thing without prayer first. I am very content to know and understand this. I can remember how heartbroken I was when Jer and I broke up after high school. I thought the world had collapsed after several months and I didn't hear from him. Then Mauge introduced the 54-day Novena to the Blessed Mother to me. 27 days of the Rosary in request and 27 days in thanksgiving.

Before I had completed this novena, I remember coming home one evening. Dad, sitting at the kitchen table said, 'Jerry called and would call back at 10:00 o'clock.' Well, I knew this was meant to be and my prayers were answered. We made a luncheon date – he picked me up promptly at 2 o'clock. I was so thrilled – I couldn't believe it. From then on we dated.

It seems as our marriage went on, I became lax in prayer, and not until my auto accident did I realize where I was lacking. Well, at any rate I am living an interesting life. Learning the language is fun. We have many laughs over it. The only language I had was one year of Spanish in high school.

Maureen recalls:

"Every twelfth of the month from May through October, we would go to Fatima. On the eve of the thirteenth, there was a candlelight ceremony to prepare for the feast day. We would watch the people with their children set up camp but they had no tents. They just slept out in the open. People would walk miles and miles to Fatima on foot, even barefoot. Because of this, Red Cross trucks would be waiting to help bandage up those who needed it."

"We looked forward to the twelfth and thirteenth of every month because then we got to miss school and go up to Fatima," Kathy remembers. "I couldn't believe it when I saw all the people carrying baskets on their heads," she continued, "many of them did not even have shoes! And some were walking on their knees! Some had a horse and wagon, but most of the people walked. I wondered why they did not have cars."

"Another time I remember going with Dad, Maureen, and Laurie to the *Cova da Iria* on the evening of May 12th," Kathy continued. "It had rained all day so the night was damp, chilly, and dark. The people were sleeping outside on blankets. Some had camp fires and were cooking. A procession was going on around them with lit candles, people praying the rosary and singing Fatima hymns. The faces on these people seemed sad as though they worked very hard all their lives. I felt so sorry for them. Still, to think that we Americans did not even want to sleep on rough hay bed let alone outside in the chilly air!"

"At the celebration of the feast day we would attend Mass," said Kathy, "which was three hours long! It was cold, and there was just enough room to stand. We would stand covered with blankets. Now we know that they were doing this as penance and reparation. At the Chapel at *Cova da Iria* where Our Lady appeared, men and women would walk around on their knees praying the rosary."

LIFE IN PORTUGAL

"Today when I think how blessed we were to be right where Our Lady appeared and to see where those children lived, I can see how little we appreciated all that. On our way back to the U.S., Dad told us that we had to share and spread the Fatima message when we got home. We really did not understand how we were going to do this. We know now that he was not kidding! A few years later the Family Apostolate was founded!"

While in Portugal, the Conikers gained some important friends. First there was Father Jerome Penero who actually baptized little Joseph Coniker! Fr. Penero would visit the Conikers regularly and would bring Jerry communion daily for a period of time while he experienced asthma. Jerry was allergic to the dampness in the Churches which made him ill. Although Father did not speak English well and Jerry did not speak Portuguese well, together, they managed to forge a friendship based on their common spirituality. It was Father Penero who introduced Jerry to St. John Bosco, founder of the Salesians and the saint's undying loyalty to the Pope, as well as his prophesies concerning the Eucharist, the Mother of God and the Papacy.

Then there was Count Graf Czernin who was a member of the Romanoff family of Austria. He also was a devout Catholic and a staunch promoter of the Legion of Mary. Through Count Graf, Jerry came to understand the vision, structure, and the organization of the Legion as well as its founder, Frank Duff. This would be an important impetus to guide Jerry later, when he founded the Apostolate for Family Consecration in helping him develop his own ideas about it and its structure and Ecclesial Teams. Jerry became very active in the Legion of Mary. The Count also told him about the amazing incident in March, 1955, when the Russians occupied the country and suddenly withdrew their army largely due to the Rosary Atonement Crusade which was propagated throughout the country by the Franciscan friar by the name of Petrus Pavlicek. The Count also taught Jerry the inner workings of world politics, education, and Communism, despite the fact that Jerry was well-read in the subject matter. Additionally, the Count informed Jerry of the situation of the Church of Portugal prior to the apparitions whereby the majority of college students were atheistic, and the rich were anti-Catholic and/or anti-American. The reason for this was that the Masons had gained control of the government in the early 1900s, expelling religious orders and inhibiting the activities of pastors. Then the miracles of Fatima in 1917 occurred. It was Masonic newspapers, much to everyone's surprise, which reported the miracle of the sun at Fatima on October 13, 1917.

Finally, there is Father Gabriel Pausback who was the Provincial to the Superior General of the Carmelites who had a keen mind. He withdrew to Fatima after Vatican II due to all the disagreements and dissensions which followed. He wrote a book called the *Saints of Carmel* which was about a Carmelite mystic by the name of St. Mary Magdalene de Pazzi. He also helped those in the Blue Army promote the Brown Scapular and was the Spiritual Director of the Marto family. He was an expert about the Fatima visions and the seers, conducting tours and pilgrimages at the Shrine. He would later become Jerry's first Spiritual Director. He obtained for the Coniker family the privilege of staying at the *Casa Beato Nuno*, which was a lodging for pilgrims run by his order, or at a home of a Fatima resident during those busy times of the month around the twelfth and thirteenth.

They also got to know the Prince of Portugal who, years later, would Knight Jerry in 2001. Gwen was made Lady Guenevere, and Jerry's son, Michael, a Squire. They met the new Bishop of Leiria-Fatima the last night they lived in Portugal, who informed Jerry that the Fatima message is really to live the gospel in a radical way. It is also a message of warning and hope. It would take Jerry twenty years to really understand the depth of this message by the Bishop.

In time, Jerry began to understand and realize that the real reason that Our Lady sent him to Portugal. It was not to necessarily raise his children as Catholics in an American Catholic community, albeit a noble reason, and once thoroughly formed, to return to the United States to evangelizing those there. It was, instead, to slow Jerry down, humble him, and to teach him about the prayer life and the message of Fatima. The Fatima message, by the way, is the message which St. Pope John Paul II saw as a message for modern times. This Pope, in his encyclical of 1984, *Salvifici Doloris [On The Christian Meaning of Human Suffering]*, says that the suffering that was experienced by those in the first and second World Wars would dwarf that of the suffering yet to come if we do not turn back to God.

Jerry was indeed humbled in Portugal. He found that the skills that he enjoyed were not valued in Portugal; skills such as efficiency, time management, or any other skills that he possessed. Jerry was unable to start a company there. Hence, he spent many hours, some nine to ten a day, in prayer, learning about Mary and her role in the economy of salvation. She is the path which leads directly to her Son, Jesus.

> "I can see now that God sent me to Portugal for what actually became a two-year retreat, and not for the purpose of starting a Catholic American community. Not being allowed to work, I spent most of my day in the Salesian chapel. Apparently God had to move me from the United States, so I would no longer be involved in political education and running a business. I had the opportunity to study the *Mystical City of God* by Sr. Mary of Agreda, in which the Blessed Virgin Mary, by way of visions, revealed her life to Sr. Mary of Agreda who recorded it. I also studied the works of St. Louis de Montfort. I found these to be treasures of Marian spirituality."

Jerry, reflecting back years later,

> "The community experience in Portugal was a failure because we allowed it to degenerate into pettiness. This pettiness is something one finds in many spiritual movements. The people in the movement start to look down on and pre-judge others; and also, in some ways, to pre-judge their children. We are very conscience of this in the Family Apostolate now and warn our members not to fall into the sin of spiritual pride and pettiness so prevalent among conservatives. We know the doctrine, but don't always have the charity which is so essential, in order to live by the doctrine the way Our Lord desires us to do. Moreover, I believe we were called to form community life

for families in the States and in the world; a life focused on the Eucharist, the Fatima message, and living the gospel in a radical way. It is to strengthen families wherever they are located; most especially, right where they are, in all their varied cities, lines of work, in their neighborhoods, and communities."

"The Fatima message is telling the modern world that unless it comes back to the simplicity of the truths of our Faith and turns itself to God – which consecration really means – and comes to Him through His Mother, it will self-destruct and bring about an age of darkness it has never seen before. However, in the end, the hope this message presents is that Our Lady's Immaculate Heart will triumph and an era of peace will permeate the world. Fatima is the prophecy of our time; and St. Pope John Paul II, who was shot on Mary 13, 1981, the feast of Our Lady of Fatima, is the one who interpreted this prophecy of *Totus Tuus* (Totally Yours), Consecrate them in the Truth."

Jerry's reflection continues as he looks back:

"The Fatima message is also a message of hope if we follow the Pope! Our Lady made a definite prophecy that her Immaculate Heart would triumph and an era of peace would be granted to the world. This will happen. The only question is when, and how much terror has to reign before we finally come to God through His Mother? Portugal, the Philippines, and the United States are under the patronage of the Immaculate Conception. This was no light matter for us, since we put so much emphasis on the Immaculate Conception in our Marian Year program, and later in the development of our Asian Apostolate through the Philippines. We also learned of the power of the bishops' consecration of a nation to Jesus through Mary, which could save a country from war. It was important to bring that message back to the United States, and use it as the base for our country's re-consecration in the Marian Year."

LIFE IN PORTUGAL

"On our last day in Fatima, June 13, 1973, we received a book containing all of Sister Lucia's letters that a Jesuit priest had put together and printed without the permission of the Bishop. Additional printings were stopped, but we were given two copies before we left Portugal. These proved extremely helpful in our work here in the United States. Now this book has been approved by the Bishop of Fatima."

Jerry came to realize through prayer that the "Success-Positive Attitude System," which he heavily relied upon for his success in business does not work in the spiritual life. In fact, it could lead one away from God. Jerry gives the following advice: "Do not rely too much on a self-assured attitude which has proved successful to me in the business world, especially through motivational speakers and positive attitude courses; for the business world is far different than the spiritual world. The spiritual world is much deeper." He continues, "The risk in this is that one depends on one's own self; confidence in one's self instead of having confidence on God and relying on God. When fighting the forces of evil, of Satan, and fighting to save souls, one is fighting against prin-

cipalities and dominions, not ordinary things of the business world. Hence, the strategy is altogether different; stronger, more powerful weapons must be employed; weapons such as the power of prayer, the rosary, the sacraments, remaining in a state of grace and so forth." He continues, "With God as our Source, anything is possible. This is how I developed the Four C's formula of Confidence [in God, not oneself], Conscience [properly formed in the Truth], Charity, and Constancy [never give up no matter what]." This "Four C" Formula would play a vital role in both

Jerry's spiritual life and in the mission he would later undertake.

Jerry's Most Complete Book on Consecration is *Preparation for Total Consecration to Jesus through Mary in Union with St. Joseph, for Families.* This book on Total Consecration includes the following:

1. Teachings of St. Louis De Montfort, St. Maximilian Kolbe, St. John Paul II, Cardinal Luigi Ciappi
2. St. John Paul II's Dual Dimension of Consecration
3. Responsibility of the Present Moment
4. Four Cs Formula of Confidence, Conscience, Charity, and Constancy
5. The Apostolate's Family Catechism
6. The Mercy of God
7. Our Supernatural House

The Coniker Family in Portugal, 1973

Chapter 6

God Leads Them and Provides

DURING THEIR TWO-YEAR HIATUS IN PORTUGAL, Jerry and Gwen returned to the United States three times. During the first trip in August, 1972, Jerry was accompanied by Gwen and Michael, and paid a visit to the company which he had sold. Since he was unable to start a business in Portugal, he had been out of work ever since he moved there. Although he was continuing to receive checks from his former company, he was feeling very concerned about his financial state because the checks would cease after the first year, according to his contract. Jerry needed a plan to continue supporting his large family.

While there, God did provide when the Chairman of the Board of their largest client, Baxter Laboratories, proclaimed, "If Jerry Coniker ceases to be a part of your company," he exclaimed, "that is the day we cease to be your client."[1] Everyone was surprised, most especially Jerry! The general manager of the company thought it wise to keep Jerry on the payroll, much to Jerry's relief!

During the second trip to the United States in December, 1972, the entire family came, and God provided again for Jerry and his family. While there, he met with Father Bernard Geiger, O.F.M., Conv. who was the editor for the *Immaculata* magazine and the National Director of the Knights of the Immaculata, located in Kenosha, Wisconsin. Jerry was hoping that Fr. Geiger would advertise

---

1   Ibid, 83.

his audio-tape on Fatima. During their meeting, Fr. Geiger introduced Jerry to the life and legacy of St. Maximilian Kolbe and the Knights of the Immaculata. Jerry was taken in by what Father had to say and quite impressed with this saint who taught and promoted consecration to Jesus through Mary.

As an aside, St. Maximilian Kolbe was a Franciscan priest who founded the Knights of the Immaculata, a movement to consecrate people to Our Lady and spread devotion to her. He experienced a vision of Our Lady of the Immaculate Heart standing over Moscow when the Bolshevik Revolution began. He had another vision of Our Lady a few days later on October 13, 1917, the day of the final apparition of Fatima when the "Miracle of the Sun" took place. He used the most modern media technology available at the time to promote the Catholic faith and consecration to Jesus through Mary to a mass audience. He was captured by the Nazis and sent to Auschwitz. When a prisoner escaped one evening, the Nazis selected ten prisoners to die by starvation as punishment and a deterrent to others considering the same thing. When a man was chosen, who was both husband and father, St. Maximilian went into action. The man was distraught and full of fear. St. Maximilian approached the Commandant requesting that he take the place of this man instead. The Commandant asked who he was in a rather interrogating manner. When St. Maximilian told him that he was a Catholic priest, the Commandant accepted his request. He and nine other prisoners went to the starvation bunker where he consoled them and prayed with them. After two weeks, when most of the prisoners had perished except St. Maximilian, they injected him with a poison which took his life. He is a martyr of charity since he gave up his life for another, the greatest act of love. The man he saved survived Auschwitz when the American military liberated them. That man went on to spend the rest of his life giving talks on St. Maximilian and what he had done for him. He was also present as a guest of the Vatican both at the beatification and the canonization of St. Kolbe.

Jerry found St. Maximilian's goals and mission of his apostolate to be perfectly aligned with his and started reading books given to him by Father Geiger on the life of this saint. What transpired later was a relationship with Father

GOD LEADS THEM AND PROVIDES

Geiger which lasted the rest of their lives. They corresponded with each other and soon, Fr. Geiger asked Jerry if he would consider returning to the States to assume the position of Executive Director of the Knights of the Immaculata.

Jerry was excited about the prospect. It would give him a chance to return to the work of leading souls to God. He would approach this mission differently than before. It would be much more spiritual, relying on God and Our Lady for strength and guidance. His family joined him in prayer for discernment, after which he decided to accept the offer and return to the States. This truly was a gift from God and he felt God was leading him this way.

Jerry returned to the United States a third time in April, 1973, this time to search for a home. Once again, God provided for Jerry when he found the perfect house through a realtor he met at Marytown. The home overlooked Lake Michigan and was located in Kenosha, Wisconsin. Although a fixer upper, Gwen had the gift of turning any house into a home! He bought it for only fifty thousand dollars! It was May 1st, the Feast of St. Joseph! It was a red brick house with three stories which was located at 6126 Third Avenue in Kenosha. The Conikers prepared for their move back to the States by selling their furniture and appliances because to ship them back would be too expensive. Just the day before they were to leave to go back to the United States, a refund check from the Internal Revenue Service showed up in the mail in the amount of four thousand dollars! This amount was just what Jerry needed to complete the down payment on the house! God provided yet again! Apparently, Americans do not pay taxes while abroad. This check was from taxes he had paid while in Portugal. He pondered the thought that had they left a day sooner, he would not have received the check. God is indeed good.

At this time, Gwen was eight months pregnant. How fitting that she was eight months pregnant when she arrived in Portugal and also eight months pregnant while leaving Portugal! The Coniker family returned home to the United States on June 13, 1973. It was a rather hectic return home: Jerry, Gwen, who oversaw the travel while eight months pregnant, eight children, a three-foot statue of Our Lady of Fatima, their luggage, and Kathy's dog, Butterscotch!

They purchased this statue while in Portugal and it was big enough to fit into a seat on the plane! Laurie was in charge of the safety of the Pilgrim Virgin Statue. Jerry took care of the luggage and the dog.

The children couldn't wait to get a real American hamburger upon their arrival! Also, when their relatives saw Gwen eight months pregnant....again.... they said, "Gwen, haven't you had that baby yet?!"

Gwen gave birth in Kenosha to their ninth child, a boy, James Francis, on July 22, 1973. This would be the first of four births by caesarean section. The position of the baby caused damage to Gwen's womb. An infection set in and the incision refused to heal. The doctor told them that future births would be very dangerous. He offered to perform a hysterectomy on Gwen but she refused. Medication finally brought about healing.

Jerry reflecting back on his time in Portugal: "Portugal was a turning point in our lives. It was a radical thing to do. We were batting our heads against the wall to protect our children from all these evils. We wanted to go to a country that would always preserve the faith. Our Lady promised that the Dogma of the Faith would always be preserved in Portugal. But what we did not realize was that Portugal was going through the same things that we [United States] were, so the reason for going there no longer existed. They may preserve the faith but the Church universal was going through trials. This is demonic and not normal. Gwen agreed with me."

Mary Ann Presberg had this to say: "Something obviously took place while in Portugal with both of them. Their two hearts had come together, whereas before it was Gwen's loyalty as a wife. It changed after Portugal. Jerry slowed down there because he couldn't work. So he was in prayer most of the time. Gwen came back and there was an outside peacefulness about her. She immediately set about making a home in Kenosha. Wherever she was, she made a house into a home. The Apostolate was in their hearts. There was something deeply spiritual upon their return from Portugal and supernatural. God gave them a mission in the truest sense of the word. It was a subtle, silent voice to do this work...as Gwen is not a mission person per se. It was as though God was guiding them to this work. It was the two of them and Gwen understood it."

Chapter 7

Founding of the Apostolate

T̲H̲E̲ ̲F̲A̲M̲I̲L̲Y̲ ̲S̲E̲T̲T̲L̲E̲D̲ ̲I̲N̲T̲O̲ ̲T̲H̲E̲I̲R̲ ̲N̲E̲W̲ ̲H̲O̲M̲E̲ and Jerry started his new job as Executive Director of the Knights of the Immaculata at Marytown. He was also the managing editor of the *Immaculata Review*. He drew a meager salary of three hundred and fifty dollars per month, but he also continued to draw a retainer from his old company. In time, he would build a lasting relationship with Father Bernard Geiger, O.F.M., who would become Jerry's spiritual director in 1973. They attended Our Lady of Mount Carmel Parish in Kenosha, WI. Meanwhile, Gwen did what she does best; turning a house into a home and being a great wife and mother.

Jerry met directors of other apostolic organizations through his work as director of the Knights of the Immaculata. He studied their approaches and their methods. They, like himself, were also very concerned about the future of the Church and society at large. He drew on his previous years of experience, prior to living in Portugal, of organizing focus groups and doing apostolic work. "I knew how to establish neighborhood teams," says Jerry, "because I had been doing it since I was nineteen years old. I recruited, organized, and trained volunteers and developed chapters or teams of people to fight against abortion and sex education without values in the schools. I had a system that I designed which was highly successful in this effort. It was similar to the system that I designed for commercial use: the Controlmaster Sales Control System. It bonded community members and built relationships. I used this knowledge and experience to design a master-plan for the Knights of the Immaculata, with Father Bernard's permission that would start with a focus group as a base and develop into other structures."

During this time, their family grew again! Their tenth child, a daughter, was born on September 4, 1974 by the name of Maria Ann. Their happy and large family consisted now of six girls and four boys!

Jerry was experiencing resistance from the rest of the Franciscan community despite his support from Father Bernard. They felt that the approach that Jerry was taking would draw them away from their present work and was not part of their charism. Jerry knew that he could not stay. He left Marytown in March, 1975. At the same time, however, Jerry had a vision in his mind of starting a family-centered apostolate. He discussed his idea with Father Bernard, who not only encouraged him, but suggested that he seriously consider moving forward. Hence, Jerry decided to go on a retreat to pray, think, and discern this decision.

Jerry made his retreat at Bellarmine Retreat House in Barrington, Illinois. Father John A. Hardon, S.J. was the retreat master. While there, he presented his vision to Father Hardon. The organization that he had in mind would be completely faithful to the teachings of the Magisterium of the Church. This was of primary concern for Jerry. It would not depend on one's private interpretation of Catholic doctrine be it a lay person, spiritual director, or clergy. This apostolate would teach, instruct, and catechize others in the authentic teachings of the Church in terms of her faith and morals. The method by which this would be done was yet to be determined. Father Hardon supported Jerry's vision and also encouraged him to proceed. That was now the second of two very good priests suggesting Jerry move forward with his plans.

The effects of Vatican II were well underway. Jerry saw this as an opportunity to quell the misinformation from the Council which was being disseminated and taking full effect in society. This representation of Vatican II's reform of the Church opened up a great opportunity to re-catechize the laity, as well as to explain the real purpose of the Council and the 16 beautiful documents which came about as a result.

With the support of his wife and blessings of two faithful priests, Jerry set about forming and founding of the apostolate. Gwen was always supportive of her husband and his noble endeavors, especially something as important as this which entailed leading countless souls back to God, a vision she too shared. For the time being, Gwen held the family together while Jerry pursued the idea of the Family Apostolate.

Jerry would start by producing catechetical programs through the use of videotapes. The difficulty, however, was that videotape was a new technology. It was filmstrips and slides which were the principal media formats. In fact, the banks told Jerry when he went to borrow money that it was crazy to think that the typical person would be able to afford a videotape recorder. That did not deter Jerry, however, who was very tenacious. Once he set his mind to something, he was determined to do it.

Jerry understood fully that, in order to keep people together and form a cohesive unit, he would have to keep feeding them new material. He would create Peace of Heart forums which are gatherings of groups of people who would meet every week or every other week, and view a video on the teachings of the faith or of a book or papal document. There would be four to fifteen programs per series. These meetings would take place either at the Conikers' home or at the local family Howard Johnson's restaurant. This format would not only instruct and catechize others in the faith but, at the same time, form lasting bonds of friendships and support for one another. "The goal was to seek out prominent teachers who knew the faith, record them, and catechize the adults so they could teach their children," said Jerry. "Evangelization begins in the home. But families don't know how or where to begin, as they themselves were poorly catechized."

Jerry compared his vision after the Legion of Mary, founded by Frank Duff. The Legion is a highly organized structure of governing which has weekly meetings, and requires two hours of assigned evangelization each week for each member called 'the work'. The assignments are given by the pastor or spiritual director of the group. "The problem is that if the priest is lukewarm, then the people will be lukewarm and the outreach programs will be lukewarm," said Jerry. He continued, "The outreach programs for this Apostolate instead would be completely organized and pre-packaged into multi-media programs." He would use volunteers to be front-line evangelizers and create God-centered parish neighborhood communities, using the videotapes as their source for solid Church teaching. He would also incorporate the charism and writing of St. Louis de Montfort to draw others to Our Lady, who, in turn, leads them directly to her Son, Jesus. Jerry had considerable knowledge between his experiences in the business world, volunteer work organizing, and as a husband and father of a large family who knew first-hand the problems that families and marriages face.

Jerry invited a few of his closest friends who were also concerned about the culture to gather on Wednesdays at the local Howard Johnson's. These friends were John Hand, who had been with Jerry in Portugal; August Mauge, Gwen's former boss at the Chevrolet dealership; Father John Richetta, pastor of Mount Carmel Church; and Bill Isaacson, a Catholic attorney from Chicago.

They all agreed with the goal and vision of the Apostolate. The family was being targeted by anti-Christian forces trying to destroy it. They also agreed that there must be a solid foundation to the Apostolate with a set of goals, a board of directors consisting of at least three people faithful to the Magisterium of the Church, and a set of by-laws approved by the Church.

The first order of business was to select the board members. These members would be August Mauge, John Hand, Bill Issacson, Father Richetta as spiritual director, and of course, Jerry. As a matter of fact, it was Fr. Richetta who came up with the name "Apostolate for Family Consecration," which was unanimously and enthusiastically adopted. So it happened. On June 18, 1975, the Apostolate for Family Consecration was founded.

Bill Isaacson, the attorney from Chicago, greatly assisted with the set of constitutions and bylaws. Gwen would be in charge of typing them up as she had a gift for typing, having done a lot of it in her previous job. Jerry used his home, specifically his bedroom, to be the first office of the Apostolate, by removing furniture and replacing them with office equipment. Later, Jerry would receive a visit to that bedroom office by the Archbishop's Vicar General, Bishop Leo J. Brust. Jerry was somewhat embarrassed to show the bishop his humble surroundings of an office. However, the bishop was greatly edified and showed great interest in the vision of the Family Apostolate. Moreover, this bishop would become a great ally of Jerry's in the years to come, even offering up his sufferings and death, due to a kidney disease, for Jerry's work.

The next order of business was to get the proper ecclesiastical authority to approve the constitutions and bylaws. This duty fell to Archbishop William Cousins, Archbishop of Milwaukee. According to Canon Law, the Apostolate for Family Consecration is characterized as a 'Private Association of the Christian Faithful.' On October 3, 1975, Archbishop Cousins approved the constitutions and bylaws. Jerry was elated. "It was not customary for approval to occur so quickly," said Jerry, "and it was not long ago that the Church would have been reluctant to give anyone such freedom to run a lay institution."

It just so happened that the St. Joseph Missionary Society, or the Mill Hill Fathers, had their regional offices just across the street from where the Conikers lived. Jerry would spend time in their chapel, and while there, came to know Fr. Cees Snoeren, M.H.M. Fr. Snoeren became interested in the work that Jerry was doing for the family and gave him encouragement. One day, Father casually mentioned that the offices on the top floor of the north wing of the building were not being used. Jerry saw this as a great opportunity for the Apostolate. "Would you be willing to rent them to the Family Apostolate?" Jerry inquired. Fr. Snoeren responded, "Not only will I let you use them but I will let you use them free of charge!" This greatly pleased Jerry, who wasted no time in taking advantage of such a generous offer.

Meanwhile, due to the good will of Frank Flick, Jerry was able to buy back part of Coniker Systems. This was because Frank wanted to see the Family Apostolate succeed and was aware that Jerry needed it in order to support both his family and the Apostolate. In fact, for the first seven years, neither Jerry nor his wife received any salary from the Apostolate.

Jerry hired a secretary and put her on the payroll of his company, Coniker Systems. It would come to pass that not all those people who Jerry would hire in the future and employ would stay, as was the case with this first hire. When the issue of birth control arose in which the Family Apostolate's teachings mirrored that of the Magisterium of the Church, some left. This sounds akin to those who left Jesus after He finished His Bread of Life discourse in chapter six of John's gospel.

Jerry started to pray that he would be able to use not just one floor but the entire building. It was an unlikely intention given the fact that the Fathers just put in a new bathroom. Still, Jerry prayed at their chapel in front of the Blessed Sacrament for this intention.

Amazingly, it came to pass that in 1975 there was a critical gas shortage which made it quite expensive for the Fathers to heat such a large house. There-fore, they decided to put the house up for sale at a bargain price of one hundred and fifty thousand dollars. But Jerry waited. As time went on and the house did not sell, they lowered the price to eighty-five thousand dollars. The Fathers were hoping that Jerry would buy it.

Meanwhile, Jerry had applied for a subsidy at the DeRance Foundation. He drove to Milwaukee, Wisconsin to inquire about it, since he had not heard back from them for his grand proposal. While waiting, he went to the library to copy some pictures from the Sacred Heart Messenger collection. In walked Mr. Harry John, president of the Foundation. He saw Jerry copying the pictures and became angry and told him to stop at once.

"You cannot make copies as those are precious books," he said in a loud voice. Jerry responded, "Well, if I cannot copy these pictures, can I have the grant of thirty thousand dollars to put as a down payment on a building for the Apostolate?" "Yes, you can have the money but you cannot copy those pictures!" Harry John retorted back. The Sister at the desk, who also was the Librarian for the foundation, confirmed with Jerry that she heard what Harry John said, and agreed to give him the grant, but not before Dr. Donald Gallagher, the vice-pres-ident, confirmed it to be true as well. After verifying it with Mr. John, he gave the check to Jerry. Jerry rushed back to Kenosha to put down the deposit on the building. The St. Joseph Center as it would be called would be the headquarters for the Family Apostolate. There was a catch however, and that catch was that the bank wanted Jerry's house as additional collateral on the loan. So Gwen and Jerry had a meeting and they pledged their home as collateral.

Jerry thanked God for the fortuitous purchase by spending the next year in the chapel of that building. He buried a statue of St. Joseph on any property he bought. He also outlined the Scripture's Four C's formula of confidence, conscience, charity, and constancy as well as writing three prayer books. Gwen was the bookkeeper for a number of years for the Apostolate.

Although the Apostolate was founded in 1975, several years of preparation was done before any presentation was made in public. Using media techniques were new to evangelization efforts. In addition, Jerry used his expertise in designing filing systems to design one for the Family Apostolate. He realized that once they got busy, there would be no time later to design it. It needed to be done now, Jerry concluded, most especially if they were to grow. So Jerry designed codes for the communications that the Apostolate would have for the basic systems. He was still earning his living with his Communication Systems from his previous company, but was spending eighty-five percent of his time with the Family Apostolate.

Jerry also worked on the material for the Peace of Heart Forums. In so doing, he realized that whatever material he provided should be checked with a theologian for accuracy. Thus, he decided to contact Fr. Thomas Morrison, O.P. who was Jerry's philosophy professor in college. He was brilliant and headed the Philosophy Department at De Paul University. Fr. Morrison was, at that point, stationed in Houston, Texas. However, his assignment for the next year was currently being discussed with his Provincial. So he asked his Provincial if he could be assigned to the Apostolate for Family Consecration in Kenosha for one year. His Provincial agreed! Within sixty days, the Apostolate had its first resident theologian!

Jerry needed to take out another mortgage against his house, in order to support both the St. Joseph Center and the Apostolate's work. Since the Family Apostolate had no credit with the banks, Coniker Systems would also loan money on a no-interest basis to the Apostolate. This financial dance between the brink of bankruptcy and just meeting their financial obligations of both home debts, as well as the Apostolate debts, would plague Jerry and Gwen for years. God loves cliff hangers and seems to operate like that quite a bit. It's His modus operandi!

In time, an Advisory Council was formed that would advise the Apostolate in the various areas of their expertise. "The first Advisory Council meeting was held at the House of St. Joseph on a very cold day in 1977," said Jerry. "It was twenty below zero with a wind-chill of even lower." One of the members of this advisory council was Dale Francis, who had a national column in most Catholic Diocesan newspapers. He would be the historian for the Family Apostolate throughout the years, by writing about the progress of the Apostolate on a regular basis. Jerry recalls, "Maureen cooked and served the meals that we ate in the dining room." Jerry continued, "There was about fifty to sixty people present including August Mauge. The chapel was full."

October 5, 1978 marked the first formal meeting of the Advisory Council which was held at Divine Word Seminary in Techny, Illinois. "It was an ideal location," said Jerry, "as it was centrally located for those attending." Bishop Leo J. Brust celebrated the Mass of the Sacred Heart. Concelebrating with him was: Fr. Robert J. McAllister, S.J. who was the director of the Apostleship of Prayer, Fr. Howard Rafferty, O.Carm., who was national director of the Brown Scapular, Fr. William J. Dorney, a pastor, Fr. John J. Richetta, also a pastor, Fr. John J. Hardon, S.J., Fr. Louis M. Cortney, O.S.M., and Fr. James J. O'Connor, S.J. The beauty of the Church was breathtaking and to see so many priest supporters of the Apostolate concelebrating together was breathtaking!

At the meeting following the Mass, Jerry presented nineteen points or phases he thought important, in order to lay the foundation for the Apostolate for Family Consecration. It would be his vision of how he saw the goal and purpose of the Apostolate for the future. Some of those present at this first formal meeting following the Mass included: August J. Mauge, Charles Scholl, Dr. Donald Cardy, Al Barone, Frank Flick, Eleanor Hand, Mr. and Mrs. William J. Isaacson, Dr. and Mrs. Thomas A. Prier, Elaine Armstrong, Dr. Richard DeGraff, William J. Jackson, and John W. Hand as Master of Ceremonies.

The following outlines these nineteen phases of Jerry's vision:

- Phase 1: The establishment of clear and specific short-range and long-range goals.

- Phase 2: Develop basic structures in order to ensure growth and stability.

FOUNDING OF THE APOSTOLATE

- Phase 3: Develop and test a volunteer system, before any major investment was considered, in order to ensure a sustainable productive activity of an international network of permanent teams.

- Phase 4: Establish an Advisory Council comprising teaching faculty.

- Phase 5: Recruit individuals and contemplative communities who will pray and offer up their sufferings for the Family Apostolate.

- Phase 6: Acquire the St. Joseph building to act as the Communications Center.

- Phase 7: Conduct necessary improvements to the property in order to advance the Apostolate.

- Phase 8: Develop basic systems and procedures for the Center's administrative and research office.

- Phase 9: Recruit qualified people to help complete formation programs.

- Phase 10: Develop a practical and scriptural formula for living a God-centered life in the modern world which will be incorporated into most of our scriptural formation programs.

- Phase 11: Write and publish prayer and meditation books which explain our spirituality.

- Phase 12: Establish local business-men's Teams to help raise funds.

- Phase 13: Write various 21-day formation programs, meditation books and audio-visual manuscripts.

- Phase 14: Produce a variety of multi-media formation programs for our neighborhood Chapters.

- Phase 15: Write and produce volunteer leader-training programs.

- Phase 16: Recruit and train key area organizers.

- Phase 17: Set up seed Lay Evangelization Teams in major areas.

- Phase 18: Recruit volunteer area organizers.

- Phase 19: Encompass total field support and produce two or three new programs a year for our neighborhood Chapters.

The Family Apostolate, which is led by the laity, takes into consideration one's state in life be it married with or without children, celibacy, widowhood and so forth, as well as one's state of health and work responsibilities. The gifts gleaned from one's state in life, as well as those given from the gifts of the Holy Spirit should be developed and utilized. In *Christifideles Laici, 56*, St. Pope John Paul II writes, "The Holy Spirit stirs up other forms of self-giving to which people who remain fully in the lay state devote themselves."

The St. Joseph Center at 6305
Third Ave., Kenosha, WI.
Headquarters to the Family Apostolate.

The Coniker home at 6126 Third Ave., Kenosha, WI.
The master bedroom served as the
Family Apostolate's first office.

Chapter 8

Second Trial: The Choice Between Life and Death

A TYPICAL DAY IN THE LIFE of the Coniker family at this point entailed the older kids helping the younger kids get ready for school. They would make breakfast for the younger ones. Gwen was always there when the children arrived home from school. She had them emptying the garbage and other chores. After dinner, the family would pray the rosary and then the children would go to their rooms to do their homework. After Portugal, Jerry would be home with the family for dinner every night. There would regularly be sixteen people for dinner which included those helping with the Apostolate such as the staff theologian, Dr. Burns Seeley. Dr. Seeley lived at the Center and was with the Conikers every night for dinner. After the family rosary, Jerry went back to work until 11p.m. - 1 a.m. almost every day.

Gwen made it possible for the Apostolate to grow. She made it possible for Jerry to conduct his work and teach while she held the family together. Like a key basketball player who passes the ball to the player who shoots, known as an assist, that was Gwen. She was somewhat in the shadows, compared to her husband, but always remained assisting behind the scenes, for she was a very key and necessary player.

This was perfect because Gwen was maintaining her primary duties of wife and mother and not neglecting them. It is very easy to put too much emphasis on things other than one's primary duty for the glamour of money, power, prestige, fame, and even spiritually good endeavors. As the children grew and got older, Gwen could focus more on the Apostolate.

Gwen loved being a mother. She was born to be a mother. As a stay-at-home mom she took care of all the children. She would say that "the first six are the hardest but then you have help from the older children." Years later, her daughter, Laurie, would have this to say about her mother: "Mom loved to cook and she knew how to make a house into a home. She never complained. She loved to be a mom. There are so many people that don't know how to create a warm, cozy atmosphere in the home, or to be a mom and be content staying home doing housework, cooking, laundry, etc. Mom knew how to make the atmosphere of the home very cozy and homey by the way she decorated it, especially during the holidays, and having music playing in the background and so forth. She would use the fine china for the holidays and knew how to entertain and cook for large parties. The interesting thing is that she made being a stay-at-home mom seem fulfilling and glamorous. If done right, there is no time for watching TV. Of course, she also never mentioned to us the stresses of the job! This was because she was not reactionary and kept silent as she was more of a listener than a talker."

Mary Ann Presberg, her sister-in-law, had this to say about Gwen, "One doesn't necessarily realize Gwen's talents because it was done in the background. One would just walk away with an impressed image, not even being able to put their finger on it but it was the ambiance, the beauty of the home, the music in the home, the food put out. It was all just done."

Gwen certainly practiced the 'Little Way of Spiritual Childhood,' as taught by Doctor of the Church, St. Thérèse of Lisieux. The little things can be the most profound, yet the most difficult. A lot of things go unnoticed and taken for granted: Meals on the table and the house kept up and made into a home, decorated nicely most especially during holidays. These things take much work on a daily basis yet a smooth running ship goes unnoticed. It's only when the ship breaks down that people take notice. Yet there is something that they sense nonetheless when the ship is smooth sailing. Imagine putting on a meal every night for 14-16 people, the traffic in and out of the house, not to mention breakfast and lunch.

Dr. Seeley was over regularly, and in addition to their children's friends, company was over all the time. Then there were life's inconveniences, hassles, irritations, dealing with children, doing the grocery shopping, the laundry, housecleaning, cleaning up after twelve children, the flowers, the candles, music, and the ambiance of the home. Gwen did it all, and to perfection so to speak!

Our crosses, no matter what they are, are opportunities to grow in holiness, love, and virtue, and to grow closer to Our Lord. One can even reach the pinnacle of holiness when one begins to actually experience joy in the midst of heavy crosses. Gwen understood these truths. She practiced the little way of St. Therese by exercising virtue to a heroic degree in the everyday irritating, frustrating things of life through silence, patience, and acceptance. She demonstrated these virtues mostly through her works and, if necessary, she spoke.

Sometimes it's actually harder to do little things with great love and patience than big things. Writing books, being on a speaking circuit, teaching catechesis, praying outside at abortion clinics, exercising one's God-given talent, although good and noble deeds, do not necessarily demonstrate heroism to the degree as withholding a sharp word in an irritating situation, dealing with a difficult person, handling physical or emotional sufferings patiently when it is so easy to complain, criticize, or condemn.

Gwen loved calligraphy and music. She played the organ and the piano and wanted her children to take music lessons. She also knew how to fix up things in the home and decorate by wallpapering, painting, and so forth. She loved entertaining and having parties. She would transform one room every year.

Gwen would correct the children by walking out of the room if they were being naughty and tell their father. Dad would punish them on Saturdays. They had a mark system and star system. If the children were bad, they would get a mark. They could work off those marks with stars by doing extra things up and beyond their regular chores. If Gwen did get upset, she would not argue or fight. She would simply walk away and it would prick the consciences of the children. She would go and tell their father. Jerry made sure that the children were doing the right thing. Gwen was the loving mother, but not the disciplinarian.

SECOND TRIAL

When Gwen would give constructive criticism, she did it in a way that the recipient was grateful. She rarely yelled but the few times she did, it was not a loud yell. Gwen's mother would always yell and Gwen said that she would never want to raise her voice in anger. She could get aggravated like anyone but she contained it. She was not reactionary. She exuded authentic and strong love which grew with time like a fine wine. Gwen also rejoiced with people and was very reliable. If her children were giving their father a hard time, she would joke by saying, "Don't talk to my boyfriend like that!"

Gwen had many virtues. She was a very humble woman. She never gave anyone the feeling they were beneath her. She would often say and really believe, "I'm just an ordinary Mom just doing my duty." It is in one's fidelity to one's daily duty that holiness increases. And so it was with Gwen. If someone annoyed her, she didn't speak badly about it. She didn't become harsh in order to correct a situation or cry over it or impose her views. She knew how to be silent so as to not provoke the situation. She listened and empathized. She had a great gift for listening. In fact, she was more of a listener that a talker. But the times she did talk, others listened with bated breath.

It is true that God will test His children. It is also true that what the world values and what God values are at odds with each other. Pressure from the world is often exerted on Catholic families to cast aside their Catholic values for the world's values. It is no different for the Conikers; in fact, even more so, given that they were founders of an Apostolate whose premise was to strengthen families and bring others closer to God. *Satan will sift like wheat those who follow God's will* (Luke 22:31).

January 22, 1973 marked the landmark U.S. Supreme Court case *Roe v. Wade*, soon followed by its companion case, *Doe v. Bolton*, whereby Roe allowed for abortion up to the third trimester before restrictions were imposed by the state. Doe then extended the right to abortion on demand all nine months up until birth. This anti-life atmosphere spread its tentacles throughout every fabric of society. The unborn were now viewed as inconveniences. The child in the womb, that was deemed to be physically disabled in any way, was encouraged by health professionals to be aborted for the "good of the child."

It was this environment and prevailing societal attitude that the Conikers were living in when Dr. Rafferty informed Gwen that her life was in danger due to her current pregnancy, baby number eleven, and felt that she would not survive the birth. It was Christmastime in 1975. Since Gwen's first C-Section, every pregnancy became precarious. Due to many stitches, the uterus became too thin and would not be able to handle another child said Dr. Rafferty to Gwen. "There is a very high probability your uterus will rupture and you will not survive," he continued. He felt that she should abort the child in an effort to save her life. Not only did Gwen experience pressure to terminate her pregnancy from the doctor but from others as well. Many kept telling Gwen and her family that she shouldn't have so many children because it was not fair to the others. "I couldn't consider abortion," said a frightened Gwen, "God allowed this pregnancy and He knows what is best, so I had to remain firm in my beliefs. The doctor felt that I was being foolish not to consider the children that I already had. So the implication is that I am being selfish to not abort for the sake of my other children. But God is the only one Who can give and take life. It is not my decision to make." So Gwen told the doctor not worry, take one day at a time. She was sure everything would work out. Naturally, Jerry and her children were very concerned.

Gwen decided to write a letter to her family in the event that she did not survive. Due to the constant harassment from others questioning her many pregnancies and her current decision to continue the current pregnancy, Gwen became concerned that the baby would not be accepted by her other children if she did not survive.

"I had been awakened at three o'clock in the morning with these thoughts in my head," Gwen said, reflecting back. "'I might as well get up,' I told myself. 'I can't sleep.' So I decided to write down my thoughts. I wanted to tell them that in case I died, not to hold it against the baby. I also wanted to share with them some of my thoughts that they could reflect upon at Christmastime."

It is interesting to note that the message that Gwen wrote to her family was multi-faceted, simplistic, and yet profound all at the same time. It encompassed cheerfulness about Christmas which was quickly approaching from a loving mother to her family, as well as a big THANK YOU to God for His goodness in blessing her already with so many wonderful children. Moreover, it demonstrated Gwen's undying obedience to the will of God and her immense faith in Him, when He was asking her to put her life on the line; to trust in Him. Gwen resigned herself to God's will, realizing that she may very well not survive. Still, Gwen reached out to God and His Immaculate Mother. The message also contained a farewell of sorts to each member of her family.

This letter was opened on Christmas morning before the presents were handed out. Gwen was to go to the hospital the very next day. Jerry asked Maureen, the eldest child, to read the letter to the family. All the Conikers had tears in their eyes. Gwen recalls, "Maureen read it on Christmas morning and everyone was in tears. I was very sad and it was not at all what I had anticipated. However, that was the feeling that came from reading it."

> *To My Precious Treasure, My Family:*
>
> *Christmas morning [1975] – Happiest day of the year! It's a special time for loving and sharing with each other. We all know we have our first spiritual happiness in that the Christ Child was born so that we may have eternal happiness. The little Babe was God's sign of His love for all of us.*
>
> *Then we know of the physical happiness – that joy of presents under the tree, the good things to eat and all the merriment of being together. But this is a special Christmas this year as we have our new little Coniker!*
>
> *I can remember the birth of each one of you and how extra special was each one. A little babe to love and take care of. And so this is number eleven. He (or she) is special too!*
>
> *A Merry Christmas to Maureen, my first baby, who fought to get out from birth and is still struggling to get out fifteen years later. You became quite a cook in Portugal; your love and kindness, your help has been greatly appreciated.*

To my dearest Kathy. Merry Christmas! I remember that cold, cold morning when you were born and I bet that I was fatter than Santa Claus. How excited I was – our little girl number two. I couldn't wait to bring you home to show little Maureen, eighteen months old. You were a joy at birth and today, a joy seeing you in eighth grade.

To my cheerful Laurie, Merry Christmas! Everywhere Laurie is, there is sunshine and happiness. I love your smile, the cheer in your heart. Keep right on cheering all the days of your life.

Merry Christmas my dear Peggy! I couldn't believe it – daughter number four. The singing, swinging Coniker Sisters. I was so happy I got my blue-eyed, blonde little baby girl, so cute.

My sweet Sheri, Merry Christmas! I thought that four daughters was terrific. But when they told me, "You have a nice new baby daughter number five," it was super: You are the Super Start of the Coniker Sisters.

To my son, Michael John, Merry Christmas! Finally, a son, a boy Coniker; how long we waited for you. Everyone was so happy! That special feeling that Dad had a son – nothing like a son. We had to tell the world that Michael John Coniker was born.

To happy Robert – Wow! Our second son – what a joy, now two boys. I remember Dad rushed me to the hospital at 1:00 a.m. after I had a root beer float.

Merry Christmas, Joe! Boy, you had to wait a long time because you are number eight. I'll never forget the beautiful birth of our son Joseph in Portugal. First going to 7:00 a.m. Mass, then taking all the children home where Mrs. Hand took care of you and our dearest Maria Jose! We raced down the Marginal[a highway] to Lisbon and right in the Hospital Particular and in a matter of minutes our little son, Jose, was born, beautiful and perfect.

SECOND TRIAL

Hi, Jimmy, Merry Christmas! Mommy has a new little baby for you. Will you take care of him (or her)? Sure you will. Be a good boy. Okay? Jimmy, our fourth son, and just like our fourth daughter; blue eyes and blonde hair and real cute.

To my baby, Maria, Merry Christmas! I love you; you are my special angel.

I made my Christmas wish for all of you but I can't forget one, and a very important one. To my wonderful husband and your loving father: a very Merry Christmas!

Mother

Gwen with 'miracle' baby,
Theresa Marie, 1975

The eleventh Coniker child, Theresa Marie, was born on Dec. 27, 1975 healthy and happy! She was known as the 'miracle' baby! Thanks be to God and our heavenly Mother, Gwen survived the operation and healed remarkably well. God is so good. Apparently, God had other plans for Gwen. Amazingly, not only did Gwen survive this pregnancy, but two more additional pregnancies after this one. In April, 1976, Gwen experienced a miscarriage of their twelfth child, a girl they named Angelica. Gwen had fallen down the stairs due to losing blood and passed out from the fall. Then on October 23, 1977, the Conikers were blessed with a beautiful blonde hair, blue-eyed girl they named Mary Elizabeth. It was Gwen's fourth caesarean section. During this birth, her uterus ruptured. The doctor performed a hysterectomy, rendering Gwen incapable of bearing any more children.

LIFE IN KENOSHA

Time went on and life settled into a routine. Jerry continued building the Apostolate while Gwen, for the most part, was busy tending to the children. Gwen worked at the Apostolate, but family always came first. Gwen helped out with the bookkeeping while little Mary would be there in her playpen. The other Coniker children shared in the work of the Apostolate, grudgingly at first, as they really did not comprehend it. However, their willingness increased as they grew to understand its mission and importance. Running the Apostolate was a lot of work. There were the day-to-day operations, keeping the Family Apostolate house clean and in order when visitors arrived, and cooking meals for retreats. Gwen was very grateful for having daughters to help in the domestic duties. She prayed to God thanking Him for His goodness and gifts.

In time, in order to serve the Apostolate better, Jerry would purchase a total of five mansions in proximity of one another, all on Third Avenue, and one twenty-five thousand square foot warehouse in Kenosha. Notwithstanding the Conikers' home, the first mansion purchased was the St. Joseph House, which was used for TV productions and as the main Apostolate Center. Next to the St. Joseph House

The Coniker Family, 1978

was the Immaculate Heart Center, which was used for conferences, retreats, dining, and housing of retreatants. Across the street from Lake Michigan were the three other buildings, the first of which was the Conikers' family home, which later would become the Juan Diego house for the Men's Catholic Corps. The Kateri House, named after St. Katera Tekowitha, a Mohawk woman who lived in the 17th century, became the residence of the Women's Catholic Corps. The third house was Gwen's 'doll house', where the Conikers lived for three years before they moved to Ohio. It was called the doll house because it was the smallest of the mansions and Gwen just loved the house. To her, it seemed like a doll house!

The Coniker children were not immune to the persecutions from other school kids and friends. As others were uninformed to the true nature of the Apostolate, they thought varying things, including the idea that Mr. Coniker must have founded another religion. Hence, they were made fun of, not only for this, but also for being part of a family which ventured far beyond the acceptable two or three children. Also, as Coniker children, more was expected from them. Being in the limelight of a 'holy' Apostolate, their behavior reflected not only on the family but the Apostolate too. In addition, children being children, it was challenging to get them to get up early in the morning on a Saturday for Mass and First Saturday devotions to Our Lady of Fatima, or to pray the family rosary every day.

Still, the time spent in Kenosha by the lake brings back very fond memories for the Coniker children. Maureen, the oldest, says:

> I loved our big red-brick home. It had lots of bedrooms and was right across from the beach and the park! Marytown, the St. Maximilian Kolbe Shrine and headquarters of the Knights of the Immaculata lent us an old truck since we did not yet have a car. People would stare at us getting out of this odd-looking truck. After Mass, we greeted the pastor, Fr. Reketa, who recognized us immediately. I wondered how that was so I asked my Mom how he knew us. I should have figured since we were the only large family taking up the entire pew and the girls wearing maxi-dresses![1] I was thirteen at the time and remember feeling embarrassed.
>
> We were all looking forward to our first Sunday Mass in English and not in Portuguese. Much to our surprise the Mass was celebrated in Italian, since it was a special feast day!
>
> At school, we went to Mass twice a week but Dad made us go every day. We were made fun of by the other kids and were called the "Holy

1   Ibid, 124.

Joes." Skirts were to be worn below the knee, as Dad insisted that it was more modest. The peer pressure was awful. I felt like I stuck out. But now, I am grateful for what my parents did to teach me what is right, even though it caused me some pain. In high school I went to St. Joseph. I was shy and not very popular. Kids would make fun of me by calling me "the nun." It hurt, especially coming from the boys. School was hard for me. I skipped school a lot and did not get very good grades. I did manage to make a couple of girlfriends, although my parents did not approve of them. After they found out that I was drinking beer at some parties, I was grounded practically for the whole year. I was also very sassy at that time being fifteen and all. I had hidden some beer in my closet. Peggy found it and told Mom and Dad. Boy, did Dad hit the ceiling! He thought I would become an alcoholic! I actually didn't even drink that much. I just wanted to be cool enough to fit in. But I was no longer allowed to attend parties.[2]

As a solution, Mom and Dad furnished the basement as a Christmas present for us, so that if we wanted parties they would be at our house,' reflects Maureen. 'Of course, Dad made sure that there was no beer. However, during one party, some of the kids and I went to the park and drank. I was a little tipsy and Dad found out. He was furious. He called a counselor to assess whether I was on drugs. But the counselor did not know beans about counseling so he didn't know the answer. I never totally gave into peer pressure and never took drugs. It didn't matter how much I would tell my parents this, they were still being very protective of me and the others. I suppose being the oldest also had something to do with it.[3]

Mary Presberg, one of the cousins, had this to say about her fond memories of visiting the Conikers in Kenosha at the big red house:

---

2   Ibid, 125.
3   Ibid, 125.

SECOND TRIAL

My sisters and I would pack a suitcase and secretly hide them in the trunk, as if we had not had it planned weeks in advance! Marie, Mary and Theresa would then egg me on to ask Uncle Jerry if we could spend the night. That overnight would turn into two weeks! Their home was always clean with beautiful music everywhere,' she continues, 'decorated beautifully, and was really cozy. Aunt Gwen really had a rhythm to the house! We all needed to do chores, which were good for us as I look back. Eating between meals was not allowed. I was starving by the time 6:30 p.m. came because we weren't allowed to eat after school. They only had healthy food, no junk food, including healthy cereal. For dessert, we would sometimes have ice-cream cones and the whole gallon was gone in no time!' She concluded by saying, "I remember also playing lots of board games and they had a pool table in the basement. My cousins (the Coniker children) were always adventurous which made for fun times!"

Laurie recounts her memories of this time in Kenosha.

We had this huge house on Lake Michigan. I used to sit and cry on the beach thinking of Sr. Amadeus, and how it would have been if I had stayed in Portugal and become a Salesian nun. Of course, Dad was ecstatic at the thought of my wanting to become a nun and teased me about it. When I had my boyfriends over, Dad would say to me, "Why are you wasting your time? You're going to be a nun in Mother Immaculata's convent!" He even went so far as to tell the Daughters of St. Paul that I was interested in them and to put me on their mailing list![4]

I was about eleven years old when Dad started the Apostolate for Family Consecration. People would ask me, "What does your Dad do for a living?" and I'd say, "He sits in a chapel in this huge house

---

4   Ibid, 126.

across the street all by himself!" Little did I know! I thought he was crazy to give up his business to sit and dream all day. But lo and behold! A number of years later, I started to understand with the first Peace of Heart Forum. Dad had us all doing various jobs to keep the Apostolate running. I had to do yard work since my brothers were not old enough to do it yet. I was eleven years old and running the tractor! I also had to shovel the snow. One winter, my younger siblings were enjoying a nice cup of hot chocolate laughing at me out the window, as I was out in the cold shoveling snow! I was so glad when Michael grew up and inherited that job!

It took time to adjust when we moved back to the States from Portugal. Mini-skirts were in style but Dad made us wear our skirts two inches below the knee. It was so embarrassing, especially when the kids at school made fun of me and called me a 'holy roller!' But once at school, I would roll up my skirt so the kids would stop teasing me. Growing up with such strict parents was not easy.[5]

Laurie continues,

In high school, I ended up getting in with the wrong crowd, mostly because I did not start at that school freshman year when all the cliques were forming. As an outsider, the only crowd that would accept me was the "druggies." As a result, I got into drugs. When Mom and Dad found out, I was grounded for months at a time.

The Coniker parents certainly had their fair share of difficulties during the teen years with some of their children, which were very typical, unfortunately. Laurie recounts:

What made things even worse is that my Dad said he was going to call a meeting with the other parents of the druggies, to inform them that

---

5   Ibid, 127.

their kids were on drugs, just in case they did not already know. Boy, did my friends hate me after that. They even threatened to beat me up if my parents called their parents.[6] Dad did make good on his word and called the parents; however, only a few parents showed up. Most of them did not like Dad making accusations against their children. The kids also made good on their word. It got to the point that it was not safe for me to go to school anymore. These kids vandalized my Dad's car and bombarded him with snowballs when he dropped us off at school in the morning. During the school day, Dad would come to check my locker and Kathy's too to see if he could find anything. It was the worst year of my life.[7] We quickly realized that we were not dealing with small drug users, that these kids were dangerous. The next year, Kathy and I went to the school called the Willows Academy in Illinois which was an all-girls' school run by Opus Dei families.

Looking back, my Dad was really courageous. If it had not been for my parents being so strict and loving and brave, I probably would still be messed up. But that shook me up so that I quit taking drugs. I loved the all-girls school I went to after that. I feel that it is a much better learning environment than being at a co-ed school.

Kathy recalls the first years of the Apostolate and her high school years:

When Dad first started the Apostolate, I thought he was crazy. Turning neighborhoods into God-centered communities? All of us kids thought it to be some sort of joke and laughed at him. I was thirteen when I started helping Dad in the office of the St. Joseph Center. I earned twenty-five cents an hour. One day, I made a big mistake when I ruined a mile-high stack of papers by three-hole punching them on the wrong side. Dad was not a happy camper! That's when I got "promoted" to cleaning lady! I worked that job all during my high school years.

6   Ibid, 128.
7   Ibid, 128.

Kathy continues,

During the latter part of my high school years, I attended a co-ed Catholic high school. Dad outlined a number of things that we needed to agree to in order to attend that school. These things entailed attending daily Mass, praying the rosary daily, and attending religion class once a week with him, as well as work to pay half of the tuition, which cost eight hundred dollars, and not to go out on school nights. Of course we agreed![8]

However, once I got to the school, I discovered there were many cliques already formed. The girls did not accept us, and there was a lot of peer pressure. There was a group of about five girls who befriended me. But within the second quarter, I bowed to the peer pressure and was smoking pot with them. Mom and Dad found out about it. Mom did not want to believe it. I'm sure Mom was thinking, 'How could this be after all we taught our children?' Dad, meanwhile, investigated and discovered it to be true.[9]

I was grounded. I couldn't use the phone, go out anywhere except to work and no one could come over to see me. This lasted over a month. Dad would take us to school and pick us up every day. No more freedom to do as I wanted. I felt like I was in prison. He would lecture us but, for me, it went in one ear and out the other. I would have to say I was a very rebellious teenager.

My friends were all mad at me. Boy, were they mad! I was very resentful of the constraints that my parents put on me. Laurie decided to give up the pot but not me. Now my friends became more important to me than my parents and family.

---

8   Ibid, 130.
9   Ibid, 130.

SECOND TRIAL

My Dad called a meeting of the other parents of my friends, but the parents showed no interest. I was so embarrassed and humiliated. I was being treated by my parents as though I was such a bad person. All I did was get high. I thought I had the worst parents in the world and couldn't take it any longer. I felt that my siblings all hated me, and felt like a criminal locked up in the house all the time.

So I decided to leave home. One day, I waited until Dad went back to work and I left. I was seventeen years old at the time. I had no plan, had no idea where I was going to go. All I knew was that I could not stay there any longer. I didn't even pack anything. I just left. I decided to go to the social worker's house about five blocks away. It was drizzling at the time. The social worker had given a talk at the school about our rights as youths and other social problems.

The social worker took me to the police station. They called my parents. I learned that in Wisconsin, minors could refuse to go home. So I did. I refused to go home. I felt so much resentment and anger.[10]

Because I would not go home, my one option was to go to the state-run group home. My parents needed to sign a paper to allow this. My Mom kept pleading and begging me to come home. But I was stubborn and refused. At that time, I did not consider how much I was hurting my parents, because I was too wrapped up in my own emotions and desires at the time. My mother was crying. She then asked me to stay with her sister who lived in Chicago, but I refused even that. I decided to go to the State Home for kids, not at all realizing what I was asking for. I just remember feeling so much resentment and I was very prideful. I wanted to show my Dad, "You can't do anything to me anymore. I don't need to obey you." I felt some of my sisters were traitors.[11]

---

10   Ibid, 132.
11   Ibid, 132.

What I didn't realize at the time, was that the State Home was full of kids who were involved in heavy drugs, stealing, robbery, and even murder! I was there for one week. The counselors, too, realized that I didn't belong there. One night, they took us bowling. One of the girls put sleeping pills in one of the counselor's drink. I later realized that they did the same thing to my drink. I was afraid to tell on them for fear they would hurt me. By the end of the week, Mom convinced me to stay at Aunt Georgia's house in Chicago.[12]

I was glad to go to Aunt Georgia's house. She welcomed me with open arms and made me feel special. My Aunt Mary had picked me up from the State Home, took me to gather my belongings from our house, along with my plants and my bird, and then dropped me off at Aunt Georgia's house. That evening after dinner and dishes, my aunt told me that whatever I did in the past stays in the past. This was a new beginning for me. I really appreciated that and it made me feel good. I felt respected by her. I spent my last year of high school living with her and going to Niles Public High School.[13]

It was seven months before I went home to visit which was also Christmas. January 16, 1980 was my eighteenth birthday and Mom and Dad came to visit me and take me out to dinner. Mom gave me a beautiful gold necklace which I still have. Then on Mother's day, which marked roughly one year since I moved out, Mom picked me up and I spent the night at home in Kenosha. It was then that Mom asked me if I would consider moving back home. I agreed and moved back home after graduation.[14]

I graduated on June 8, 1980. Those that celebrated with me were my family, my Aunt and her family. We went to Kenosha for a little party. Later that night, I returned to my Aunt's house. She let me attend

12   Ibid, 133.
13   Ibid, 133.
14   Ibid, 133.

a graduation party at some friends' house. There, we were drinking and getting high. I still had not given up my druggie lifestyle. I battled drugs until 1984. It was very late and the only person left at the party who could drive me home was Dave. He was also the most drunk person there.

He had a little Pinto car. We were driving down a two-lane road at 45 MPH when Dave turned to look at me. "Congratulations, Kathy!" he said to me. "It's our graduation!" All of a sudden a semi-truck was barreling down on us ready to hit us head on. The next thing I knew, we were suddenly in the other lane, and I saw the rear lights of the truck behind us.[15] My guardian angel made me grab the wheel and turn it just in time to miss the truck by inches! That night, all I could do was think about how close we were to being killed. If I had not reacted so quickly, I wouldn't be here to tell this story and I would be in Hell for all eternity! God is good. The next day, Dave thanked me for saving his life. Years later, he became a Catholic priest! I guess God had plans for us. God is good.

After graduation and after thirteen months of living with my Aunt Georgia, I moved back home in Kenosha to the basement which my parents had refurnished for me. It took me some time before I would feel comfortable sleeping in the bedroom with my sisters. Aunt Mary picked me up and took me to confession. It lasted for two and a half hours! My knees were numb!

Then a month later, I was in another serious car accident. I was knocked out when my head hit the windshield. Although the car was totaled, I recovered with no serious injuries. It was as though God was trying to get my attention. But I still did not listen to Him.[16]

Over time while living at home, I came to realize that my family did

---

15   Ibid, 134.
16   Ibid, 134.

in fact really love me. It took a long time for me to feel comfortable with them again. My friends continued to mean a lot to me even though my parents still did not care for them. I remained persistent in smoking pot while my parents did not know.

I finally started to wake up after five long years and began to believe what my Dad had been trying to teach me all along, that the key to my life was God, and I was just throwing away the key. I began to pray to St. Joseph to help me as I had no inner peace. I quit kidding myself and decided to kick the habit. I gave up smoking pot for Lent. My whole family and extended family were praying for me. Lord knows I needed it! I became very devoted to Our Lady. God surely has been good to me.[17]

Today, Kathy is the Director of Religious Education at a Catholic parish in Kenosha and has a very successful program. The bishop was commenting on the letters from her students. They would write letters such as why do I want to be Catholic, etc. He couldn't get over the letters from her students. It's the second year in a row that he has been reading them. She has to battle the liberals along with other difficulties. She's doing phenomenal work and is a very active Catholic!

The following are some insights from Gwen and two talks given by her sometime during the early years of the Apostolate:

Eight words describing the Apostolate for Family Consecration: Helping you Heal Families through the Catholic Faith [through the media and the Sacraments.]

Consecration – giving all our efforts, good works and possessions to Jesus through Mary in union with St. Joseph. Prayers, works, joys, sufferings – everyday – very powerful in living out daily life.

Faith and Family – Family (the Domestic Church) is the cell of the new Evangelization. Where our treasure is, our heart is also.

---

17   Ibid, 135.

SECOND TRIAL

IN THE MIDST OF DAILY LIVING

We know we live in a fast-paced, goal-orientated society where there is a deep spiritual hunger. We need to satisfy this hunger and grow spiritually through commitment to the ordinary events of everyday life.

We want to learn the role of love and commitment in the midst of daily living while serving families and consecrating them in the truths of our faith. We do this through the Apostolate for Family Consecration in union with Jesus through Mary, in union with St. Joseph.

This family ministry is God's work, blessed by the Church and we are His instruments in building up the kingdom of God, with the sole purpose to reach our eternal salvation and to bring as many souls as possible with us. No small task, it is one of great responsibility for all of us.

Let me assure all of you that this is our intent, and we take it very seriously. Just as we aim to raise our children with their families for heaven, we have the deepest desire and goal to spiritually guide and walk this journey through life with you.

Evangelizing Families Scripture:
Go forth and teach all nations…

We have learned that our Faith in God gives us strength. It is within family life that we get to know God, and through knowing Him, we come to love Him, and when we love Him we are all eager to serve Him.

As Pope John Paul II said, "The Christian family is the first community called to announce the Gospel to the human person during growth, and bring him or her through the progressive education, to full human and Christian maturity."

As we all know, education in the faith is a life-time task. It has to be a daily and constant part of our lives.

Once this is realized, your efforts to evangelize become a part of your family and a way of life to share with other families.

Let me share our experience of how a family evangelized and opened our minds and hearts to a new way of life. It was a family that invited us to their home once a week to study and learn about "True Devotion to Mary" by St. Louise de Montfort. We learned about consecration of our lives to Jesus through Mary.

We knew nothing about consecration, in fact never heard of that word. We were asked to read a few pages every day and then meet once a week in the home of our friends.

Through this know, love and serve method, we became excited about it, and our lives began to change. Things that we thought were important were not so important to us any longer.

We began to realize that God was our source and our strength. And it was to Jesus through Mary in union with St. Joseph by consecrating our lives, our family, all we had, and all that we did was willingly given to Mary our Blessed Mother.

Once we started living a consecrated family life, family prayer became an integral part of our lives. We wanted our children to have this spiritual richness, so our Faith became alive in our family.

In an interview with Mother Teresa she said, "We must really bring prayer back into the family. All the rest will be all right because prayer deepens faith…and the fruit of faith is love, and the fruit of love is service, and the fruit of service is peace."

So you see, to know, love and serve brings peace. Therefore, our mission in this Apostolate for Family Consecration is to bring this peace of heart to all families with the goal of winning souls for Christ in order to build God's kingdom.

So remember the letter code: W S F C = Win Souls For Christ!

SECOND TRIAL

Scripture tells us in Matthew 5:14 'Let your light shine before men that they may see your good works and glorify your Father who is in heaven.'

Chapter 9

A Special Relationship
with a Saint

TIME WENT ON AND THE APOSTOLATE GREW and developed. On May 1, 1976, Jerry attended a meeting in Chicago, Illinois consisting of six hundred heads of religious communities and their staff, along with a number of bishops. It was held at the Felician Sisters' Motherhouse. Present at this meeting was Mother Teresa of Calcutta, now known as St. Teresa of Calcutta! Naturally, being a world-renowned figure, everyone would want to get some time with her. But Jerry was specifically requested by Fr. John Hardon, S.J., a member of the committee and who invited Jerry to the event, not to ask Mother for private time because no private interviews were being granted. If he was granted that privilege, others would want the same he told him.

"At the time, I was building our Advisory Council," Jerry said, reflecting back, "and Fr. Hardon invited me to come but told me not to try to record anything or to try to get a special meeting with Mother, because of the number of superiors and bishops there and her time being so limited." Jerry continued, "Fr. Hardon took me in the line to meet Mother. I shook her hand, gave her my card and moved on."

She took Jerry's card, looked at it and pulled him back, and said, "This is the most important work in the Church and in America." She continued, "In America, it's not so much physical starvation which is the biggest problem but spiritual starvation, especially in the family. I want to know more." She then said she wanted to talk to him during lunch. What a happy event! "Thank goodness Fr. Hardon was with me because he would never have believed it!" Jerry chuckled. They met for forty-five minutes privately over lunch! This relationship, which began as a seed with God's design, was planted that day and would grow to fruition into a long and intimate friendship over time, and last the rest of their lives.

Mother Teresa carefully read Jerry's complete presentation and the Advisory Council application form. He asked her to join his Advisory Council and she agreed! She signed the form. This was amazing because Mother rarely joins committees or organizations. Fr. Hardon, who knew her very well and taught her nuns all over the world, said to her, "Well, Mother, you should be a member of the Institute of Religious Life's (IRL) Advisory Council. That's the meeting you are at today and it would be good for you to support them by joining their Advisory Council." She simply said "No," and that was it.

"Mother, what besides prayer is the most important thing that I must do," Jerry asked, "in order to succeed in this mission?" Without any hesitation and looking at Jerry intently, she responded, "For every active member in the Family Apostolate, find someone to suffer for the work in the Apostolate. We do this in the Missionaries of Charity," she continued, "and we call them our 'second selves.' This suffering member," she advised, "should offer his or her sufferings to the Holy Family for the apostolic work of a specific active member. This union," she went on, "would be the source of the spiritual power that would make the active member's work more fruitful. An active member, in turn, offers his or her work to the Holy Family through the suffering the (Sacri-State) member incurs. This is one's second self." She also told Jerry that there was nothing more important than the offered suffering for each active member of her order.

Jerry would heed to Mother Teresa's advice. He started searching for his own Sacri-State member or 'other self.' In August of 1976, while in Florida, Al Barone exposed Jerry to a set of talks given by Sr. John Vianney. Sister was located in Elm Grove, Wisconsin at the Notre Dame Health Care Center. He was impressed with her talks and decided to ask her if she would be willing to do a set of catechetical programs for the Apostolate. She agreed! It would be a children's version of *The Apostolate's Family Catechism*. Most of the Coniker family would also participate in this series, being children themselves at the time. It became a valuable resource for children. In time, Jerry also asked Sr. John Vianney if she would become his Sacri-State member, and she agreed to that as well!

"Every day for three weeks," Gwen recalls, "Sister John Vianney was videotaped at St. Joseph's Carmelite Nursing Home in Kenosha. The programs were produced from her bed side. My children went with their dad to do the programs. It was Robert, thirteen, Joe, eleven, Jim, ten, Maria, nine, Theresa, eight, and Mary, six. The children would prepare Catechism questions ahead of time to ask Sister. Sister would then give her answers, always citing an example or story from her own life, to make the lesson easier for the children to understand."

This series was also made available years later online for anyone with internet access to view. There were some three hundred questions.

Later in 1976, the Coniker family went to St. Louis, Missouri for a convention. The Family Apostolate had its own little booth. A big sign decorated the booth outlining the Four C's: Confidence, Conscience, seed-Charity, and Constancy. Mother Teresa was also there. The Coniker children met Mother for the first time! "When she spoke," Kathy said, "you could feel a holy presence."

In June of 1977, Jerry meets again with Mother in the Bronx of New York, where she shared her Constitutions from her own order with him. Jerry had written her, asking to see her again, in order to consult with her about a particular problem. So after Jerry spoke to Mother about his issue, he then outlined for her the spirituality of the Family Apostolate. When he had finished, she responded with, "The spirituality of the Apostolate for Family Consecration is the same as our own spirituality. I would like to share with you our Constitutions, which I have never given to anyone else outside our own Congregation." What an honor for Jerry to be given such valuable insight, and brought into the inner workings of an Apostolate of a woman who would one day become a Saint!

With that, she dug into her satchel and drew out her tattered copy of her Constitutions on mimeographed sheets and handed them to Jerry. He would include excerpts from them later in a book entitled, *Peaceful Seed Living, Volume II*.

A SPECIAL RELATIONSHIP WITH A SAINT

On April 22, 1978, Jerry and Gwen would again meet Mother Teresa at a meeting in St. Louis, which was organized by the Institute of Religious Life. "Cardinal Carberry, then Archbishop of St. Louis, and Advisory Council member was the host," remarked Jerry years later. "At that meeting, Mother signed a letter in which she spiritually united the Apostolate for Family Consecration with her Missionaries of Charity. It was the greatest gift she gave to the A.F.C.," said Jerry.

That Letter of April, 22, 1978 is the following:

On April 22, 1978, she wrote:

Dear Mr. Coniker,

Let every member of our community be a Sacri-State member of the Apostolate for Family Consecration. I wholeheartedly pray for the success of the A.F.C. and its marvelous work in renewing the family through the systematic transformation of neighborhoods into God-centered communities.

God bless you
Mo Teresa m c

Mother Teresa, Foundress and
Mother General of the
Missionaries of Charity

Jerry and Gwen would see Mother Teresa again in the summer of 1981. On June 13, 1981, Jerry invited Mother to Kenosha to do some video programs. She accepted! The plan was that she would arrive in the morning, stay overnight, and leave the following morning.

The TV studio was readied. Gwen took care of the backdrop of the studio. She decorated a room with wallpaper, paint, pictures, chairs, curtains, carpeting, and flowers. Meanwhile, Jerry hired a professional TV crew for $25,000.00 a day. They planned to produce four programs. This also would be the first programs produced by the Family Apostolate in their own studio! The topics for the programs included the Sacred Heart of Jesus, the Immaculate Heart of Mary, St. Joseph, and the Holy Family. One can see why they bought their own television studio on credit.

Then there came a glitch in the plans. Mother sent word that she could not come down for an entire day and a half. The best that she could manage would be seven hours at the Center, since she had to give a talk in Chicago that evening. It was a bitter disappointment for Jerry.

It seems that for every joy, there is a cross that accompanies it. Mother Teresa would indeed visit them in Kenosha and record the four programs intended. She would even baptize the Family Apostolate's television ministry at the St. Joseph Center.

Gwen traveled to Marquette University in Milwaukee to pick up Mother to bring her back to the Apostolate Center in Kenosha. "Gwen had a considerable amount of time to spend with Mother in the car on their way back to Kenosha," Jerry said. "They really hit it off! Gwen was really relaxed with her. Over time, once Mother got to know Gwen better, she came to really love her." Jerry continued, "In fact, when Gwen was with me, the meetings were far more productive!"

In the meantime, however, someone had leaked to the press the news of Mother's visit even though it was to be kept strictly quiet. The phones began to ring, reporters began to appear, crowds began to gather, and even the Mayor and other dignitaries began to arrive. It became quite a fiasco and a security problem. The local police were called to handle the crowds.

As this was happening, the TV crew that Jerry had hired were put to work on other programs while waiting for Mother to arrive. They finished several TV programs for the Peace of Heart Forums before Mother even arrived. "We rigged up TV monitors outside in our back yard to accommodate the people who came," said Jerry. "When Mother first walked in the door, she immediately said, 'I would like to meet with Jesus in the chapel.' We took her to our chapel, spent a few minutes in prayer and started the day in the TV studio."

"We had four teams of people that were to be interviewed with Mother and arranged to produce four programs. We successfully completed those programs. However, the sound track was less than ideal. Even so, the result was still good enough for the programs to be shown for years to come. All of the programs that we produced with Mother over the years became the most popular productions that we had," said Jerry.

A SPECIAL RELATIONSHIP WITH A SAINT

"When the work was completed and the filming over, Gwen had all the children assemble in the back yard around the St. Joseph statue. We walked Mother out to the back and many were crowding around her. Someone said, 'Would you pray for my son's vocation?' She stopped, walked back to her and said, 'Only if it is going to be a good vocation.' She was all about loyalty to the vows that one takes, either marriage or religious life."

Jerry continued, "We took a family picture in the back yard with Mother. That picture became part of our opening TV program for thousands of programs produced throughout the years." At that time, Maureen was 21 years old, Kathy, 19, Laurie, 18, Peggy, 17, Sheri, 15, Michael, 13, Robert, 10, Joe, 9, Jimmy, 7, Maria, 6, Theresa, 5, and Mary, 3. Some of the Presberg children were also present. Mary Presberg, one of the cousins of the Coniker children said years later, "Mother Teresa grabbed my sister's hand [Ann Marie Presberg] and held it the whole time!" Mary Ann Presberg, Jerry's sister, had twelve children of her own and was a member of Opus Dei.

Mother Teresa addressed the Conikers: *"For all works of love are works of peace. I will pray for you that you make your family life something holy, something like Nazareth. The love, peace, and joy, and from that you can spread that love, especially father and mother. Be one heart full of love in the heart of Jesus through Mary. Keep the joy of loving each other and share this joy with all you meet. Let them look and see how you love each other. How do they know you are a Catholic family? How do they know that you love one another, as Jesus said? By your love for one another, they will see that you are His disciples."*

"It was really Mother Teresa who inspired our TV ministry," Jerry remarked. "She coined a phrase to explain her work and the spiritual life:"

"The fruit of silence is prayer. The fruit of prayer is faith. The fruit of faith is love. The fruit of love is service. The fruit of service is peace."

"I noticed throughout the years as we were videotaping Mother, she developed this formula. It was gradual but it really summarized the spiritual life. Mother would tell us to give God permission; permission to act in our life, permission to drive."

No sooner had Mother left and the crowds dispersed when Gwen began to experience violent headaches. Jerry also became ill with the flu. He had been fighting off the effects of the flu all week. He literally collapsed and had to be helped to bed. These were all part of the cross in order to bear fruit. Although a high price to pay, it was well worth the wonderful graces and blessings received from the events of the day.

Mother Teresa at Coniker home in Kenosha,
WI. June, 1981

Dr. Wahlig, O.D. and the Image of the Immaculate Conception

In June of 1985, Jerry, Gwen, and the Coniker boys went to New York to meet with Mother Teresa at her Missionary of Charity home in the Bronx. Since they did not have any money, Jerry used the Coniker boys as the camera crew. Moreover, all the hotels in New York were on strike, so there was no ability to stay at one of them. However, Jerry had a friend who lived there by the name of Dr. Charles Wahlig, O.D., an optometrist and widower. He was eighty-two years old and his house served also as his office.

Dr. Wahlig was a prominent author and eye doctor who discovered the images in Our Lady of Guadalupe's eyes, and he was an expert on the history of that shrine. A figure of a bearded man had been already discovered in the eyes of the Virgin in 1929 and 1951. In 1962, Dr. Wahlig discovered two more figures in her eyes and, also, succeeded in reconstructing the exact circumstances under which the celestial portrait had been created. Dr. Wahlig invited them stay with him.

They were able to videotape Mother Teresa's talk on "The Right to Life." They also conducted a private TV interview of Mother while there. The trip was a huge success! They were adding to their library of programs to be viewed through the Apostolate's "Be Not Afraid Family Hours" conducted in hundreds of churches across America. It also seemed that Our Lady brought them there also to learn more about Guadalupe and to videotape Dr. Wahlig.

Dr. Wahlig knew well the history of the Shrine at Guadalupe. He delivered talk after talk to Jerry, Gwen, and the crew. He told them that Our Lady of Guadalupe, Patroness of the United States, should really be honored under the title of "The Immaculate Conception," since this is how she declared herself to Juan Diego in 1531. He said she is being called by the wrong name. She herself declared to Juan Diego, "I am the Immaculate Mother of God who crushes the serpent's head."

"Just a few months ago," he told them, "at the International Conference on the Sacred Image, the Archbishop of Mexico, who is also over the Shrine, gave me an award for being an expert on Guadalupe. Yet none of them will listen to me when I tell them that they are calling the Sacred Image by the wrong name. It should be called the 'Image of the Immaculate Conception.' It is, besides, the one and only image we have from heaven of Our Lady. It is the most powerful sacramental we have in the history of the Church. This sacramental was active when the Church bridged the gap between the Old World and the New in 1531."

He insisted that there is no such thing as "Guadalupe" in Mexico. Guadalupe was a major Marian shrine in Spain which had nothing to do with this image. Scholars are divided as to how the term was applied to the apparition. In 1668, Pope Clement IX had declared Our Lady of Guadalupe to be the Immaculate Conception. So why is it so difficult to have the Sacred Image properly identified? Why, after seventeen years' campaigning for this had he not succeeded in his effort?

This interview with Dr. Wahlig was videotaped. It became one of the most powerful Peace of Heart Forum series they had ever done. It is entitled, "Our Lady of Guadalupe, known as the Immaculate Conception, Patroness of the Americas." This message was broadcasted across the country during the Marian Year of June 1987 through August 15, 1988, by the Apostolate.

A few days later, the Conikers were on their way to pick up Cardinal Silvio Oddi, who was visiting in Green Bay, Wisconsin. He was prefect of the Congregation for the Clergy and a member of the Family Apostolate's Advisory Council. On their three-hour drive back to Kenosha, Jerry discussed his visit with Dr. Wahlig, and shared the information of the doctor's research on the Image of Our Lady of Guadalupe. He then asked the Cardinal if he would do a TV program on the subject. Cardinal Oddi, a great Marian Cardinal and well-versed in all that relates to Mary, responded without hesitation, "Sure, I will!" Jerry told this to Dr. Wahlig, who could not believe that a Cardinal of the Roman Curia, was so interested, since he had been unsuccessful getting any priests or catechetical teachers interested!

A year later, Jerry stayed again with Dr. Wahlig in New York. "Jerry," he said, "your Apostolate has done more to promote the true title of the Sacred Image of Our Lady than anyone else in the world, and that includes myself! Now I want to pass the torch on to you. I can go home to my God and to my wife." They said their goodbyes to each other, but Jerry had a sense that it was the last time he would see his friend. In fact, he wasn't even bed ridden but he suddenly died later that very night. His daughter called Jerry two days later to tell him the news.

Dr. Wahlig insisted that graces had flowed through the Aztec Empire on their recognition of Our Lady as the Immaculate Conception. Similarly, he believed, that graces would also flow through the United States when they came to recognize Our Lady of Guadalupe as the Immaculate Conception, and entrusted the country to her under that title. Jerry felt that Our Lady had her hand in this all along when they went to New York to interview Mother Teresa.

In June of 1988, the Conikers had the privilege of yet another visit with the saintly nun. "We had a last minute notice of an opportunity to video her while she was visiting her sisters in the Bronx, and we didn't have time to wait for a plane" said Jerry. Gwen remarked, "Our friend, Fred Hill, came from Canada in his private jet to Kenosha to pick us up and flew us to the Bronx." Gwen continued, "This was my first experience of flying in a small jet plane, and I was really nervous. But I thought, 'the Blessed Mother will take care of us since this journey was to give her honor.'" Mother was supposed to arrive from St. Louis at 8:00 p.m. but was very late and did not arrive until 11:00 p.m. Sr. Nirmala, her assistant, said it would be impossible to videotape her this late as she had a heart condition. However, Jerry had his crew set up the equipment nonetheless, and had a studio ready within an hour's time in hopes of still being able to interview her upon her arrival.

In the meantime, the sisters were scurrying about getting ready for Mother's arrival. They were all in their bare feet as they do not wear shoes in the home. When Mother did finally arrive, the sisters rushed to greet her and welcomed her with flowers, ringing bells and singing hymns! She greeted each sister with a kiss and then, finally, welcomed the Conikers and those with them with her usual warmth.

"Although she was obviously very tired, Mother insisted on being videotaped," said Jerry. "The TV interview lasted for an hour and a half!" Mother looked at Mike, Jerry and Gwen's son, who was putting the microphone on her, and said, "Did you ever thank your parents for having you?"

"We must really bring back prayer to the family," Mother exhorted. "Then the rest will follow. Because prayer deepens faith, and the fruit of faith is love, and the fruit of love is service, and the fruit of service is peace."

"After the interview," Jerry said, "we accompanied Mother to their little chapel. It was a very bare room with the exception of an altar, a crucifix, and the tabernacle with a single lit candle. There were no pews or kneelers or chairs. The sisters kneel on the floor to pray. On the wall were the words, 'I thirst.' One could feel the presence of God in this chapel. Afterward, we left for the hotel and flew back to Kenosha the following morning."

There were numerous other interviews throughout the years. One time she was interviewed by the Apostolate in Rome. "Mother invited us to come over to her Mother House in Rome but, by the time we arrived, her time was up and she needed to be somewhere else," recalls Jerry. "She told us that we could stay and she would be back in four or five hours, and then we could do the interview. We spent that time getting the studio ready and all the equipment set up. In the end, it worked out well and we succeeded in interviewing her."

"The interesting thing is that Mother did not grant any interviews at all to others but always granted them to us," continued Jerry. "In fact, Sr. Fatima, who was head of Mother's orders for contemplatives, said to me, 'She considers the Family Apostolate very special.' She would always make time for us. She also loved Gwen. They really hit it off."

At Studios in Kenosha

Mother Teresa embracing
Gwen in New York

Mother Teresa with Gwen and Jerry
Coniker in Rome.

A SPECIAL RELATIONSHIP WITH A SAINT

"Our last meeting and interview with Mother was just days before her death," said Jerry. "She was in Washington D.C. and was not granting any interviews because she could only sit up for five minutes at a time. I knew it would be impossible to get permission in advance to interview her. So I sent our video team with a letter drafted to her to get permission to use her famous prayer breakfast video, since the cable company owned the footage. I had tried unsuccessfully to obtain a videotape from C-SPAN of Mother Teresa addressing the National Prayer Breakfast in Washington, D.C. C-SPAN refused, saying the tape would only be given to unbiased media outlets, not a pro-life organization like the Apostolate. I later contacted Sr. Nirmala Joshi, Mother Teresa's successor, and asked whether she might read her address for me, so that I could have it on videotape. However, Sr. Nirmala rejected my request, citing the poor health of Mother. But Mother interjected, 'Is this for Jerry?' she asked Sr. Nirmala. 'Then we'll do it,' she said.

"It was a miracle because nobody was even allowed to visit with her let alone interview her," said Jerry. "She sat up for the entire interview, which was over 45 minutes, and read her entire speech so we could have our own copy. This was when she was dying. She got a  burst of energy. At the end of the reading of it, Mother added, 'That ought to get 'em!' she said. She was brought back to Calcutta and, in a few days, died on September 5, 1997."

Jerry continued, "Gwen and I were privileged to narrate Mother's funeral with Fox News TV. We would rotate between 2-3 people until 4:00 a.m. It is noteworthy that Mother had a state funeral in a country that did not believe in Christianity."

ANOTHER SAINTLY FIGURE, MOTHER MARY ANGELICA OF THE ANNUNCIATION, PCPA

Not only did Jerry and Gwen Coniker rub elbows with two super saints, that of St. Mother Teresa of Calcutta and St. John Paul II the Great, but they also had a personal encounter with what could very well be a third one in the future, that of the holy, tenacious, and extraordinary cloistered nun who founded a multi-million-dollar network called Eternal Word Television Network; Mother Mary Angelica from Irondale, Alabama. Mother Angelica, as she was known, was also a Franciscan Nun of the Poor Clares of Perpetual Adoration.

Jerry discovered Mother Angelica while watching TV. He heard her tell her audience that she was about to start her own TV network. The light bulb went off in Jerry's mind. He had been wanting to create the Peace of Heart Forum formation programs, using state-of-the-art technology at the time—VCR tapes. He believed that although currently VCRs were cost-prohibitive for the average household, they would someday be in every household, he envisioned, and wanted to be ready for that. So against the advice of some members of the Family Apostolate, who advised him to use filmstrips or slides, as well as the objection of the bank from whom he was trying to obtain a loan, Jerry stuck to his intuition to go with the VCR tapes. Jerry contacted Mother Angelica and arranged with her to be able to use her studio facilities for one week.

It was June 1980 when Jerry and Gwen and some of their children went to Our Lady of the Angels Monastery in Birmingham, Alabama, in order to produce the Peace of Heart Forum video programs. "We dropped off Jerry and Laurie, seventeen years old, in Birmingham," said Gwen, "and then I went to visit my mother, Rose Billings, in Brooksville, Florida with Maria, six, Theresa, Five, and Mary, three."

"We worked tirelessly that whole week," said Jerry. "Those who were in the video programs were Dr. Burns Seeley, John Hand, Monsignor Alphonse Popek, Father John Hardon, Mother Immaculata of the Mt. Carmel Hermitage in Minnesota, Father Lawrence Lovasik, Mother Angelica, Father William Dorney, Laurie Coniker, and Richard DeGraff."

"We did programs on such topics as the Spirit of St. Teresa of Avila, the Rosary, and one series each on the Gospels of St. Matthew, and St. John, and two series on St. Paul's letters." Jerry continued, "We went to the studio with prepared scripts, but Mother Angelica said, 'You don't need those scripts, just speak naturally, and let the Holy Spirit speak through you.'"

When Gwen came back after the week to pick up Jerry, Mother Angelica said to her, "You can have him back! He's all yours! He's some worker! He worked us to death!" They had produced fifty shows in one week and had completely exhausted her TV crew. Gwen said, "We are all aware that Jerry knows how to use every minute of every day!"[1]

As time progressed, more and more programs were created by the Apostolate. There were also changes in Board members as some were called to do other things. Some of the Board members and Advisory Council members were very generous with their time, talents, and/or treasures. For example, August Mauge, longtime friend, board member, and Gwen's former boss at the car dealership, was a very generous man, both with his time and his finances. Bill Barnett, who travelled the country promoting devotion to the Sacred Heart of Jesus, impressed Jerry and influenced him to devote himself to the important cause of Consecration to Jesus through Mary, which Jerry believed to be the most powerful means to renew family life. Then there was Advisory Council member, Father Lawrence Lovasik, S.V.D., who was a very key member. He was a prolific writer and author of *The Apostolate's Family Catechism*. He helped the Apostolate most likely more than any other. He wrote many of the materials which the Apostolate uses.

---

1   Ibid, 140.

Mr. Pat Maher was a most generous benefactor. Mr. Maher assisted the Apostolate in funding many things, not the least of which was funding the salaries of three employees for a year as well as paying for the down payment for the Apostolate's lake-side Immaculate Heart Retreat Center.

Lloyd V. Conant, President of Nightingale–Conant Corporation, was the largest distributor of audio-cassette motivational tapes in the world. He was well known in business circles and a customer of Jerry's. Lloyd admired Jerry for his fresh ideas and skill in selling. As a young man, Lloyd gave Jerry a contract for supplying their record albums because Jerry gave Lloyd ideas which helped his business. They ended up becoming close friends. Jerry was much younger than Lloyd but that did not matter to Lloyd.[2]

There was a time in which Jerry was in desperate need of seventeen thousand dollars, for the Apostolate, and he asked Lloyd to help him. However, at the time, Lloyd himself was in dire financial straits. Nevertheless, he gave Jerry the advance as he knew he was using the money for the Family Apostolate. "I just know Our Lady would bless him for his generosity," said Jerry. "He always was generous to us, donating desks, chairs, and other items to us. He was not Catholic but was baptized as a Lutheran and a morally good man."

When Lloyd was dying of cancer, Jerry visited him and brought some holy water, to baptize him in the event he was not already. It turned out he had been baptized. Then Jerry sat down with him and read him some Scriptures. While reading to him, Lloyd fell back, as if sleeping, and passed away. Jerry was asked by his wife, Hazel, to give the eulogy at his funeral. "I was much honored to be asked this of his wife," Jerry said. "I really believe that God blessed him for his faithfulness to his family and friends, and for his extreme generosity to others and, especially, to the Apostolate. The most important thing for Lloyd was God in the end."

---

2   Ibid, 137.

Chapter 10

Faith, Hope, and Trust

It was 1980 and the Apostolate was beginning to be heard about far and wide most especially, because of the Conikers' good fortune of making friends with others, and coming into contact with people who knew the kind of people, who could promote their work; people like Mother Teresa of Calcutta, Mother Angelica from EWTN, and Mario Luigi Cardinal Ciappi O.P. to name a few.

The Conikers came to know Cardinal Ciappi through Father Thomas A. Morrison, O.P. a Dominican, who had stayed in Kenosha for one year in 1977 as their resident theologian. Father Morrison taught philosophy and theology at De Paul University. Cardinal Ciappi was also a Dominican and had served as the Pope's theologian since the pontificate of Pope Pius XII. When Pope Paul VI became the Vicar of Christ, he chose to ordain Father Ciappi a bishop and to elevate him to the College of Cardinals, in the same week! Father Thomas wanted to witness this momentous occasion of his fellow brother Dominican, so he flew to Rome to be present. Before he went, however, Jerry asked him if he would take an invitation to the new Cardinal to become a member of their Advisory Council.

Cardinal Ciappi was well loved in Rome by members of the Roman Curia. This was most evident at the ceremony to elevate him to Cardinal. When the other cardinals-elect received their red hats, applause broke out by members of the Roman Curia. However, when Cardinal Ciappi received his red hat, the Curia members broke rank to surround and embrace him.

Fr. Morrison did keep his promise to Jerry and gave the new Cardinal his invitation to become an Advisory member for the Apostolate. He told him about their work and the wonderful things they were doing for the family. At that time, the Cardinal declined, replying, "I'm still the Pope's theologian attached to his personal household." He continued, "I am also the Master of the Papal Palace. Consequently, I don't think I could ever lend my name to another organization. However, I shall pray for them and read their books and literature."

Three papal theologians who have made invaluable contributions to the Church: St. Dominic, O.P., founder of the Dominican order and first theologian for the pope; St. Thomas Aquinas, the Angelic Doctor, fourth papal theologian; and Mario Luigi Cardinal Ciappi, O.P. (foreground), the eighty-fifth successor to St. Dominic as papal theologian, the primary theological advisor for the Apostolate for Family Consecration since 1979. His Eminence, Cardinal Ciappi, O.P., is one of the greatest theologians and Mariologists of our time.

FAITH, HOPE, AND TRUST

Cardinal Ciappi did in fact start reading the Apostolate's literature. He was so impressed that he even showed Jerry's book on St. Joseph and several of their other books to the Holy Father. He sent Jerry a letter telling him of this. Now the Apostolate's work has reached the very top, all the way to the Pope, who at that time was Pope John Paul II! Also, in 1979, Cardinal Ciappi came to the United States, met with Jerry, and agreed to join the Advisory Council! Mario Luigi Cardinal Ciappi would later become a key asset to the Apostolate for Family Consecration, a friend of Jerry's, and be the Family Apostolate's theological director from 1979-1996.

Father Rodrigo Molina, S.J., a Jesuit priest from Spain visited the Apostolate Center in 1980. Father Molina founded *Lumen Dei*, an apostolate of consecrated laymen, laywomen, and priests. He was on his way from Chicago to Milwaukee to visit the archdiocese and wanted to pay a visit to the Apostolate for Family Consecration. Although he did not speak English, his traveling companion did and translated for him.

The first thing Father Molina did, upon his arrival at the Apostolate Center, was to go into the chapel to pray for several hours. When he emerged from the chapel, he instructed his traveling companion to cancel his plans for the rest of the day, as he wanted to stay for the evening.

Jerry and Father talked until 2:00 a.m. in the St. Kolbe studio about the spirituality of the Apostolate and the similarities between the Family Apostolate and *Lumen Dei*. Father Molina advised Jerry to have one particular and definite spirituality which inner core members could focus on. He did not, however, suggest which spirituality should be adopted. In his opinion, this was essential if the Apostolate was to survive, notwithstanding the fact that it was teaching all of the spiritualities of the Church in its Peace of Heart Forums. The other advice that Father gave for the Apostolate to succeed was the importance of having priests who were imbued with the Apostolate's spirituality. These priests would also need to guide its leaders in the spirit of the founder; otherwise, it would always lack in unity of purpose.

Jerry took Father's advice very seriously as he considered him to be a wise and holy man, akin to the depths of Mother Teresa. Father Molina led a very austere life, sleeping a mere three to four hours a day, and spending a minimum of four hours in prayer. He considered four hours of prayer daily to be a necessity for himself as well as the members of *Lumen Dei*.

Father offered to Jerry his willingness to form someone in their seminary for the priesthood should Jerry send someone to him. Jerry would, indeed, send someone by the name of Kevin Barrett. Kevin was given permission by Bishop Juan Torres Oliver, the Bishop of Ponce, Puerto Rico to go to the *Lumen Dei* Seminary in Spain, since *Lumen Dei* already had a house in Puerto Rico and was known to the Bishop. In time, Kevin Barrett would be ordained to the priesthood and become the first priest ordained specifically for the work of the Apostolate.

Jerry also agreed to allow Father Molina's priests to come to the Apostolate Center annually, to have a retreat given in Spanish according to the Ignatius spirituality. Some from their community have even stayed there for extended periods of time.

Father Molina asked Jerry for his assistance in getting *Lumen Dei* into the Archdiocese of New York. So Jerry sent a letter to Cardinal Cooke, Archbishop of New York and member of the Family Apostolate's Advisory Council, introducing Father Molina and his society. The Cardinal was very agreeable and permitted them to establish a house in the Bronx of New York.

Needless to say, this visit would have a very positive impact on the future of the Family Apostolate. Jerry and Father Molina made a spiritual pact which took place at a formal meeting of the Order in Spain. There, the members of *Lumen Dei* spiritually united themselves with those of the Family Apostolate, a pact they also both signed. "Please do not sin," Father exhorted Jerry, "because if you do, you will hurt our work, too."

One day while praying in the chapel, Jerry had a thought that he should adopt the spirituality of Pope John Paul II. After all, they were already studying him and doing so many programs about him and his writings. They also were using his writings, such as *Familiaris Consortio,* and adopting as their own the Marian and family spirituality aspects of Pope John Paul II. Some of the great teachers of the Church have been St. Augustine, St. Thomas Aquinas, and Pope

John Paul II (Karol Wojtyla). Pope John Paul II is a contemporary and the man for these times. It seemed such a logical choice, given that consecration to Jesus through Mary via the St. Louis de Montfort charism is the foundation of the Pope's spirituality, and he was also influenced by Saint Maximilian Kolbe's Militia Immaculata spirituality. All of this Marian spirituality was also that of Jerry's and Father Bernard Geiger, OFM Conv. So it was. The Apostolate did indeed adopt the Marian spirituality of Pope John Paul II.

The pace at the Apostolate started to gain speed. There was a professor of philosophy at Xavier University in Cincinnati by the name of Dr. Richard E. Dumont, who was friends with Dr. Burns Seeley. They used to teach together at the same university. Dr. Dumont specialized in the philosophy of Pope John Paul II. He helped at the Apostolate to produce seventy-three programs on the philosophy of John Paul II.

The interesting connections continued. It just so happened that Dr. Dumont found out that there were a couple of priests coming to the United States from the University of Lublin in Poland, who had close personal ties to Pope John Paul II. The first priest was Fr. Meiczyslaw Albert Krapiec, O.P., who had known John Paul personally and intellectually, ever since he was a young priest and was instrumental in John Paul's formation. Fr. Krapiec had been the rector of the University of Lublin for thirteen years and currently held the Chair of Metaphysics.

The other priest was Fr. Andrej Szostek, who represented John Paul in the Chair of Ethics for eight years at Lublin University. Fr. Szostek was young and very Marian. In fact, the final act that Pope John Paul II did as Cardinal Karol Wojtyla, before going to Rome to become pope, was to approve this priest's doctoral thesis. John Paul had held the Chair of Ethics there and, as Archbishop of Krakow, was responsible for the University. Hence, these two priests knew his thinking most intimately.

They were coming from Poland in order to attend a philosophy seminar in Baltimore, Maryland. Dr. Dumont exhorted them to come to the Apostolate's St. Joseph Center in Wisconsin for one day during their stay in the United States. What happened, however, is that they ended up staying an entire week!

"We produced forty video programs with them on philosophy," says Jerry, "and also produced a series called 'Be Not Afraid' based on Pope John Paul II's book. We focused on the teachings of the Pope, because we saw that this Holy Father understood in a profound way, Mary's role in the economy of salvation, the laity, and family life as no other person we had studied."

After deciding to focus the Apostolate on John Paul's spirituality, they released Dr. Dumont's tape which declared the importance of this day in the history of the Family Apostolate; because most new movements in the Church spend most of their early years prospecting for a particular spirituality. By choosing to use John Paul II's spirituality, they could focus on the gold mine of John Paul's brilliant writings and teachings and stress consecration of families, parishes, and communities in the Truth.

The Apostolate was producing more and more programs and written materials to disseminate. Dr. Burns Seeley, the staff theologian, had written meditation books on the Gospel of St. John, St. Matthew, and a couple on the writings of St. Paul.

The Apostolate used these materials for their Lay Ecclesial Teams and at the Retreats that were held at the Apostolate Center. The Coniker girls would cook for the retreats that were held in Immaculate Heart Retreat House, one of the buildings they purchased on Third Avenue in Kenosha. These retreats would last from Thursday to Sunday. Before the purchase of the Immaculate Heart building, the retreats were held in the St. Joseph Center. "The first Retreat began in February of 1982," said Gwen, "with twenty-six people. Women slept in the north wing and men in the south."

They were large rooms so bunk beds were set up to accommodate more people. The house had six bathrooms, a large kitchen, and a dining room. "The leaders were so delighted with the St. John's video Scripture series that it was shown several times," continued Gwen. "At that time, it was the only Peace of Heart Forum we had."

One huge benefit of the Retreats was to expose the Family Apostolate to people. It served as an unexpected marketing tool! They averaged two retreats a month with twenty to thirty attending.

The Apostolate gained the attention of a well-known columnist by the name of Dale Francis. He wrote two articles on the Family Apostolate, which were published in diocesan newspapers and in *Our Sunday Visitor*. Dale was a syndicated columnist; therefore, his articles were distributed throughout the nation. This was a piece of great fortune for the Apostolate in getting their name out there and recognized. The result from this excellent publicity was that thousands of people wrote in for more information and asked how to start Chapters in their own neighborhoods.

"With the first Peace of Heart Forums," says Jerry, "we would draw people into homes for weekly meetings about books which they agreed to reflectively read during their daily prayer time. We learned that people do not like classes, nor to be formally educated. So the Forums helped people get together and start learning almost without effort. In the Family Apostolate, we are really looking for peace of heart. The method we decided to use to spread the news about the Chapters," continued Jerry, "was to send out releases to the *National Catholic Register* and other Catholic papers. We did have good printed material produced, and we also organized our weekend retreats and training programs."

The first Chapter was started by Charles and Sue Van Hecke in a suburb of Milwaukee. Like many others, they had had some very difficult experiences raising their two older sons, who were now in their late twenties. They had gotten into drugs in high school and suffered serious after-effects. Of course, their parents did not know what to do to help them. The influence of the Peace of Heart Forums began to show in the family. Twenty or so people would meet in the Van Hecke's home, studying the Gospel of St. John. Soon, their thirteen-year-old son started to get interested in it, as well as their seventeen-year-old son. They then started to attend the meetings. The seventeen-year-old started inviting his friends who came, and they, in turn, invited their parents. It was amazing!

Then there was the St. Joseph Businessmen's Chapter in Lake Forest, a suburb of Chicago. It was comprised of about twenty or so businessmen, including the President of Walgreens who met once a month on Saturdays. They met in an elegant dining room where breakfast was served, and Jerry would give a talk on the mission of the Family Apostolate. They would, in turn, advise him as to how he could spread this work throughout the country and how to finance it. Some members in this Chapter included: John Hand, Frank Milligan, Bill Isaacson, Charles Scholl, Bill Spencer, Ray Cross, Fred Canning, President of Walgreens, and others.

As with any Apostolate, things are tried and do not always work. So there is a time to check and adjust. One such learning was the failure to instruct leaders not to ask new members to take on an assignment at a Peace of Heart Forum meeting. The leaders should speak to the new members individually and then ask them to accept some responsibility after giving a general presentation on the Apostolate. The effect of not doing this is that one person with influence who held a negative opinion at a meeting could shut down a Chapter.

Another adjustment was necessary, when it was revealed that some members were using the videos to provide spiritual nourishment for themselves and other members solely. This is not necessarily bad; however, the apostolic nature of the movement was not being promoted. So the result was that the non-committed were being accepted on the same level as the committed and no apostolic action was being done outside the Chapter.

Jerry and the Board of Directors came to understand that the members were not aware of what the Second Vatican Council was asking of the laity. That is to say, the laity have an obligation to evangelize and catechize not only their own families, but others to whom they come in contact with as well. Hence, the laity needs to be formed.

Because of this revelation, the Board made some changes and enhancements. The first thing they would do is to promote to a greater extent the "Be Not Afraid Family Hours" as their main method to evangelize and consecrate families in the truth.

Secondly, they would expand upon the Apostolate's Family Catechism, which was approved by the Vatican, and use it as an important tool to unite families with parish schools, and to assist and enable parents to fulfill their roles as the primary educators of the faith for their children.

The third change they would employ would be to greatly expand their television ministry, in order to reach a much greater audience. Lay Ecclesial Teams could be formed from this enhanced audience whose purpose would be to creatively use the media in homes, schools, and churches to strengthen families by systematically transforming neighborhoods into God-centered communities.

Finally, they would work toward forming the consciences of families. This would, in turn, better dispose them to receive abundant graces from the sacraments of Penance and the Most Holy Eucharist.

THE FINANCIAL DANCE

As mentioned previously, God seems to press upon His disciples a 'financial dance' so to speak, so as to build their trust in Him. This Apostolate and the Conikers were no different. It will be elucidated some of the financial stresses placed upon this family of fourteen, so faithful to God, and open to life.

In the early 1980s, Jerry bought from Frank Flick the copyrights, patents, tools, and inventory back for the Control Master time-master management system that he had sold him previously. They did not understand the system anyway nor how to market it, so Jerry was able to buy it back for a reasonable price.

Coniker Systems also donated valuable inventories to the Family Apostolate, which they were then using for Control Master and office supplies. All of the copyrighted systems of Coniker Systems were freely being used by the Family Apostolate.

Jerry needed to use his personal credit and Coniker Systems' credit to advance the early works of the Apostolate. The St. Joseph House was purchased with a thirty-thousand-dollar down payment, through the kind donation of the DeRance Foundation. However, Jerry still had to personally guarantee a mortgage for fifty-five thousand dollars from the First National Bank of Kenosha. For six years, he was paying faithfully the Family Apostolate's bills. But they were also not drawing any salary from the Family Apostolate those years.

They would use the Coniker Systems' money to pay bills. But there were a number of occasions where they ran out of money, not having enough to cover themselves or Coniker Systems. Their personal credit was stretched to the limit and no funds were available for the Family Apostolate. Many times, Jerry faced financial collapse. However, God came through at the last moment. Like an action-packed movie which keeps one on the edge of one's seat! This was very stressful for them.

There was one time when Jerry needed four thousand dollars to meet the basic bills for just one week, when an elderly couple from southern Illinois came to see him with a check for the exact amount. "We never received money in advance for any project we initiated," says Jerry. "We always had to go out on a limb to finish it. Through the grace of God, it would be completed, and then funded, but only after a period of unbelievable stress. Since Gwen helped me with the bookkeeping during those years, she also suffered the pains of financial insecurity."

Another time, they needed two hundred thousand dollars to pay absolutely necessary bills, in order to avoid lawsuits. Jerry was meeting with a particular benefactor from Minneapolis, who was not quite on board with the Apostolate, given its very Marian spirituality. He also had only met Jerry once. Still, she decided to give Jerry the two hundred thousand dollars, just at the very moment that they were starting the First Saturday videotape in the chapel.

"The strange thing is," Jerry recalls, "that the woman who gave us this money is very charismatic and strong on evangelization, but not in agreement with our Marian spirituality and some of the traditional practices of the Church. When I gave her the Apostolate for Family Consecration's prayer book, she opened it up at the one page which would have upset her; the page of indulgences! I could see that we had a problem on our hands. Since I had to stand my ground on Marian devotion and the Church's teaching on indulgences, I thought for sure that she would not give us a dime. But she kept on talking, and then suddenly stopped in the middle of her conversation. 'I can see that you're hurting,' she said, 'I will make a commitment for two hundred thousand dollars, even if I have to take it out of my principal.' The check was written on a First Friday, received on a First Saturday, and spent on the following Monday.[1] Even more compelling is that she

---

1   Ibid, 164.

gave from her need instead of her surplus. God will surely reward her generously as He is never outdone in generosity."

Still another time, they needed three hundred and fifty thousand dollars. Jerry had launched a project without the funds necessary to pay for it. Jerry had heard of a man by the name of Pat Mauler in Denver, Colorado, who wanted to help apostolic organizations like "Campus Crusade for Christ." He had already heard of the Family Apostolate from the DeRance and Raskob Foundations. He said that he wanted to see Jerry, who flew out at once to meet him at the airport. After the meeting, Pat loaned the Apostolate $350,000. Pat would later write it off. Pat ultimately gave over a million dollars to the Apostolate.

Jerry commented, "When I go into a new area, I try to look for potential benefactors and start to plant seeds. Because of previous drastic funding needs," he continued, "I would be doing fundraising that I would not normally do. For example, I would try to persuade people to give substantial grants before they were fully aware of the aims of the Family Apostolate. This works on some people but not on others."[2]

"I'm well aware that I am not raising funds the way I should be, by building up slowly on a firm foundation. However, we are ministry oriented, and only fundraise when absolutely necessary. I believe with all my heart that, unless a donation is given out of one's need, and not one's surplus, it does not have much merit. I discovered that in most cases, a donor steeped in Scripture understands this key principle and conditions required for a donation to be pleasing to God, and that it should be given from one's need, and not from one's surplus. It seems to me that God always wants us to be dependent on Him, and not on ourselves," says Jerry.[3]

The heaviest financial burden was the funding of the Marian Year of Consecration in 1988. Jerry was attempting to obtain a two hundred and fifty thousand dollar guaranteed loan from Carl Karcher from California. Gwen and Jerry flew to California to meet with him. There was great pressure to keep the momentum

---

2   Ibid, 165.
3   Ibid, 165.

of the program for the Marian Year going on, and Jerry knew if that he did not get this funding, he would never be able to push the program to its fruition, which cost a total of over two million dollars of borrowed funds. This grand Marian Year of Consecration will be explained in greater detail later but, for now, Jerry was pushing himself physically to the point where he was not feeling well, and was taking heavy doses of vitamin C tablets.[4]

During the presentation to Carl Karcher, Jerry was using all his energy and persuasive techniques, in order to plead his case when he started to feel faint. He thought he was about to experience a heart attack and began to back away. Gwen, aware of what was happening, firmly held Jerry's hand and stepped forward, following through with great enthusiasm. Carl did not even notice Jerry's condition. He was so impressed by Gwen's enthusiasm that he guaranteed the loan! What a great partnership Gwen and Jerry have together and what wonders God can do!

Jerry went to the hospital when he arrived back at home for a check-up, but the doctors could not find anything wrong with his heart. It seemed as though there was an overdose of adrenaline combined with heavy doses of vitamin C that had brought on the attack.

It was typical that if the Family Apostolate had enough money in the bank to cover expenses for one week, they felt safe. One time they had owed two hundred thousand dollars and had only thirteen thousand dollars on hand. Again, the Apostolate never started any project with money needed in hand already. The money always came later. It was pure trust in God to see them through.

"Perhaps it was not the best way," says Jerry, reflecting back. "It was most certainly not the way I preferred. However, it was God's way. We got funds from foundations and wealthy individuals, who understood and appreciated the work of the Apostolate. About fifteen percent of our income came from the sale of books and the rentals of the videos to our Chapters. We even obtained funds through no-interest loans. The main source of income was from calling people and asking them to help us. I think to myself, 'I wonder if I'll have any friends left after I have asked them for their money!' These folks know why I

---

4   Ibid, 166.

am calling them. It sure helps when they still want to talk to me knowing why I am calling them!"[5]

Most founders had very difficult financial needs. The founder of Opus Dei, St. Josemaria Escriva, St. John Bosco, and St. Mother Teresa of Calcutta always had financial problems in fundraising. In fact, St. John Bosco would say, "If the work is for the glory of God, spend all you have and even borrow more. If it isn't, don't spend a cent, for Providence will not help you."

It's particularly difficult to raise money in the Catholic Church, if you are not a religious order or institution run by a religious order. As for laymen, it's easier to receive loans compared to donations to be paid off at a later date.

---

5   Ibid, 167.

Chapter 11

Extraordinary Holy Year, 1983-1984, and Scaling the Heights!

POPE JOHN PAUL II DECLARED 1983-1984 to be an Extraordinary Holy Year. Jerry had a strong desire to go to Rome during this year. He consulted with Mario Luigi Cardinal Ciappi about this desire and he suggested to Jerry to come in November of 1983, because the Synod would be over but everyone would still be in Rome before they left for their home countries.

So Jerry wrote to all the cardinals of the Roman Curia as well as the prefects and presidents of pontifical councils. Jerry had learned at an early age to go to the top in order to accomplish his goals. So this was no different. He also discovered that the people at the top were easier to deal with than people below. The only appointment he had secured for his trip to Rome was with Cardinal Ciappi. So he asked the good Cardinal if he would assist him, by asking him to contact the other cardinals to see if they would meet with him. Jerry would have a letter for each of them, once he arrived in Rome, stating he was currently in town and that he would be calling them.

Jerry, Gwen, and son Robert set off to Rome, with video equipment and all. In fact, there were eighteen boxes of equipment! It was their first pilgrimage to Rome. Gwen remarked, "We had our own idea of what we wanted to do and to accomplish, but we were ready to let God lead us."

There was much red tape with the trip and with the equipment they brought, from clearing everything with the American and Italian Embassies, and the Vatican, to all the paperwork and other requirements that were necessary to fulfill. Moreover, upon arrival in Rome, customs confiscated all of the cameras and video equipment! The language barrier added to the struggle because the Conikers did not speak Italian. Added to this stress was Jerry's uneasiness with their securing of their equipment or lack thereof. All of their expensive equipment was placed in a glass enclosed room to be seen by all. Jerry complained about the lack of security and that his whole life savings went into purchasing this equipment but they simply responded with, "Don't worry! Don't worry!" For Jerry, the situation was unreal. "We were filled with anxiety about the equipment, but we had no choice," said Gwen. "We took a bus to the Michelangelo Hotel, six blocks from the Vatican."

Jerry took a cab to the Vatican and explained the matter to some Vatican officials. He got nowhere. Exasperated, he kept pursuing his options and finally was able to phone the Archbishop in charge of the Vatican City-State services. Fortunately and much to Jerry's relief, this Archbishop took care of the situation. He contacted the airport and was, to put it mildly, very assertive with them about the camera equipment and the situation at hand. Immediately, three limousines were dispatched from the Vatican to the airport where the equipment was picked up and brought directly to the hotel. Jerry was greatly relieved!

While in Rome, they interviewed several cardinals and Roman Curia bishops. The most important interview was with Cardinal Ciappi. "The distance was not far from the hotel to the Vatican which was important since we did not have a car," said Gwen. "But we did have a big metal cart for the equipment," she continued, "and we wheeled that cart back and forth from the Vatican to the hotel with the Italians staring at us!" They had to also carry the equipment up long flights of stairs which was not an easy task. When they went to interview Cardinal Ciappi, however, nothing happened when they pressed the button. A fuse blew in the recorder and it would not work. There was so much disappointment experienced, especially after all the trouble bringing the equipment all the way to Rome. They then decided to take still photographs. However, when they developed these, they discovered that a number of them came out blank. Their crosses did not end.

When they went to record Archbishop Gagnon, pro-president of the Pontifical Council for the Family, Jerry made it a point to remind the camera man twice to check the second recorder that they brought to ensure it was working. "It's all set," he assured Jerry. They taped the shows with the Cardinal and inconvenienced everyone by turning the reception room into a studio. However, it would be well worth it, they thought. They recorded three shows. But alas, upon reviewing them, they discovered that the audio was turned on but the video was not. It was the last straw of a very disappointing trip. All the effort, hassle, security risks, and money, to lug all that equipment to Rome ended up being for nothing.

Despite these bitter disappointments, there were many things for which to be grateful. Jerry did meet all of the cardinals except the Secretary of State with the assistance of Cardinal Ciappi, spending about an hour with them. Jerry did not realize this then, but later found out that this was rather unusual. He also was able to get many cardinals to join the Advisory Council. He met with William Cardinal Baum and was told he could only meet with him for a few minutes. However, the visit ended up being over an hour with the Cardinal signing on to the Advisory Council, encouraging Jerry, and lending his name to the Family Apostolate.

Other cardinals he was able to spend time with included: Silvio Cardinal Oddi, prefect of the Congregation for the Clergy; Augustin Cardinal Mayer, secretary of the Congregation for Religious and Secular Institute; Edouard Cardinal Gagnon, pro-president of the Pontifical Council for the Family; Simon Cardinal Lourdusamy; Angelo Cardinal Rossi; and Opilio Cardinal Rossi.

With respect to Angelo Cardinal Rossi, prefect of Evangelization and of the Propagation of the Faith, Jerry did not have an appointment with him. He decided to try to "pop" into his office to see if he was there. When Jerry arrived, the Cardinal's secretary agreed to take a letter in to him. The Cardinal emerged from his office to greet Jerry. He was both gracious and supportive.

When the Cardinal learned about the Family Apostolate, he was impressed and really liked the idea of the Sacri-State members. He said, "Any organization which puts a high priority on finding people to suffer for its work will bear great fruit." He then signed the Advisory Council membership form and gave Jerry a large medallion.

Jerry arrived back at the hotel. A message was waiting for him from Cardinal Agostino Casaroli, the Pope's Secretary of State. The message said that he would visit with Jerry for a five-minute courtesy visit because of Cardinal Ciappi. Jerry went alone to see him since Gwen was exhausted from all the day's visits. The five minutes turned into fifty-five minutes! The Cardinal showed a genuine interest in the Family Apostolate.

Before Jerry left, the Cardinal grabbed his hands and had this to say: "The genius of your apostolate," he said, "is that it uses the media in controlled conditions: in homes and in churches to create community and motivate people to read, meditate, and learn their faith. I want to see that encouraged."

THE EXTRAORDINARY MEETING

Jerry's end goal, of course, was to meet Pope John Paul II. So he asked Cardinal Ciappi if he could make that happen. Jerry also met with Monsignor John Magee, Master of Papal Protocol and private secretary for three popes: Paul VI, John Paul I, and John Paul II. He was the only cleric to hold such a position in Vatican history. He gave the Monsignor a letter from Mother Teresa. Monsignor Magee was able to arrange a meeting between Jerry and Monsignor Stanislaw Dziwisz and Monsignor Emery Kabongo, the two secretaries of the Pope. Monsignor Magee joined the Advisory Council and would prove to be one of the Family Apostolate's most powerful teachers and friends.

Monsignor Kabongo, later Archbishop of Zaire, Africa, assured Jerry that he would speak with Monsignor Dziwisz to see if he could arrange a meeting with the Pope. It was the seventh day and they still had not seen the Pope. Then that night, he called Jerry to tell him that the Pope would receive him after his private Mass at 7:00 am the next morning. "Be at the bronze doors with the letter from your bishop," he told him.

But Jerry did not have a letter from his bishop. It just so happened that Jerry's bishop was providentially in Rome at the time. So Monsignor Kabongo contacted Jerry's bishop and then informed Jerry that everything was settled and he could come. Later that evening, Monsignor Kabongo called Jerry again, saying to him, "That presentation binder you showed me the other night," he said, "I'd like to go over it with the Holy Father tonight. Can you bring it here?" So Jerry walked through the rainy streets of Rome to the bronze doors of the Vatican to hand over the presentation binder to the Swiss Guard.

The next morning, Jerry, Gwen, and their son Robert, who was also their photographer, got up at 5:00 a.m. and trucked through the dark and the rain to the bronze doors at the Vatican. They were led into the Pope's small chapel into his private apartment at 6:45 a.m. to attend his Mass. It held about twenty chairs. The Holy Father was already kneeling in front of the altar. It was an amazing experience for them, having been deeply edified by the Holy Father's solemn posture of prayer.

After Mass, the Pope emerged out of the chapel to greet all his twenty or so guests in the parlor. He first received some Koreans and had his picture taken with them. He proceeded down the line until he arrived at the Conikers who were last. He approached the mother of thirteen children who worked for the Church while raising a family. He stared into the eyes of Gwen and she, in turn, was quite moved by him, while taking hold of her hands. He then spoke with Robert for several minutes. Finally, he turned to Jerry, saying, "I have read your book and I bless this most important Family Apostolate." He discussed the structure of the Apostolate, suggesting if one could structure correctly the use of the laity for the Church, one could unleash their tremendous potential.

It is standard practice that when one gives the Pope something that his secretary takes it from him. However, when Robert gave the Pope the Family Apostolate's *Prayers and Recommended Practices* book, he would not let his secretary take it from him. The Pope also made it clear that he wished to have a picture taken with them, while admiring Jerry's book displaying the Sacred Heart on the cover. The meeting lasted for about ten minutes.

EXTRAORDINARY HOLY YEAR

Gwen, Jerry, and Robert's first encounter with Pope John Paul II,
November 1983. Extraordinary Holy Year of 1983-84.

So the Extraordinary Holy Year did indeed become extraordinary for the Conikers! They had a private meeting with a great Pope, and signed many cardinals of the Roman Curia to their Advisory Council; all of these cardinals had direct contact with the Holy Father!

Later that same morning, Jerry went to a meeting with Cardinal Oddi. Meanwhile, Gwen and Robert attended the General Audience at ten o'clock and enjoyed a second surprise meeting with the Holy Father. When they arrived at the Audience and presented their tickets given to them by Cardinal Ciappi, they were unexpectedly escorted to the front row! The Pope greeted Gwen and Robert again for a rather lengthy moment for a general audience; and to think that Gwen almost did not attend the audience because she did not feel well. For the second time in one day, Gwen received the Papal blessing! "The Pope looked into my eyes like he was reading my soul. He had so much compassion in his eyes!" said Gwen. The Pope recognized Gwen immediately and said to her, "I just saw you!" When the Pope came to Robert, he held his head and pulled him close in an endearing manner. He then assured them of his prayers.

Jerry met once again with Cardinal Oddi on *The Apostolate's Family Catechism*. Later, he met with Cardinal Ratzinger (who later became Pope Benedict

XVI), and Cardinal Gagnon, who had approved *The Apostolate's Family Catechism* on behalf of the Holy See. The trip lasted for nine days and was filled with appointments, crosses, and excitement!

For Jerry the trip, although it had its share of crosses and disappointments, had graces beyond compare. Jerry said that things had never been quite the same, since the Holy Father's encounter and blessings, during that extraordinary Holy Year of Redemption! The pace of the Family Apostolate accelerated very quickly after that trip. Jerry realized that support of the Pope and the Roman Curia carried with it a great responsibility that he would never take for granted. Jerry prayed to follow God's will and consult with his spiritual director, Father Bernard Geiger, O.F.M., Conv., before making any major decisions.

The Archbishop who originally helped the Conikers retrieve their TV equipment from security at the airport said to them, "As long as I have been at the Vatican, I have never seen Cardinal Ciappi so excited about any apostolate. He doesn't usually lend his name to organizations. People expect me to do things for my friends but that's not so with Cardinal Ciappi. Yet the word around here is, 'Who's this American with the Family Apostolate that Cardinal Ciappi is calling everybody about and encouraging them to help?' That means a lot here because Cardinal Ciappi is careful, super careful you might say, about what he endorses. After all, he is the Papal Theologian and Master of the Papal Household."

Jerry believes that it was the endorsement of Cardinal Ciappi that opened the doors of the Vatican for him. In terms of getting the TV equipment back to the airport, Jerry sought the help of the Archbishop in charge of the Vatican Bank. This is not something they do very often, but they were more than kind to provide three limousines for themselves and their equipment to take them back to the airport.

Chapter 12

Marian Year Consecration
1987-1988

THE FAMILY APOSTOLATE GREW to such a point that they needed to use a very large Episcopalian complex a block away on the Lake Michigan side of the street to run the larger training sessions. They created more and more video programs with some of the top teachers of the faith including Father John Hardon, S.J., Dr. Scott Hahn, Mother Teresa of Calcutta (now St. Teresa of Calcutta), Francis Cardinal Arinze from the Roman Curia, Cardinal Ciappi, the Pope's theologian, and many other Roman Curia members, renowned figures, theologians, and experts in the faith. Their library of catechetical material would grow immensely in the coming years which will be elucidated later, and would branch out on an international scale.

Cardinal Ciappi, O.P., The Pope's theologian

The mission of the Family Apostolate was to join with Pope John Paul II's belief that Christ will conquer through Mary in union with St. Joseph. Moreover, the way to arrive at the reign of the Holy Family is through the dual dimension of John Paul II's consecration: *Totus Tuus* (meaning Totally Yours; giving everything to Jesus through Mary, all in union with St. Joseph, according to the charism of St. Louis de Montfort, St. Maximilian Kolbe and John Paul II, all in union with St. Joseph), and *Consecration in the Truth* (cf. John 17; consecrating our families in the Truth through continuous formation). This is truly the "Catechesis of the New Evangelization" that Pope John Paul II said could renew the world; family by family, parish by parish, and diocese by diocese.

Through this Total Consecration, an ever-growing spiritual army is being assembled by the Holy Family to bring all of society to God. It is truly a "Gideon's Army," where the consecrated few can be powerful instruments of atonement by giving their meager efforts to Blessed Mary, so that she can increase their value and then present them to her Son. The great Message of Hope is that a consecrated few can offset the effects of the sins of many, and usher in a civilization of love and life!

THE CATHOLIC CORPS

In 1986, eleven years after the Apostolate for Family Consecration was founded, the Holy Spirit inspired Jerry and Gwen to found a community of lay consecrated celibates–the Catholic Corps–to serve the Church in the work and mission of the Family Apostolate. The Catholic Corps is a growing community of loving, faithful, dedicated men and women who promise to be single and make private vows of poverty, chastity, and obedience for life. It is a vocation, similar to a religious order, in that it is done in stages, so as to ensure that both the community and the individual are sure there is a true calling to this life.

The Catholic Corps would also help with the various works pertaining to the Family Apostolate in whatever capacity that was needed. It became, for the Conikers, an extended family, so to speak. Gwen, known by her Catholic Corps members as "Mamma C," would always have an "open door" policy, to meet with any member to speak privately about any matter that was a concern for them. They loved being with her and would often seek her out for advice.

THE IMMACULATE CONCEPTION

In 1986 it came to Jerry's attention that the Holy Father was planning a trip to the United States before it had been publicly announced. This revelation was also confirmed by another source in August 1986, by Sister Hayat Marie from Haiti, who came to the Apostolate Center. "Did you hear that the Holy Father is coming to the United States?" she asked Jerry.

"Yes," Jerry replied.

"And do you know that the United States' Patroness is the Immaculate Conception?" she inquired further.

"Yes," Jerry replied again.

She continued on, "But did you know that when the Holy Father visits a country, he usually consecrates that country to its Patroness?" This Jerry did not know. Jerry had witnessed how powerful a consecration of a country can be, when the bishops had consecrated Portugal prior to World War II. The powerful effects of this consecration spared Portugal from the Second World War and the takeover of Portugal by the communists in 1974. The wheels starting spinning in his head! He realized that they had so much video material on the Immaculate Conception, having interviewed Mother Teresa and Dr. Wahlig's study of the matter, that he began to formulate a plan in his mind.

He thought, "Hmm, should we launch a national campaign for the Consecration of the United States to the Immaculate Conception, and tie this in with the new idea of the image of Our Lady of Guadalupe? But that would be a major undertaking and we already have so much to do," still thinking to himself.

It just so happened that a couple days after Sr. Marie left the Apostolate Center, Cardinal Ciappi paid a visit. Jerry confided to the good Cardinal his idea. He asked him if he would do a television show explaining why the image of Our Lady of Guadalupe should be called the Immaculate Conception. The Cardinal thought for a moment and responded affirmatively. Jerry suggested that it be in Italian to be more clear, and then to translate it into English. This they did and a top theologian from Rome, Fr. Brian Harrison, who was also staying at the Apostolate Center for the summer, did the voice-over translation. The Cardinal edited the consecration formula prayer and the campaign literature for the National Consecration, prior to the Pope coming to America. The goal of this project for the Apostolate was to use the Papal visit to gain enough support to bring about the consecration of the country. They coined this project the "Immaculate Conception, Teach the Children Campaign."

Then on January 1, 1987, the Holy Father announced a Marian Year which would begin on Pentecost Sunday, June 7, 1987, and end on August 15, 1988, the feast of the Assumption of Our Lady. Their campaign would develop into the Marian Year Consecration Program. Jerry would use the Marian videos that they produced already, with key figures and create a program that would combine and incorporate a National Consecration Campaign coupled with public recognition, by the hierarchy of Our Lady of Guadalupe's image of the Immaculate Conception, calling it a "Marian Year National Consecration Program." It would entail a video novena package of nine days or nine weeks of one-hour videos for churches, homes, and Mother Angelica's "EWTN" International Cable Television Network.

Jerry solicited and successfully obtained the approval of all four Cardinals in the United States: John J. Cardinal O'Connor, Bernard Cardinal Law, John Cardinal Krol, and Joseph Cardinal Bernardin. They also agreed to be videotaped on the subject of the Immaculate Conception, with the imagery of Our Lady of Guadalupe for the campaign together with Archbishop Anthony Bevilacqua of Philadelphia, Father Patrick Peyton, Mother Teresa of Calcutta and others. Cardinal O'Connor wrote to Archbishop Thomas C. Kelly, who was organizing the Papal visit, to inform him of the campaign and what it entailed.

"It is very unusual having a layman coordinate a campaign of this magnitude, and having all the bishops of the United States consecrate the country to Our Lady," said Jerry. "It's hard getting the bishops to agree on anything, let alone a project as vast as this one," he continued.

MARIAN YEAR CONSECRATION

In fact, a prominent Dominican priest called Jerry and was livid that Jerry was upsetting his work to consecrate America to Our Lady, for which he had been working to accomplish for five years. He felt that his work was threatened by Jerry's project. Jerry ignored the priest's outrage and went about his work of continuing on with the effort.

In addition, it just so happened that when Jerry was in Rome in June of 1986, he had interviewed and videotaped Monsignor John Magee, Master of Papal Ceremonies. All of these programs would be utilized in the campaign to bring clear understanding of the spirituality, of Pope John Paul II and Our Lady of Guadalupe as the Immaculate Conception.

Jerry also contacted all the "Lay Evangelization Teams" asking them to conduct "Be Not Afraid Novenas" in the local churches. The Family Apostolate promoted novenas in churches, in order to get as many people as possible to support the Consecration, during such a grace-filled period. The first novenas were presented on June 17, 1987 and continued all throughout the Marian Year. These novenas on videotapes were extremely successful. The Apostolate sent out mailings, news releases, and announcements in all the diocesan newspapers at the time of the Papal visit. In addition, various Catholic TV networks agreed to put two different versions of the Novena on their television network [thirty-minute and one-hour programs]. The hope, naturally, was to reach as many people in the shortest time. It also served to expose their Apostolate, and their Lay Evangelization Teams initiative, as well as the good work by EWTN that was showing the Apostolate's novena program several times a week on their Global Television Network. It was a huge and expensive undertaking. Two hundred thousand dollars were used just to do the mailing. Two million dollars was incurred, however, to pay for extra television time, TV equipment, computer equipment, inventories and so forth for the Marian Year program.

For Jerry, the expense and debt incurred was well worth it. "The importance of the Marian Year lay in its unrepeatable opportunity for obtaining powerful graces for our country, for the Family Apostolate, EWTN, and for Franciscan University of Steubenville, with which the Family Apostolate is officially associated," said Jerry with firm conviction.

Another unusual thing that the Family Apostolate did was to create 'dated' programs, which it tends to shy away from, given that they desire to produce programs which can be shown at any time and replayed. Given the importance of the Marian Year which was preceded by the news of the Papal visit, they decided to produce hundreds of dated TV programs in order that people would act during a period that was so filled with grace.

Jerry experienced enormous pressure to drop the Marian Year project with criticisms of it taking too much time, enormous amounts of money, and effort. However, in Jerry's mind, it was important that the country come back to God, by such a great outpouring of grace and to not miss such an opportunity. He again discerned and sought comfort in his decision by reaching for a book in the St. Joseph Center's library that he had not looked at in years. It was a book of the letters of Sister Lucia in her own handwriting. Jerry had obtained two copies of this book on his last day in Fatima on June 13, 1973 when he had an audience with the Bishop of Leiria and Fatima. After the audience, a Jesuit priest met with Jerry and gave him the books. This book had been released by another Jesuit priest, whose blood sister was a nun in the Dorothean Order to which Sister Lucia had belonged, before she became a Carmelite.

During the years of 1926 and 1939, Our Lady appeared to Sister Lucia and revealed to her the First Saturday devotion with its respective promises, as well as the consecration of nations to the Immaculate Heart of Mary. In 1940, Sister Lucia had written a letter about these messages to then Holy Father, Pope Pius XII. When the Bishop of Fatima found out that these letters had been published, he stopped all further publications.

So when Jerry was perusing through this book, he came across a letter from Sister Lucia to Pope Pius XII, in which she tells him that Portugal would not be involved in the Second World War; precisely, because the bishops had consecrated Portugal to Our Lady during that time, and this tremendous grace would have been granted to other nations had they done the same.

Well, that was all the encouragement that Jerry needed to carry on with the Marian Year Campaign! Even if the two million dollar debt was in a sense crushing him as was the opposition from within, he carried forward with firm resolve and courage, conviction and confirmation that he gained from the words of that letter, despite attacks from the highest level within the Apostolate. Only in the next life will we know and fully realize the wise decision made by Jerry and its good effects, if he had not pursued such a noble effort for the sake of millions of Americans! Many will be thanking him later for this. Jerry sent out a letter to all the bishops in the United States before this campaign had a chance to wither.

It was important for the Marian Year Committee to have the support of Cardinal Bernard Law of Boston, as they wanted him to act as co-Chairman, in order to give the campaign momentum. Tom Monaghan, founder and owner of *Domino's Pizza*, arranged a meeting with forty or so prominent Catholics with Cardinal Law to be the keynote speaker. Jerry was invited to this meeting by Tom.

The guests needed to take a ferry boat to Monaghan's exclusive resort on Michigan's Drummand Island in northern Lake Huron. They were late because the boat broke down on the way there. Upon arrival, Jerry noticed that the Cardinal was already surrounded by some prestigious people, one of which was the Ambassador to the Vatican. However, when the guests were sitting down at the table, Jerry noticed an empty seat right across from the Cardinal. He jumped at the opportunity and sat down across from him. Divine Providence paved the way and Jerry was able to speak with the Cardinal for an hour! Jerry asked him to act as Chairman of the Committee, elucidating how important his name would be to the Campaign. He also asked him if he would write to Cardinal Bernardin, asking him to join the committee. Jerry's tenacity paid off! The Cardinal accepted the invitation! Of course, Jerry's tendency is to seek the last bit of juice from a piece of fruit, lest some be lost. So he invited the good Cardinal to become a member of the Advisory Council too, but he said, "Let's see after the Marian Year." One can't blame Jerry for trying! But then he turned to him and said, "Oh, I'll do it now!" and he signed the form!

Jerry and Gwen went to see Archbishop Bevilacqua of Philadelphia, another key figure. Jerry was told that the Archbishop could give them only one hour of his time. However, they spent three hours with him, including creating a videotape!

He had no intention of giving Jerry a letter. However, he started off the meeting correcting Jerry's grammar in the letter that he wrote and got so involved with the corrections that he ended up giving Jerry a better letter, along with printing it on his letterhead including envelopes for all the bishops of the U.S. and the mail merge software to boot! The Archbishop also wrote to every bishop in the United States, asking them to support the campaign and to sign the consecration form, to be presented to the Holy Father at the end of the Marian Year. The support from Archbishop Bevilacqua was very important because he was the archbishop of the city where the American Constitution was written, and the Family Apostolate was having its letters signed during the year of the 200th anniversary of the signing of the Constitution. Additionally, Bishop Thomas V. Daily of the Diocese of Brooklyn agreed to bring to the Bishop's conference this letter as a point of discussion.

The Family Apostolate also contacted over a hundred contemplative communities asking them for their prayers for the success of the Campaign, and for Archbishop Bevilacqua's letter which was put forth before the Bishop's conference. On the day of the Bishop's conference, Jerry tracked down Mother Teresa, who was providentially in Mexico at the Shrine of Guadalupe, in order to solicit her prayers. She assured him not only of her prayers, but would also solicit the prayers of the poor for the success of that meeting and for the Consecration of the United States to the Immaculate Conception.

During the Bishop's meeting, favorable comments were made by those bishops who had experienced the wonderful effects of the Novena. One bishop from California, in particular, told Cardinal Law how enthusiastic one of his pastors was about the "Be Not Afraid Family Hour" novena videos. The Bishop's conference was a huge success and planted very good seeds.

GWEN'S CARE OF HER MOTHER

Gwen's mother, Rose, went to live with the Conikers in January of 1987 because she had terminal cancer. Gwen and Jerry's room was set up for her with a hospital bed on the second floor of their home. Rose had a beautiful view from her window of Lake Michigan. She was also able to watch spiritual tapes and programs on Catholic topics from her hospital bed. Gwen and the children tended to her every need for the next eighteen months or so until she went to the hospital.

On July 2, 1988, which was a First Saturday, the Coniker family was preparing to go to Mass when Gwen received a call from the hospital telling her that her mother was not doing well. Gwen and the children headed immediately over there. Fr. Mauro Ventura met them there as well. Jerry was in Steubenville, Ohio at the time, giving a talk at Franciscan University on the First Saturday devotion of Fatima and the Sabbatine Scapular Privilege.

As an aside, the Sabbatine Scapular Privilege is a tremendous grace. It is a promise given by Our Lord to St. Simon Stock in which anyone will go to Heaven the First Saturday after his or her death if the following conditions are met: Wear the brown scapular; be chaste according to one's state in life; pray daily the family or community rosary or pray the rosary in the Eucharistic Presence of our Lord; and become a member of the Carmelite Brown Scapular Confraternity. Membership into the Confraternity is only done once per lifetime.

Rose Billings fulfilled all these requirements. Fr. Ventura celebrated Holy Mass and the family prayed the family rosary by her bedside. Rose breathed her last, three hours later, at 3:45 p.m., in peace. What a wonderful privilege she had to be surrounded by loving family and filled with all of God's graces.

DIVINE PROVIDENCE

Money was always in scarce supply and the Conikers faithfully relied on God's Providence to see them through. At this point in time, the Conikers had eighteen hundred dollars in their savings account and an inadequate amount going into their I.R.A. Their investment was in their children, they believed, and a good form of social security, they thought!

By July of 1988, only a fourth of the one hundred and eighty-six diocesan bishops had signed the consecration form. On the surface, the project looked like a dismal failure. But so did the death of Jesus to His apostles at first. The Apostolate for Family Consecration, however, was in Our Lady's hands. Fourteen days before the end of the Marian Year on August 1, 1988, the Apostolate Center sent out another Federal Express letter to every bishop in the United States with copies of Cardinal Law's original letter and Archbishop Bevilacqua's letter asking them to sign the consecration form and return it, in order for it to be presented to the Holy Father at the end of the Marian Year. One hundred and one more responded, making the total of one hundred forty-one out of one hundred and eighty-six bishops who signed the consecration form or about two-thirds!

WGN, a cable superstation out of Chicago that had cable affiliates all over the U.S., accepted the one-hour TV special to be aired on Sunday morning, at 9:00 a.m., August 14th. This was the day before the end of the Marian Year and the feast of St. Maximilian Kolbe, a great Marian Saint who promoted Marian Consecration. NBC, CBS, ABC, and others also picked it up in many major areas. Many of the videotapes that the Family Apostolate made for this occasion were included in a one-hour special and shown on national television. Many millions of people joined Cardinal O'Connor in the act of Consecration of the United States to the Immaculate Conception—Our Lady of Guadalupe on August 14, 1988!

Jerry contacted Cardinal Arinze in Rome to see if he would present the letters, now in binder form, to the Holy Father. The Cardinal declined, stating the inappropriateness of the fact that he was not from the United States. With this thought, Jerry decided to present it to the Holy Father himself!

Jerry contacted Cardinal Ciappi on August 10, 1988 in Rome to see if it would be possible to have another private meeting with the Holy Father, in order to present to him the bishops' signed consecrations of the United States to the Immaculate Conception, under the image of Our Lady of Guadalupe. The Cardinal's response was thus: "Yes, the Pope would receive Jerry and his family privately after the general audience on August 17, 1988." The Pope was trying to fulfill Our Lady's request to consecrate not only Russia but the world to Immaculate Heart of Mary, not an easy task to accomplish. Cardinal Ciappi arranged for Jerry, Gwen, and the entire family to meet the Pope in a private audience; however, politics got in the way. Somebody got the audience canceled. Cardinal Ciappi interceded and he got Jerry, Gwen, and his family into the public audience hall which holds 10,000 people.

So Jerry then contacted Fred Hill, a generous benefactor, to ask him if he would like to accompany Gwen and him to Rome for the ceremony. Not only did Fred agree, but he wanted and felt it appropriate that the entire Coniker family go to the ceremony on his expense, including in-laws and grandchildren! Before Fred's kind offer, the Conikers were only planning on taking two children to Rome because of the cost.

Gwen went about getting everything ready for the trip, passports and all! On August 13, 1988, the entire Coniker family was airborne to Rome! Upon arrival in Rome, they hired a TV crew. Jerry had hoped to meet with Monsignor Peter Elliot, a priest in the Roman Curia of the Pontifical Council for the Family and whom Jerry had met through Cardinal Gagnon, President of the Pontifical Council for the Family. But Jerry could not find his telephone number. Cardinal Ciappi, on the other hand, spent the whole day with them, giving them all a tour of the Vatican and showing them places that were prohibited to the general public. They discussed the procedures for presenting the letters to the Holy Father which were bound in a large, thick ring binder. They were also going to present to him the Holy Family Portrait, nine week video novenas, the program on the image of Our Lady of Guadalupe and other materials.

On August 15, 1988, they attended the Mass at St. Peter's. On August 17, 1988, Cardinal Ciappi arranged for the Conikers to meet the Holy Father in a private room after the general audience at 10:00 a.m. The Conikers went to an early Mass and, afterward, were met by the Cardinal's secretary who told them to hurry because the program had been changed and the Pope was to arrive earlier.

The doors were to be closed at 10:00 a.m. and it was already 9:30 a.m. Jerry gave the binder of letters to Gwen to take with her, while he made sure that the family arrived at the Vatican on time. Upon arrival, the guards were already on the verge of closing the doors. Meanwhile, Cardinal Ciappi persuaded the guard to hold open the doors to the auditorium until the rest of the Coniker family had arrived.

SERVANT OF GOD

The new arrangement no longer allowed for the Conikers to meet with the Holy Father in a private room; however, Cardinal Ciappi had twenty chairs put up on the side of the stage for them. It turned out to be a better situation than before. They were at the end of the line which meant there would be more time with the Pope. Jerry then looked over to Gwen and asked her for the binder of the bishop's letters. To his astonishment and dismay, she told him that she did not have it! She had assumed that he took the binder with him. They wondered where it was and surmised that it still must be in the car.

"When the Pope comes in," a Swiss Guard warned Jerry, "security takes over. If you leave, then you won't be able to get back in to see the Pope."

"But what am I doing here?" Jerry asked himself. "The only reason I am here is to give the Holy Father the bishops' letters consecrating the U.S.A. to the Immaculate Conception under the image of Our Lady of Guadalupe." With that, he immediately got up, crossed the stage, left the auditorium, and exited, in order to go back to the car in hopes of finding the binder. "Walking across that huge auditorium of ten thousand people," he recalls, "was the longest walk I ever took in my life!" The Swiss Guards were calling him back as he walked off.

Upon arrival at the car, he saw the binder lying there in the back. He seized it and hurried back to the auditorium. When he arrived, the doors were closed, so Jerry pounded on them. Then Cardinal Ciappi opened the door with one hand while holding back the Swiss Guard with the other. Once inside, Jerry found that the Holy Father had already arrived and was speaking to the people. Jerry slipped in and was heading back to his seat when two guards grabbed him, and told him that he would have to wait until the audience was over, to get back to his seat. Cardinal Ciappi then stepped in and guided Jerry to a tunnel that led to the other side of the auditorium where Gwen and the rest of the family were located. So Jerry crawled the full length of the auditorium. He was able to get to his seat with Gwen and their family as the Swiss Guard looked on. He slipped into his seat unnoticed in front of a crowd of ten thousand people.

Jerry was anxious, not knowing how much time he would have with the Pope to present the bishops' letters and introduce his family. But Gwen had her own agenda; she wanted to make sure all twelve of her children were introduced to the Pope. Just as the Pope walked over to Gwen and Jerry, Gwen grabbed the Pope's arm and swung him around and away from Jerry and started introducing her family first. The Pope was aware of what Gwen was doing, and he went along with her priority with meeting her family. To Gwen, her family was most important, even if the Pope ran out of time before Jerry could give him the binder of letters!

Fortunately, there was enough time to present to the Pope the binder of letters. Jimmy, their youngest son, was also holding the holy family portrait and Kathy, their second daughter, presented the nine one-hour videotapes that were used in over 300 parishes for consecration, shown on television on August 14, 1988 and shown on EWTN regularly throughout the Marian Year. The Holy Father seemed very pleased and accepted this act of humility and solidarity.

The Pope turned his attention to the Coniker family where he gave a short talk and then held the hands of Gwen and Jerry and prayed over them, thanking the Apostolate for Family Consecration for the entire Marian Year Program that no doubt brought many graces and continues bringing many more graces to the United States. This was a very significant event, because over two thirds of the bishops in the United States consecrated their dioceses and all parishes in their dioceses, under the image of Our Lady of Guadalupe–the Immaculate Conception.

It's sad to say, not many countries in the world consecrated themselves to Mary during this grace-filled period during the Marian Year. The ones that did were the United States, Portugal, Philippines, and Poland. Portugal was spared from World War II because of their consecration and was spared again from being taken over from a Communist government in 1974. "I am sure we have avoided many chastisements for the United States because of this Consecration by the bishops in 1988," said Jerry.

A special note should be made here. Gwen had her priorities correct and her family came first. Even if they didn't have the time to present the Marian Year program, her family was a priority. This is a testament to her holiness in which she followed God's will first, which was her daily duty as a wife, and as a mother tending to her family.

SERVANT OF GOD

All this happened in front of the entire general audience which to Jerry was far more impressive, than if the letters had been presented to the Holy Father in private. This was one of the most important events in the history of America and to the Family Apostolate. "I shudder to think," says Jerry, "what would have happened if the Holy Father had not been thirty minutes late!" This, he believed, was all according to Divine Providence.

Jerry and Gwen meet Pope John Paul II again in
Rome August, 1988 during the Marian Year of 1987-88.

The entire Coniker Family in Rome to meet Pope John Paul II during the Marian Year
of 1987-88 including, in-laws and grandchildren, eighteen in all!

Chapter 13

Attempted Takeover and New Pastures

AFTER SUCH AN EXHILARATING EXPERIENCE and one of great euphoria, the Conikers returned to their hotel room. Gwen talked about their agony and ecstasy. They had just experienced the ecstasy. Now, their agony would soon follow. Upon arrival, there was a letter waiting for Jerry from Cardinal Law. The letter, essentially, was about Cardinal Law laying down the law by telling Jerry that he must work with Archbishop Weakland, as it pertained to the work of the Apostolate and the TV programs that they were creating. He thought that Jerry had too much exposure on worldwide television and he should be under the leadership of Archbishop Weakland who headed the Archdiocese of Milwaukee, the diocese where the Family Apostolate was located. Archbishop Weakland had brought his concerns to Cardinal O'Connor about the Apostolate gaining too much power which prompted a response by Cardinal Law. Archbishop Weakland felt that communicating through the media with no bishop to synthesize their work, along with too much influence, power and exposure than bishops had in the Church, was problematic. It appeared that Archbishop Weakland wanted to control the Family Apostolate. This letter started what would be a two-year ordeal and exchange of letters with Archbishop Weakland.

SERVANT OF GOD

ARCHBISHOP WEAKLAND

There was a bishop's meeting in the United States where both Cardinal O'Connor, who was the guardian of the Family Apostolate, and Archbishop Weakland attended. During the meeting Archbishop Weakland walked over to Cardinal O'Connor and said, "How would you like to have a major apostolate in your diocese where you have no control over it and the founder doesn't come to talk to you?"

"I wouldn't like that," Cardinal O'Connor responded.

Archbishop Weakland pressed on, "Well, if Jerry Coniker's Apostolate moves into your diocese, that is what is going to happen. Jerry Coniker does not submit his teachings to me."

Cardinal O'Connor said nothing and walked away.

The Apostolate was growing by leaps and bounds, so Jerry had asked Archbishop Weakland for his permission to take over a large facility in Racine, Wisconsin. The Archbishop would not approve of it. The fact of the matter is that Archbishop Weakland wanted to control the Apostolate. He even admitted that he wanted control of their theology and their money. Everything else they can do. But the interesting thing to note is that the Apostolate was not wealthy. In fact, they often depended upon Divine assistance to meet their daily needs…literally their daily needs.

Archbishop Weakland was known to be one of the most liberal bishops in the United States. To protect families from the far-left theology in the Church, Jerry had a full-time staff theologian, Dr. Burns Seeley Ph.D., check everything before it left the studio. This is why The Apostolate for Family Consecration has over 500 of the top theologians in the church teaching on over 15,000 24 ½ minute video segments. "One of the benefits of being in the Apostolate is to be assured that all teachings follow the Magisterium of the Church," said Jerry.

The Apostolate for Family Consecration advisory council is very active in teaching the faith. Cardinal Oddi, the Vatican's prefect for the Congregation of the clergy in Rome, meaning prefect over all the clergy in the world, advised Jerry to ask Cardinal O'Connor of the Archdiocese of New York if he would allow his diocese to sponsor the Family Apostolate's Canonical Center. "Cardinal Oddi felt that it would better serve the Apostolate to have the Canonical Center in New York instead of Pansey, Puerto Rico, and" shared Jerry, "Puerto Rico does not have the muscle that New York has." He continued, "Archbishop Weakland could put pressure on the diocese in Puerto Rico, in order to get jurisdiction, but he can't do that in New York. New York is one of the most influential dioceses in the world and is unique, in that it has a lot of international orders. That way one apostolate would not stick out, but be one of many."

So Jerry contacted Cardinal O'Connor, asking him permission to move their Canonical Center from Puerto Rico to New York. Cardinal O'Connor called his canon lawyer, Bishop Egan, and asked him to look into the situation and to see if it was possible. Bishop Egan researched the subject and said the Canonical Center can be located anywhere in the world, as long as the bishop of the diocese approves and the Board of the Directors of the Apostolate also approves. So Cardinal O'Connor told Jerry, "Yes!"

Archbishop Weakland did not receive the message well. During this time, he wrote Jerry, wanting to see him and Gwen on December 23rd. It was going to be a show down. Gwen didn't want to go to the meeting because she felt it would ruin her Christmas with her family. Jerry contacted Cardinal O'Connor about the meeting. The Cardinal responded with a request that Jerry and Gwen to come see him prior to the meeting, and to bring one of their daughters with them. So Jerry, Gwen, and Laurie, who was seventeen at the time, went to see Cardinal O'Connor in New York. Gwen expressed her concern to the Cardinal of her apprehension of seeing Archbishop Weakland before Christmas, for fear it would ruin her Christmas with her family. The good Cardinal laughed at Gwen and said, "Don't worry!" The Cardinal then proceeded to grill Laurie and Gwen about the Apostolate and on the faith for quite a while. "Laurie was not timid at all," said Jerry. "She was very outspoken." The Cardinal was impressed. When he was done, he turned to Jerry and said, "You have nothing to worry about."

Jerry and Gwen went to the meeting with Archbishop Weakland as planned.

It lasted thirty minutes and nothing was mentioned about jurisdiction. "It was the strangest meeting," said Jerry, "the meeting was a lot of small talk about nothing."

Another serious issue occurred when the Archbishop wrote a letter to all the Apostolate Advisory Board Members, strongly accusing Jerry of abusing the reservation of the Blessed Sacrament at their St. Joseph's Center in the Sacred Heart chapel. At first, Jerry did not know about the letter, so he was not able to defend himself from such allegations. "Bishops don't normally share letters with lay people, most especially when it concerns the laity," said Jerry, "however, I was tipped off about the letter from Cardinal O'Connor's office in New York. The letter stated that, *'Jerry did not have permission to have the Blessed Sacrament reserved in their chapel.'*"

This is a very serious offense because the bishop of the diocese has total jurisdiction over the Eucharist, which at the time was Archbishop Weakland. However, Jerry had already received permission from Archbishop Weakland's predecessor, Archbishop Cousins, and was not as of yet informed by Archbishop Weakland that permission was suspended. The Archbishop also wrote other negative things about Jerry in the letter, such as accusing Jerry of being disobedient.

The Advisory Council members who received the letter told Jerry that the Archbishop has total authority over the Eucharist, and that the accusations were very serious. Jerry immediately contacted Bishop Leo Brust, the Vicar General for the Milwaukee archdiocese, under Archbishop Weakland, sharing the situation and that the accusations were false.

"Archbishop Cousins of Milwaukee approved our bylaws in 1975 at the time," said Jerry. "Auxiliary Bishop Brust took the Apostolate under his wing, who gave us permission to have the Eucharist in our chapel. Bishop Brust then became Auxiliary Bishop to Archbishop Weakland when the Archbishop succeeded Archbishop Cousins. Bishop Brust was kept abreast of everything that the Apostolate was doing, including retreats in the chapel and formation programs." Jerry and the Catholic Corps were given permission to expose the Eucharist at that time by Archbishop Cousins, and Bishop Brust was the liaison between Archbishop Cousins (later Archbishop Weakland) and Jerry.

ATTEMPTED TAKEOVER AND NEW PASTURES

Archbishop Cousins called Jerry and, during their conversation, shared that Archbishop Weakland's statement was not correct. At that, Jerry quickly responded, "Would you please put that in writing?" When the Archbishop responded in the affirmative, Jerry and his secretary left for Archbishop Cousins' office, in order to have his secretary draft a letter admitting that Jerry had always been obedient. The Archbishop dictated the letter while the secretary typed on his letterhead. This was on September 14, 1988. It turned out that Archbishop Cousins died a few days later unexpectedly.

Jerry contacted Cardinal O'Connor, the Archbishop of New York, which was the diocese that had jurisdiction over the Apostolate, seeking his help to resolve the issue about the Eucharist. The Cardinal informed Jerry that the diocese where the Apostolate is physically has jurisdiction when it comes to reserving the Eucharist even though the New York diocese had jurisdiction over the Apostolate. The jurisdiction over the Eucharist was a different matter. Therefore, the good Cardinal could not override Archbishop Weakland's permission regarding the Eucharistic in this matter. Bishop Brust called Cardinal O'Connor and told him about the situation with Jerry, and that he was obedient with everything the diocese asked of him. "Jerry did not abuse the reservation of the Eucharist," he told Cardinal O'Connor. In calling the Cardinal, Bishop Brust essentially went over his boss' head which is not typically done in the Church.

During this time, Rome's Cardinal Luigi Ciappi, the Pope's theologian, agreed to become the Apostolate's primary theological advisor. The Vice President of the Council for the Laity also agreed to be primary Spiritual Director for the Apostolate.

Suddenly, almost miraculously, the issue of the Eucharist in the Apostolate's chapel went away and jurisdiction pertaining to the Eucharist continued under Bishop Brust, who gave permission for Jerry and the Apostolate to reserve the Eucharist in their chapel. Jerry received no letter but Cardinal O'Connor informed Jerry to abide by the authority from Bishop Brust, the Vicar General of Milwaukee in this matter pertaining to the Eucharist.

Jerry was present, during a retreat for Benedictines, in order to meet with

Cardinal Arinze, the retreat master. Archbishop Weakland, passing Jerry in the hallway, appearing upset, addressed Jerry, saying, "I understand that you have received permission to reserve the Eucharist in your chapel."

"Yes I did," responded Jerry. The Archbishop then, with no further words, walked away. That took the wind out of Archbishop Weakland's sail, because he no longer had jurisdiction and could not control the Apostolate or Jerry, in any way.

ROME TRIP NOVEMBER, 1989

Grace and mercy walk together, and the joys and crosses of the Apostolate continued. Jerry and Gwen went to Rome again from November 5 to November 17, 1989 in order to document the Marian spirituality of Pope John Paul II. This would serve greatly the Apostolate for Family Consecration in their Marian Era of Evangelization Campaign, and also because they had adopted the spirituality of Pope John Paul II. With them were their two youngest children, Theresa and Mary. Also with them was one of the Catholic Corp men who was in charge of videotaping.

Jerry interviewed members of the Roman Curia including Cardinal Gagnon, Cardinal Arinze, Cardinal Pironio, president of the Pontifical Council for the Laity, and many other high-level members of the hierarchy and laity. Cardinal Pironio approached Gwen, mother of thirteen, and placing his hands on her shoulders, looked at her and said, "Mrs. Coniker, I have to tell you that I am the last, not of thirteen children but of twenty-two!" Wow! A Cardinal in the Roman Curia is the last born of a large family. Just think if his parents had one less child, there would be no Cardinal Pironio!

Jerry interviewed Father Patrick Peyton, known for the adage, *"The family that prays together stays together!"* This, by the way, is no cliché! It happens to be quite true. Father and Jerry discussed Father's world-wide campaign for the rosary, for which Father highly exhorts families to pray the family rosary. He agreed to assist Jerry with his Apostolate in any way he could.

One interesting thing that Jerry discovered while in Rome was that the Romans don't quite work like he does; around the clock, that is! Jerry is and always has been a man on a mission, a very hard worker, out to accomplish as much as possible in the shortest period of time. This trait of Jerry's was in high gear even more so in Rome, given the short span of time while they were there. However, the Romans were not so anxious to give up their two-to-three-hour siesta!

One day, Jerry was reviewing the tapes in the Vatican archives and decided to run two machines at the same time which had never been done before. Jerry had a knack for discovering and correcting inefficiencies in the workflow process. That did not bode too well with the Vatican staff. Then when the one o'clock hour came around, naturally Jerry kept working. At one-thirty, much to the impatience of the people in charge, they reprimanded him for not going along with their customs and shooed him out the door.

Despite the slow moving atmosphere of the Eternal City, Jerry was able to interview thirty-three people during their stay in Rome, making a whopping one hundred-thirty 24 ½ minute video segments all focused on the Marian spirituality of the Holy Father, Pope John Paul II! What an accomplishment!

Jerry was unable to interview the Holy Father personally, as was hoped; however, he did manage to be present at the general audience. Pope John Paul II was consumed with historical events happening in Eastern Europe, with the lowering of the Berlin Wall and its ensuing upheavals. Nevertheless, they were still able to present to the Holy Father the program and the logo of the Marian Era of Evangelization Campaign. The Pope blessed the work of the Family Apostolate, and personally blessed Jerry by placing his hand on Jerry's forehead, with Gwen by his side.

Monsignor Dziwisz, the Pope's personal secretary, promised Jerry that both he and the Holy Father together would review the Marian Campaign program in preparation for the Year 2000. He also promised that a formal Apostolic Blessing would be forthcoming through the Secretary of State's Office. The letter was written a few days later and forwarded to Jerry through the Apostolic Nuncio's office in Washington, D.C. A copy of that letter is as follows:

SERVANT OF GOD

November 18, 1989

No. 250.418

Dear Mr. Coniker,

The Holy Father was pleased to learn about the "Marian Era of Evangelization Committee" of the Apostolate for Family Consecration, and he wishes me to convey his cordial greetings and good wishes to you and to all those associated in this worthy initiative.

His Holiness hopes that as a result of the Committee's activities many Catholics will be led to a deeper appreciation of their faith and to a renewed commitment to Christ and his Church. The wise use of the communications media in the service of teaching and pastoral guidance creates new possibilities for evangelization. By focusing on family life in the home, neighborhood and parish, the committee's efforts strengthen the very foundations of Christian living for the benefit of the Church and all of society.

As the Apostolate for Family Consecration works for a spiritual and moral transformation of society, the Holy Father commends all of you to God's loving care. In particular, he joins you in asking the intercession of the Blessed Virgin Mary so that all you do may be inspired by her shining example of faith and trust. With confidence in her powerful protection, he willingly imparts the requested Apostolic Blessing.

With every good wish, I am

Sincerely yours,

+ S. Cassidy

+E. Cassidy

Under-Secretary of State

Gwen and Jerry meet Pope John Paul II again in November of 1989.
Accompanying them are Theresa and Mary Coniker.

Jerry receiving a papal blessing from Pope John Paul II,
November of 1989.

SERVANT OF GOD

Missionaries of Charity
Calcutta, India

May 20, 1989

Jerome and Gwen Coniker
Founders
Apostolate for Family Consecration
6305 Third Ave., P.O. Box 220
Kenosha, WI 53141
U.S.A.

Dear Jerome and Gwen,

I want to encourage you and all of your members and friends to faithfully support Our Blessed Mother's request to come together in the churches on the First Saturday of the month, to receive Our Lord in Holy Communion, pray the Rosary and meditate for fifteen minutes and go to confession if at all possible, all in reparation for the sins that offend the Immaculate Heart of Mary and the sin of abortion in our world.

Your videotaped presentations are excellent; they hold the interest of the entire family and focus them on the Holy Eucharist, Our Blessed Mother, and the teachings of the Holy Father, the Pope.

It is so important that we be loyal to the Holy Father during these confusing times. On the First Saturday is a very special time for the parish communities to come together to honor and thank Our Lady.

I assure you of my continued prayers for your family and for all the members and co-workers of your Apostolate for Family Consecration.

Keep the joy of loving Jesus in each other and share this joy with all you meet.

God bless you.

God bless you
M Teresa mc
M. Teresa, M.C.

334-100

Another letter from Mother Teresa to Gwen and Jerry from May, 1989:

New Pastures

The Apostolate kept growing and it was apparent that their current facilities were no longer suitable to support its growth. They needed to branch out into new pastures. Jerry had asked Archbishop Weakland if they could occupy a large facility in Kenosha, however, he would not approve it. More than likely, his response was from losing the battle to control the overseeing of the Apostolate. So Jerry went to see a piece of property in Racine, Wisconsin, yet, it too was not suitable.

At this time, the Apostolate was becoming an affiliate of Franciscan University of Steubenville, Ohio, and was collaborating with them. Fr. Michael Scanlon T.O.R., the President of the University, was trying to blend the University's charismatic spirituality with the more traditional Marian spirituality. So they called on the Apostolate to assist them in doing this. One of the priests had a dream of the Apostolate coming out there.

While vising Franciscan University of Steubenville during a retreat, Bishop Albert Ottenweller, Bishop of the Diocese of Steubenville, made an announcement that the Diocese was selling their seminary and if anyone was interested, to come and see him. The seminary sat on 850 acres and was located not far from Franciscan University. Jerry recognized its strategic location between two big cities, New York and Chicago. Jerry thought to himself, "Hmmm. It would be difficult to draw people from New York, if we stay in Kenosha." Jerry approached the Bishop inquiring about the property and how to go about seeing it. The Bishop told him that he would take him himself. Jerry went out to take a look at the property. Divine Providence was manifested again.

Gwen hated the whole idea and was not happy at all. Nevertheless, Jerry and Gwen went out to Ohio to Franciscan University to meet with Fr. Scanlon and to take a look at the property together. He had a member of his staff show them the property. The property was large with many buildings that were dilapidated, and the place was in shambles. Gwen didn't see the vision Jerry did of its potential. She just saw work and a lot of it! The auditorium was a giant bird cage. "There must have been 10,000 birds in there, most of them DEAD!!" Jerry chuckled as he looked back years later. "However, I saw potential in the large auditorium which could fit about 2,000 people. One priest even visualized a great conference center."

At first, Gwen didn't take Jerry too seriously about the idea. But when Jerry went back to Ohio again, this time without her and then sent her pictures, she became increasingly numb to the idea. Gwen never fought Jerry before on his decisions, but she did on this one. It was very rough. She didn't say *no* but didn't say *yes* either. This would be for Gwen the heaviest cross yet if such a move came to fruition. It would mean having to leave behind her most endearing treasure, her family.

It was Jerry's birthday (November 2nd). Gwen wanted it to be very special for him. So she set up a chair with a lamp. She also set up a stage. When he walked in, she turned on the light and began to lip sync the song "You Light Up My Life"! Even after she was asked to give up all to move to Ohio, she sang her heart out to him as he walked in the room! This was true love and the way Christ wants us to love each other…not just out of commitment, but out of love.

Chapter 14

The Third and Most Difficult Trial and the Bridge

IT TOOK GWEN A FEW MONTHS to accept the fact that they had to move. She wanted Jerry to commute between Kenosha and Ohio, but in reality, that simply was not feasible. For Gwen, this move was far worse than even the move to Portugal, a foreign country, because at least in Portugal her entire family was with her. Now she is being asked, for the good of the Apostolate and according to God's will, to give up her most priceless treasure; her children, by leaving some of them behind. To add to this pain was the fact that some of her children were now married with children of their own. Hence, Gwen also was being asked to leave her grandchildren too. The irony is that her married children had bought property in Kenosha specifically to be close to their parents. Now, their parents were moving. Privately, Gwen would cry tears of anguish. At this point, her children did not know what was forthcoming.

THE BRIDGE

However, Gwen had one more trick up her sleeve. A problem arose with the plans to buy the old seminary when it came to the attention of Jerry and Gwen, that there was a bridge leading to the property that was condemned by the state. The poor condition of this bridge prohibited trucks from getting onto the property.

This could be a deal breaker! Gwen was so happy at this news! She began to storm heaven with a novena that this whole move would ultimately *not* come to fruition.

However, it would come to pass that her glee was short-lived. The county had decided to fix the broken bridge situation by building a new one. Jerry saw this as a sign to go ahead with his plans. Gwen cried, and it was hurting her very soul at the realization that the move was actually going to happen.

What made things even worse was the unbelievable amount of work ahead of them that would be required of the property, in order to get it to the way they needed it to be; a daunting task that would take years to accomplish.

The Bridge!

The move to Ohio was a process that, over time, came to fruition. In the end, Gwen gave her consent to Jerry. "I can't emphasize enough how traumatic the move was for Gwen," Jerry recounted years later as he reflected back. "She had to sacrifice so much for the good of the Apostolate by leaving much of her family behind, which was her truest treasure. It was the hardest cross Gwen ever faced up to that point. Nothing could compare to that. I feel that the decision was good for the growth of the Apostolate, however, the family paid a heavy price." It could be said that the lack of cooperation from Archbishop Weakland, the Archbishop of Milwaukee, where the Apostolate's center was located, to not allow them to occupy more space, facilitated their move to Ohio.

The move to Ohio would also involve selling their five properties in Kenosha! This, of course, included: the St. Joseph House, the Immaculate Heart Center, the Kateri House (home of the Women's Catholic Corps), the Conikers' family home, and the Juan Diego home of the men's Catholic Corps. "Gwen loved those homes," said Jerry. "Two of the mansions were right on Lake Michigan! The other three were across the street with a lake view. We sold them for roughly $200,000 - $300,000 each. Today, they would be worth between one to one and a half million!"

BREAKING THE NEWS TO THE CHILDREN

The children did not know about the move until the day before the process of moving would get started. Gwen called everyone to the chapel in the House of St. Joseph and gave a presentation and talk, both of which were also videotaped. Everyone was present, except Jerry, who was out of town at the time in Ohio, and four sons, who were away at school. Included also were some of the Presbergs (Jerry's sister's family), such as Peggy and Sue, and Jerry's sister, Mary Ann.

Gwen explained to her children that she, Jerry, and the youngest children, would be moving the Apostolate to Ohio. She expressed her feelings and regrets of leaving Kenosha, most especially her children and grandchildren. However, she is accepting what her husband wants her to do. She expressed much compassion in trying to explain this to her children. She emphasized that she did not want to go but had to. All the kids sat in stunned silence. No one wished her luck. No one was willing to accept it; however, they had no choice. One thing that Gwen did say to them was this: "I love you so much…but I love your father more." She was correctly placing her priority, of her beloved spouse, over her children. After all, she made a life-long, sacramental vow to her husband on their wedding day: God first, spouse second, children third.

When the news was finally starting to sink in, they started crying. Mary Ann stepped in and asked the girls to be brave. At the time, Mary was 13 years old, Theresa, 15, Maria, 16, and Jimmy, 17. These were the children who would move with them to Ohio.

"So Mom called all of us to the chapel to tell us," reflects Laurie. "Dad was not present, as he was in Ohio. It was the most horrible thing imaginable. I never thought they would leave Kenosha. I hated Dad for five years."

SERVANT OF GOD

Five daughters would be left behind in Kenosha. Mike, Robert, and Joe would go to Franciscan University in Steubenville, Ohio, and eventually, meet their wives there. Maria, Theresa, and Mary Beth would also, later, attend Franciscan University, and meet their future spouses there too. Jimmy went to Ohio State for a time and studied for a certification for Information Technology.

One of Gwen's best talents was to organize and host true celebrations for the family! These included birthdays, holidays, and feast days, particularly, St. Patrick's day. Not many young women know how to organize and cater special gatherings. All of the Coniker girls were taught this skill. In specific, Maureen, the oldest, turned this skill into a business called Maureen's Cuisine, "Home cooked catering to perfection!"

In 1990, the Apostolate for Family Consecration moved to Bloomingdale, Ohio, where it acquired a diocesan seminary in the Diocese of Steubenville. The canonical name is the John Paul II Holy Family Center, also known as, Catholic Familyland. The seminary sits on 850 acres with over 300,000 square feet of buildings. The Apostolate continues its work of nourishing families with the Catholic faith through its multi-media catechetical programming and resources, Family Fests, conferences, retreats, television productions, and Lay Ecclesial Team Evangelization Programs.

Gwen Coniker's farewell address to her family in Kenosha, Wisconsin, in 1990, just before the move to Bloomingdale, Ohio:

We switched, Mom tapes instead of Dad. He doesn't know anything about this, by the way, because this grace came to me this morning, and he's busy on a retreat in Ohio at the Holy Family Center. So, I just know how he thinks and says: 'If you're gonna talk, tape it!' That is why I wanted to put it on tape, so that our four sons who are away at school could have a chance to hear it.

This Sunday evening at our family holy hour, I have all of my children here, and my sister-in-law, and some nieces and nephews, which were a surprise too; I wasn't expecting them.

I'll just start with the Memorare.... Well, I'm not sure exactly where to start, but, this is the day before our family of four children living at home with us here are going to be leaving for the Holy Family Center [now known as Catholic Familyland] in Ohio. It's been a constant struggle, needless to say, because the dearest thing to my heart is family and our children. I seem to be just torn and tossed back and forth. I'm not at peace so I feel like something just isn't right. I'm not letting go and letting God work in my life like I have in the past; I can just feel it.

I know that my place is at the Holy Family Center in Ohio where Dad is, and the children aren't married, and I just know that in my heart all of you here have each other and your spouses – by the way, five of the best son-in-laws anyone could ever have – they are each very unique and different and they are with the Lord. I feel our family is united in prayer, maybe not in sports, but we are united in prayer and that is the most important thing.

Doing God's will is not easy. His ways are not always ours. When we want to know God's will, there are three things which always concur. First is the inward impulse, which are the inner feelings that you feel you should be doing. The second is the Word of God. As it says in Scripture, St. Mark, where Peter begins to say to him, "Behold we have left all and follow Thee." Answering, Jesus said, "Amen I say to you, there is no one who has left house or brothers or sisters or mother or father or children or lands for my sake and for the Gospel's sake who shall not receive or know in the present time a hundred fold as much houses, brothers, sisters, mothers, children, and lands, along with persecution, and in the age to come life everlasting."

So those words are inspiring to me, and I felt like I had to share them because I'm torn at this time. I feel God is asking this of me. I say to Him, why? Why are you asking this; you've blessed us with twelve, beautiful children and a little angel in heaven, and now you are calling on me to be separated from them?

The third thing that you know when you are doing God's will is to try the circumstances. There have been so many, but just to name a few that have to do with the property in Bloomingdale, Ohio, known as the John Paul II Holy Family Center [Catholic Familyland]. We have the miracle of the bridge, the bridge itself, in order to get onto the property, was not up to capacity for large trucks and shipment so Dad had said there is no way he could even think of bidding on this property. We wouldn't have been able to bring our trucks in, so I thought everything was pretty safe. I didn't think anything would happen. But lo and behold, just a few months later, the county had started tearing down the bridge and built a new one. It said "no limit" on it, so any size truck can come at all, so we laughed about that for a little bit, and we went on.

There were a few more circumstances. The warmth and welcome that we got from the Bishop (Albert H. Ottenweller) in the Steubenville diocese; he just opened up his arms to the work that we are involved in – bringing the Gospel message and the love of Christ to other people.

We had the rejection of our own family that we felt right here in Kenosha with the school systems, and it put us in a situation now where we have our younger children in home study. This allows us to travel back and forth to Ohio and Kenosha. These are just a few of the circumstances that I feel are perhaps really showing what God is asking of our family.

God's will is there for each of us. If we listen and are watchful and pray, He will show you the way. This is a little book called, God's will; You Can Know it. *And it just says in here, "in those who walk in His way today, He will reveal His way tomorrow." In John 14, the Lord promised to manifest Himself to those that keep His commandments. Proverbs 3: "In all your ways acknowledge Him, and He shall direct thy path."*

The Christian must live faithfully, obeying in responsibility that is now, near, and next. And also, this is about what we are going into, as we are not sure what is going to happen next. I know the great faith that Abraham must have had when God called him to sacrifice his son. It must have taken tremendous faith to have to offer his son. But because he went that far and was willing to do it as God asked him, God told him, "Now that you have followed Me, I ask you not to take your son's life."

I also have a little modern love story that I wanted to share with you right now. When a college quartet sang in an Illinois church for a two-week campaign, a girl in the church and a member of the quartet, Ruth and John, became enamored with each other. The rule in courtship was to be subjected to a year separation when the quartet was on an around-the-world trip. If still in love at the end of the year, they would become formally engaged.

The reason I shared this is because there is another love story that comes to mind, and that's my own, with your father! Dad and I met in high school. We had a couple of years of courtship, and we were enamored with each other. Then at graduation time, we decided to separate. We had a year and a half separation, and there wasn't much I could do about it. I lost my sweetheart; I felt that was the end of the world. I lost my appetite, and I was grumpy. My mother always said I was hard to live with, but I just felt like my whole life was lost because I really had strong feelings for Jerry.

The only thing that helped me along was the Rosary. When a friend of mine introduced me to a Rosary Novena, I thought, well, now I'm going to bring this to God. I'm going to ask Him, if it is His will, that I would hear from Jerry again. Like I said, it was a long year and a half. The point that I'm trying to make is, I felt that I was doing God's will; I was asking for God's will and nothing could happen without it. It's better to go to Him and go His way and find happiness.

And so it was–I got the phone call from Jerry eighteen months later! I felt He (God) really listens. He answers my prayers! So after six months of dating and then six months of engagement, we were married on August 15, 1959, on the feast of Our Lady of the Assumption.

It was then when I said, "I do." I picked Jerry. I wanted him. I asked for him, and with God's help, he became my partner, my provider and protector for life. Right at this time, I feel like I can share this letter. We went on a Marriage and the Holy Spirit weekend. We were asked to write a letter to our husbands that I'd like to share with you now:

My dearest husband,

I don't know where to begin; I only wish we learned about, and realized what the Sacrament of Marriage was long ago. I feel we have lived it somewhat, and know our dear Lord and Savior with His most beloved Mother Mary has carried us along the way–our journey through life.

It feels somewhat strange to be writing you. I believe, in fact, I don't know when I have ever written to you, but as I am writing you, tears are flowing down my cheeks, and I don't know why. Why is the Holy Spirit allowing me to cry? I know I love you dearly with all my heart; I respect, and honor you. You have always had compassion for me and are always thoughtful of me. You are a great protector and guardian for me and our twelve, beautiful children – our heavenly treasures that God has given us.

I know there have been many times I have ignored you or got upset with you but how I want to say I'm sorry for my shortcomings. This blessed weekend has opened my eyes to many things. I do want to be one with you, I treasure you, your life, and that God has allowed us to be united in the sacrament of love. I made a commitment to you on that great feast day, the Assumption of Mary, August 15, 1959. And 30 years later–wanting that commitment to become even stronger.

I have put my trust in you. Remember our move to Portugal? Total trust in what our Blessed Mother and Jesus her Son has shown us. My trust in you as my protector, guardian, provider, dear, and faithful husband, and father to our twelve living children and our angel in heaven. I thank God every day for you.

Love you always, your Devout wife and sweetheart.

Those are very touching words for me. Part of my struggle right now is that I need to be with Dad, where he is, and I need to have support from my daughters that are here, especially Maria, Theresa, and Mary, who are living at home.

It all boils down to one word that I can leave you, and I hope you will remember it for the rest of your life, and that is; faithfulness. Faithful to God first, to your spouse, and to your children. I'll tell you that whether I am here or in Ohio, I will always be there for you. I will be most faithful to each and every one of you and only a phone call away.

But I am asking for your support in helping me, because the last thing I'm asking for is to leave here, to leave Kenosha. I love it here! I am comfortable; we have a nice home; our family is here. And yet I'm torn.

These are the feelings that I wanted to share with you today. I hope that when we leave on Tuesday, we all can leave in peace and with a peaceful heart and love. I would just like to ask you to take the <u>Family Consecration Prayer Book</u>, number 4. This is the prayer that was developed and approved by the Church for the Apostolate to say every day. It says it all right in that prayer about our life here, and thinking about our loved ones who have gone before us, the poor souls. At this time, I would like to read it together with you, and perhaps you can read it daily just as a reminder to know that this is one way we are going to be united.

Heavenly Father, grant that we, who are nourished by the Body and Blood of Your Divine Son, may die to our own selfishness and be one spirit with Christ, as we seek to fulfill Your distinctive plan for our lives.

Form me and all the members of my family, community, and The Apostolate into instruments of atonement. Unite our entire lives with the Holy Sacrifice of Jesus in the Mass of Calvary, and accept our seed sacrifice offering of all of our spiritual and material possessions, for the Sacred and Eucharistic Heart of Jesus, through the Sorrowful and Immaculate Heart of Mary, in union with St. Joseph.

Our Father, let Sacred Scripture's Four "Cs" of Confidence, Conscience, seed-Charity, and Constancy be our guide for living our consecration as peaceful children, and purified instruments of the Most Holy Family.

Let us live our consecration by remaining perpetually confident, calm, cheerful, and compassionate, especially with the members of our own family and community.

Please protect our loved ones and ourselves from the temptations of the world, the flesh, and the devil. Help us to become more sensitive to the inspirations of Your Holy Spirit, and Holy Family, our Patron Saints and Guardian Angels.

And now, Most Heavenly Father, inspire us to establish the right priorities for Your precious gift of time. And most of all, help us to be more sensitive to the needs and feelings of our loved ones.

Never let us forget the souls in Purgatory who are dependent upon us for help. Enable us to gain, for the Poor Souls of our loved ones and others, as many indulgences as possible, We ask You this, Our Father, in the Name of Our Lord and Savior Jesus Christ, Your Son and the Son of Mary, Amen.

Okay. I have selected a song I just want you to listen to. I have been playing it several times at home, praying and thinking of what is going to be coming. I just want to play it now, and end on a very joyful, peaceful note with this song which is called, "I Am Forever Grateful."

Let us sing together:

You did not wait for me to draw near to You, but You clothed Yourself in frail humanity.

You did not wait for me to cry out to You, but You let me hear Your voice calling me.

And I'm forever grateful, Lord, to You.

And I'm forever grateful for the cross.

And I'm forever grateful to You, that You came to seek and save the lost.

That You came to seek and save the lost.

The Saint John Vianney Chapel at the John Paul II Holy Family Center, aka, Catholic Familyland in Bloomingdale, Ohio

Chapter 15

The Crooked House

THE DIOCESE HAD SOLD THEM THE PROPERTY for one million dollars, but it was rundown. "The benefactor that was going to purchase the property for us backed out of the deal," said Jerry. "He had a survey made of the property and it was short by 150 acres. 850 acres was the total. During the negotiations, the benefactor told the Bishop of Steubenville at the time, Bishop Albert Henry Ottenweller, that he wanted to have a price reduction due to the shortage of acreage. But the land was worthless, and it was the buildings which were worth all the money, so that did not happen."

The bishop refused to lower the price, so the benefactor pulled out of the deal and walked away, leaving Jerry to find one million dollars. "We had to make a decision," recounted Jerry, "if we wanted to go forward and take on the one million dollar mortgage or walk away. We decided to do it and bite the bullet. The diocese had a contract on the property that their lawyers drew up and it had no closing date on it, which was an oversight of the attorneys on both sides of the deal. So there was no date when we had to pay for it even though we could move in," said Jerry. "Both parties overlooked these facts."

Jerry sought the help of Tom Monaghan, founder of Domino's Pizza, to help him with the financing. Tom had his attorneys write up a new land contract, voiding the previous contract. In it, Tom agreed to put down $100,000 of his own money and the Apostolate would pay roughly $8,000 per month, and a $100,000 balloon payment at the end of each year until the debt was paid off.

In terms of payments on the property, Jerry had this to say: "The contract read that if we didn't meet the payments, the diocese would foreclose on us. So every year, $100,000 was due. There was a monthly payment and a yearly balloon payment. Every year, we never knew how we were going to pay that balloon payment," said Jerry, "but God opened up the heart of someone every year at different times to pay the balloon payment for that year. One member asked me to come see him about one of the balloon payments. When I did, he went and borrowed $100,000 on his own property and gave us a check on the day it was due. Another time, we would sell a building in Kenosha just in the nick of time to make a payment." Again, the Conikers played the financial dance trusting in Divine Providence to see them through each time.

In terms of the property, large buildings were shut down, and the heating system frozen over. There was so much to the property that was just not right. Almost 300,000 square feet of buildings needed to be refurbished. They needed to go building by building and restore large parts of them.

The move to Ohio was quite an extensive ordeal that would take over a year and require forty truckloads to move. The Ryan brothers, who were very kind benefactors, owned a trucking company called Ryan Trucking. They donated the trucks and covered the cost to move the entire Apostolate to Ohio. The drivers also donated their time.

The Family Apostolate had a warehouse of 25,000 square feet where the printing presses and inventory were held. They also had the contents of the five mansions. The TV Studios were in the St. Joseph Center. This building was also filled to the brim, including shelving on all the walls.

Jerry drove the U-Haul with the master tapes in it. When they arrived that first night, it was dark and eerie. There was a lot of fog that night which gave a very spooky feeling against the backdrop of the dark back hills of Ohio. The house that the Conikers moved into (which was located on the property) was very rundown. It was literally a crooked house! It was so bad that one could roll off the bed!

At the time of the move, five of children were already married, starting with the first wedding, which was in November of 1981. There was, on average, a wedding every couple of years after that. There were also eleven grandchildren born by 1990 when the move took place.

If there is one thing Gwen cannot stand is snakes! She is deathly afraid of them. Shortly after arriving, a person came to the door of the crooked house holding a three and a half foot snake he had shot! If that was not bad enough, Gwen personally had up-close encounters at least four or five more times with snakes just in the first few days there! The devil was doing everything he could to spook Gwen! Gwen hated it. She left five palatial homes, some right on Lake Michigan with a spectacular view, to live in a crooked house with snakes and cows nearby, not to mention leaving some of her loving children. The contrast was extreme. Moreover, it had a detached garage so in inclement weather, while unloading groceries with multiple trips from the car to the house, it would only add to the inconvenience and hardship. These crosses would become yet more flowers to add to her garden of life; a gift she would offer to Him, her Spouse, and a treasure which would yield in time astounding rewards. "Mom cried over that crooked house," Maria recalled. "She left her best friends, which were her daughters, to live in a dirty carpeted, bad crooked house with snakes!"

Nevertheless, Gwen proceeded to do to that crooked house what she did with every other house that she moved into; to make it into a home no matter how challenging that might be! She painted it and fixed it up. She put pictures on the walls. She always made sure that food was available.

In terms of the seminary property in Ohio, every portion of the property had a different story. Most of the buildings needed extensive work done to them, as they had not been maintained well in years. One building was the Sacred Heart Center which was the second largest building. The diocese leased part of the building out to a mental health operation. One wing was totally gutted by a fire that occurred ten years prior. The lease on that building was a mere one dollar a year. The lease was also not due to expire for another two years! The inhabitants were not at all cooperative with the Conikers, so it was quite a challenge for them.

THE CROOKED HOUSE

Here is one example of the resistance experienced in taking over the property: One flatbed truck came in with the Family Apostolate's printing press on it, and the inhabitants would not move their cars to let the truck in. After much time and consternation, the truck driver went into their office and told them that he is going to push their cars over to the side if they didn't move their cars in five minutes. Finally, they listened and moved their cars!

To the good fortune of the Conikers, during this time, there was a high school in Steubenville going on the auction block, and offering to sell the entire school for $50,000. The mental health bought it and moved out of the Sacred Heart building, much to the joy of the Apostolate members.

The Catholic Corps, as well as others, rolled up their sleeves to tackle the magnitude of the work that was involved. The members started to come and help restore the property. They even received outside volunteer help from other Catholic families, who would visit the property for Family Work Fests.

Things started to improve with time. In 1992, the Conikers moved off the property, out of the crooked house into a warm two-story home with a big yard and a swimming pool. They lived there about three to four years. Then they moved back to the property into a white trailer house, which they named the Fatima House. It was literally two trailer homes put together. One felt as though he or she was standing in a camper. However, when Jerry wanted to give $150,000 from the sale of their home in Kenosha to the Family Apostolate, Gwen insisted that it was not right for them to have nothing while giving everything to the Apostolate. So Jerry agreed to use $50,000 of that money to build a basement onto the trailer home, which became a very big family room with a brick fireplace, large enough for gatherings for their growing, extended Coniker family, as well as the Men and Women's Catholic Corps members. It would be used for family functions for years to come, and would be the room in which she would pass away.

Gwen Coniker's letter written to her married daughters and their families living in Wisconsin from Catholic Familyland in Ohio, July 16, 1990:

SERVANT OF GOD

To All My Dear Children,

Here is it Monday morning, the 4ᵗʰ day of my "Cursillo." What a powerful and most wonderful weekend with Jesus, our Redeemer and Savior – all loving and merciful! I say this as I came to know Jesus even better than I did before. I cried a lot this weekend, both tears of joy and sorrow. I experienced so much love and wherever there is love there is sacrifice.

My heart is longing to be with you right now and I can't be. I love you all so much! I know now that God, our Good and Great God, is calling me to be detached from those that are most dear to me. All of you; daughters, sons, son-in-laws and grandchildren. **Oh, how I wish that God wasn't asking this of me, but I must surrender all to Him.**

I know we are all God's children, and He only gave you to me on loan, you are His special children and I pray you will all understand.

Now I can feel only some of the pain Mary, our Blessed Mother, felt at the loss of her only Son. God has given me four sons and eight daughters and a beautiful soul with the Lord. All wonderful and beautiful children, and my constant prayer and hope is that you all will continue to grow in Jesus' love and share it with your children.

I was with a lot of mothers this weekend that have shared their sorrows in their life, and yes, we shared their feelings of love and cried with them. We all knelt next to our Lord in the Tabernacle in the St. John Vianney Chapel at the John Paul II Holy Family Center in Bloomingdale, Ohio [now known as Catholic Familyland].

I want each of you to understand that where there is love there is sacrifice. Just as there was at the cross where Jesus suffered so totally for each one of us and His Holy Mother, Mary, by His side. What pain she felt.

I can remember when each one of you was born and **I was told, I am only God's babysitter. You are mine on a loan – take care of each**

one and teach, lead and guide them to Me. So my tears are tears of
joy for you and your families.

I love you! Mother

Gwen Coniker's Christmas letter written to her family,
December 25, 1990:

To My Greatest Treasure, My Family

It has been fifteen years since my last Christmas message to you. A lot
of changes in our lives has taken place. And during this tender, loving
season of Christmas when the Jewish family of Nazareth showed us an
inexhaustible source of inspiration and strength, since it was the birth of
the true family.

"A child has been born to us; a son has been given to us." The family has
been given to us. With the first Christmas, God entered into the human
family, and the family of man entered into the Trinity of God. St. Paul
wrote that the love of man and woman is a figure of the love of Christ for
His Church, "the mystical idea that the man and the woman had become
one sacramental substance."

Now that our five daughters: Maureen, Kathy, Laurie, Peggy, and Sheri
are united in the sacrament of marriage with their beloved spouses Matt,
Mike, Kevin, Peter, and Joe, I can refer to the thought from G.K. Ches-
terton when he said, "Of all human institutions, marriage is the one
which most depends upon slow development, upon patience, upon long
reaches of times, upon magnanimous compromises, upon kindly habit."

One thing the marriage ideal did and did alone: it took love seriously.
Chesterton said, "You shall not have this secret and super human happi-
ness unless you give up all for it."

We have shared love, faith and hope in each other and I feel so grateful to
each of you as a treasured gift from Almighty God.

SERVANT OF GOD

Each one of you, Maureen, Kathy, Laurie, Peggy, and Sheri have filled my heart with love and joy. May the ever-loving Christ Child and His holy mother Mary be ever present with you always.

Our first son Michael now 22, you have touched my heart in a wonderful way. I see all the goodness in your young life as you approach graduation. I see your friendship with God growing in you and your faith coming alive. My message to you is keep growing in God's love and share His love with others.

To our dearest son Robert, you have been a shining light to me. Your generous loving heart has sparked me on so many times. My prayer and every wish is you continue to grow close to our Blessed Mother, as there is nothing she wouldn't do for you. You need only to ask. Remember this little prayer: Lovely Lady dressed in blue, teach me how to pray. God was with your little boy, please show me the way.

To our special son, Joe — You have always been there for me in trying times. You have made motherhood a delight. A bit of cheer said by you has always brought joy to my heart. You are anxious to reach success in your life and the ladder to reaching that success is trust in Jesus through Mary.

My most precious son, James. You are now in the prime of your teen life of 17 years. There have been so many tears of joy and sorrow that we've shared. But it all has been good. You have tested my patience time and time again. You continue to be a real challenge to me, but with God's grace and strength, we will continue to grow together. I pray that Our Lord will touch your mind, your heart, and your life so that your faith will grow deeper every day.

Next is our dearest Maria, so beautiful, and sweet sixteen. Your charm and all your dedicated efforts to do what is right has filled my heart with great joy. Keep your beautiful smile glowing for all to see.

To our dear sweet Theresa my teen angel and that you are. Fifteen years ago we were expecting an angel and that's what we got. I see you trying to adjust to teen life, to grow in love of the Christ Child and our Blessed Mother. You are a real support to me at his difficult time of growth in the Family Apostolate leaving some of our family in Kenosha, as we strive to bring God's love to other families at the Holy Family Fests in Ohio. I thank you from the bottom of my heart, Theresa.

The last and very special gift of the life is our sweet daughter Mary Beth (Mary Elizabeth). You have filled me with overwhelming joy. You have reached the great time in life of 13. Now is your chance to learn about our great gift of faith. How rich is God's mercy, and you have an unrepeatable gift to give, and that is yourself so sweet, kind, and loving. I pray that the Blessed Mother will ever be at your side to guide you through the journey of life.

Most of all Merry Christmas to my loving spouse, Jerry. Remember the day we united our life in the Sacrament of Love on the great feast day of Our Lady the Assumption, August 15, 1959. We stood at her feet, and prayed, asking her to watch over us and guide us in our marriage. We gave our life to Jesus through Mary in union with St. Joseph and they have always been with us in good times and bad. It's been our Lady that has shown us the way in all our joys and sorrows. And now, may I say sincerely, and with great love, thank you for everything, my dearest husband.

A blessed and Merry Christmas in Christ's love to each of you –
my treasured gift of family.

Love, Mother

Darkness Envelopes Gwen

In May of 1991, Jerry and Gwen were again in Rome during the time of the Fatima feast day of May 13th, in order to produce a series on both the Fatima apparitions and the Holy House of Nazareth. The Holy House of Nazareth, by the way, is also known as the Holy House of Loreto because it is now located in Loreto, Italy. This is the *actual* house where the Annunciation took place, and where the Blessed Mother, St. Joseph, and Our Lord Jesus lived while in Nazareth.

According to Catholic Tradition and testimonies of Popes and Saints, in the latter part of the 13th century, the Holy House of Nazareth was miraculously transported by Angels from Palestine to Tersatto, which is located in modern day Croatia, due to invasion by Muslims. The Angels again miraculously moved the Holy House three more times to its final resting place in Loreto, Italy.

Just one example of confirmation of the *actual* Holy House of Nazareth is that when is appeared, the pastor of St. George Church in Tersatto, Fr. Alexander Georgevich, puzzled by its appearance, prayed for enlightenment. His prayers were answered when the Blessed Virgin Mary appeared to him in a dream, and told him that it was *indeed* the Holy House of Nazareth, and it was brought there through the power of God. She also told him that as confirmation, Fr. Georgevich would be cured from his illness which he had suffered for many years. Immediately, he was healed.

The Holy House of Nazareth is the most treasured and venerated Shrine of our Lady in the world. More than two thousand persons, who have been canonized, beatified or made venerable by the Church, have visited the Holy House. Some of these include St. Therese of Lisieux, St. Alphonsus Liguori, and St. Francis de Sales. St. Francis of Assisi visited the Holy House in 1219 when it was in the Holy Land. Many, many miracles have occurred there; so many in fact that they are no longer recorded. There have even been three popes who have been miraculously cured at the shrine of the Holy House of Loreto.

At the airport going to Rome, Gwen was noticeably not herself. She was quiet and seemed very sad. Jerry was very puzzled by her behavior and wondered what it might be. So he asked her what was wrong. She answered, "My whole life has changed and I'm not happy." Jerry just listened and didn't know what to say. Then on the plane ride, Gwen seemed disturbed and she wouldn't sit down. She kept walking up and down the aisle. She was experiencing a very low point and was overwhelmed with the realization of her life without half of her children, particularly her five married daughters. This caused her great anxiety. She started to experience regrets moving to Ohio…deep, deep regrets. Satan was taunting her through her thoughts. She deeply missed being away from her children. In fact, she did not want to continue with the Apostolate unless it was in Kenosha. She wanted to move back to Kenosha to be with her family. During this attack, which would last several months, Jerry experienced Gwen's first lack of trust in him and felt rejected by her. It was such a difficult time for the both of them.

When they arrived at the hotel in Rome, there was a letter waiting for them from Pope John Paul II's private secretary, Monsignor Stanislaw Dziwisz. Much to their delight and surprise, it was an invitation to a private Mass with the Pope and a visit with him afterward. This blessing would be granted to only twenty people. The wonderful news temporarily lifted Gwen's spirits since she so very much loved this Holy Father.

"Typically, I would have to jump through hoops to get an audience with the Pope," said Jerry. "In fact, I had the Papal visits down to a science. Even still, Papal visits are very uncertain because the Pope needs to leave time open for other official visits, and visits with certain dignitaries. Also, Wednesdays are the only day that the Holy Father receives members of the laity." Jerry continued, "My system was that I would first send letters out to all of the members of the Roman Curia, which would entail dozens of letters. I would tell them that I am coming to Rome, when I would arrive, and that I would be calling them for an appointment once I arrived there. After I arrived in Rome, I would send another copy of the letter to them, followed up by a phone call stating that we were in town and asking them if we could meet." Jerry would continue calling until he received a response. This process would continue until he had all of his appointments set up. If Jerry was unsuccessful in meeting with some Curia member, upon leaving Rome, he would send a letter with a different cover letter expressing sorrow for having missed them, and inviting them to call him if they came to the United States.

Jerry would also time his arrival in Rome so as to arrive on a Monday, in order to give him two Wednesdays at a shot of meeting with the Pope. Since the Pope only met with the laity on Wednesdays, Jerry would usually miss the first

Wednesday to meet with him, and focus on the second Wednesday. However, this time, the Pope met with the Conikers on the first Wednesday instead of the second!

Gwen and Jerry went to the Pope's private Mass. After Mass, Jerry made sure he was last in the receiving line to visit with the Pope so he would have the most time with him. While conversing with the Holy Father, the Pope asked Gwen and Jerry about the Family Apostolate and its latest happenings. After updating him, the Pope continued to encourage them in their work of the Apostolate, particularly, the work related to *The Apostolate's Family Catechism* book.

When their visit concluded, they went back to the hotel room. Gwen was very silent. It was as though she used up all her energy just to carry on and show good spirits for the Pope.

Jerry contacted Fr. Sebastian, who is head of Mother Teresa's order for contemplative brothers located in Rome. She had an order of priests, and another of brothers. The purpose of the call was to ask Fr. Sebastian to accompany him and Gwen to the Holy House of Loreto, in order to record a series on it. He agreed! It was roughly a three-hour bus ride to Loreto, Italy, from Rome. Fr. Sebastian noticed that Gwen was torn to pieces, and was hurting, as she had a depressing disposition about her. However, he did not comment. They completed the programs with Fr. Sebastian and returned to Rome.

The next day, Fr. Sebastian told Gwen and Jerry that Mother Teresa was in Rome and would meet with them. Gwen lit up with excitement! They gathered their equipment and went to see Mother. However, when they arrived, Mother was just leaving for an appointment. She thought they would get there sooner. Jerry asked her if they could video tape her later in the day, after she returned. She said, "Yes." Mother Teresa did not grant interviews, but she had a close relationship with Gwen and Jerry and allowed them this special privilege.

So they took time to scout out the facility and find the best place in which to video tape. While waiting for Mother to return, they produced some television programs with a friend of Jerry's, Monsignor Peter John Elliott, from the Pontifical Council for the Family. When Mother did return, they produced a 45-minute show. "The production was exceptional!" recounts Jerry. "Gwen really rose to the challenge, and took over beautifully as we interviewed Mother. It is really amazing how Gwen carried on given her state of mind at the time. She lost all enthusiasm for the work of the Apostolate, but when she had to perform, she did. Afterwards, she was very positive for a time." However, this would not last long. Jerry continued, "For our trip to Rome to start off in such a negative way, grace poured forth and we were able to receive a message from the Pope, produce an exclusive interview with Fr. Sebastian, Monsignor Elliott, and Mother Teresa, and do so much more!" In retrospect, the delay in waiting for Mother Teresa to return actually ended up being better in the long run, and resulted in a better production.

"The entire trip for Gwen was very difficult," said Jerry. "She was so distraught that when we returned home she couldn't even balance a checkbook. She lost all enthusiasm. It was the only time in our marriage that we were not united. When Gwen came out of it a few months later, she wrote me a beautiful love letter."

Gwen's Love Letter to Jerry

My Dearest Spouse, Hubby and Lover. Darling! I love you!

I always get excited when I have thoughts of our past. I can remember and I still feel that tingle in my heart when you picked me up for a date. It was always such a good feeling. I remember our honeymoon and all our tender moments we've shared. A big turning point in our lives was attending Our Lady of Fatima novena every Wednesday night at Queen of All Saints Basilica. The prayer, songs, candlelight and love we both had for the Blessed Mother.

Remember how extra caring you were when I had that car accident which took us deeper into our faith and love of Our Lady?

You were always my strength and support at each one of the births of our children, each one special.

SERVANT OF GOD

Today you do many kind things for me such as make a hot bath, hang your clothes, keep the house tidy, fold laundry, and I just want to say "thank you" for these and all your kindnesses you show to me.

And I want to ask you to forgive me for my offenses, dislikes, pettiness, or any hurts I have caused you. Just know I pray every day for you and thank God for the gift He gave me in you.

I can remember praying to God, begging that God's will be done and asked to have you as my friend, and spouse forever and ever. Amen. My motto has become, one heart full of love for Jesus crucified and our Blessed Mother Mary, our Mother of sorrows and joy, and united with an ever-lasting love for you.

Thank you, for I'm forever grateful. Love you, your sweetheart!

Catholic Familyland
Bloomingdale, Ohio

Jerry and Gwen Coniker
St. John Vianney Chapel
at Catholic Familyland
Bloomingdale, Ohio

Chapter 16

Life in Ohio, Life of the Apostolate

ONCE THE CONIKERS SETTLED into a routine, after the initial culture shock, as well as the overwhelming amount of work that was required to get the property and the Apostolate in good working order, life in Ohio began to improve. Gwen acquired five dogs, being the dog lover that she was. She would also periodically write love letters to Jerry, expressing her deepest love and feelings for him. Here are two such letters:

Gwen's Love Letter to Jerry – March 8, 1992

To My Sweetheart, Today, tomorrow and forever...

I love you. We are traveling the journey of life together with all its ups and downs. We pray every day, asking St. Joseph to help us with our earthly strife ever to live a pure and blameless life. From the bottom of my heart, I give all my love to you. You are special in my life. After 37 years of knowing you, my heart still tingles for you. I especially like it when you do come home. Some days I wish you were here in the afternoons. I get these inner feelings or "attacks" to have you with me.

Mary, our Mother is so wonderful to us. Remember when we had the "Pil-

grim Virgin" stay in our home for one week after which we adopted the family rosary? That was the most important thing we did to protect our family life.

Our journey to Portugal...to Fatima...Birth of son Joe....Return to USA...Birth of Jim...Working with Fr. Bernard...so many, many things. And now our journey with the John Paul II Holy Family Center.

Thank you for all your love, cares, and concerns for me. You are an absolutely wonderful partner and together we will walk through this life, in prayerful hope we will be one in eternal life, Forever and Ever Amen. With a heart full of love for Jesus and Mary in union with St. Joseph, I am yours my love, Gwen.

GWEN'S LOVE LETTER TO JERRY – FEBRUARY 14, 1998

My Dear Husband,

It was 39 years ago today that you asked me to be your bride. How excited I was. You came to pick me up, and as soon as you stepped in the door, you pulled the ring, still in the box, out of your pocket. I was just 19, you were 20 (then we were two skinnys)!

So we vowed our love for each other and have grown to a much deeper love. You were always Mr. Handsome and my heart was always beating for you. Even today I love being with you. As the song goes "You Light Up My Life."

Love bears all things, believes all things, hopes all things, and endures all things. On this Valentine's Day, my prayer for you is that your happiness will always be my loving wish and prayer. So on this day and always, may God keep you in His care. And may He find a special way to make your hopes come true, and fill the coming days and years with all good things for you.

To be more specific, you have always shown me your love and concern in my weaknesses and faults. Remember when your outstanding love for me *after my auto crash? You were at each birth praying and waiting for our little treasure to be born.*

Oh so many, many more, but now you're helping me make our bed, set my vitamins out, do dishes, laundry, shop, take me to the doctor, and all mean so very much to me.

You will always be my honey!
Your "Sweetie Pie" Gwen

Gwen liked one-on-one time with the Catholic Corps men and women. She viewed them as an extension of her own family, and was a wonderful mother figure as well as mentor to them. Gwen made sure she had an office, so she could have her one-on-one time with them, and anyone else who needed her time and attention. She would even make appointments with the Catholic Corps members. To her, it was all about building relationships and nurturing those relationships; of course, all in an effort to draw those she came into contact with toward Christ through Our Lady.

The Apostolate in Ohio would come to be known as Catholic Familyland, a place set apart where entire families can come, parents and children alike, to spend quality and spiritually enriching time together, as well as enjoy simple family fun. At Catholic Familyland, there is 850 acres of woods for hiking, a pool for swimming, horseback riding, cabins, camper hookups, bonfires, tennis and basketball courts and baseball fields, and chapels in every major building. It is a week-long getaway of faith, family and fun! Gwen and Jerry had about seventy-two wooden cabins built at St. James Field. Four more wooden cabins were added to the restored eleven cinder block cabins built at Holy Family Park. There are also camper hookups and about sixty sites for RV and tent camping at Holy Family Park.

Each of the wooden cabins have a double bed, two sets of bunk beds, and a loft where two to four children can sleep, depending on their age and size, totaling enough to house eight to ten people. There is also a table, changing room, refrigerator and microwave. The cabins are ready for summer or winter with heat and air conditioning.

Family Fests, which actually started out as Family "Work" Fests, are one-week events held five times in the summer. Each Fest draws as many as 150 families. They were initially work fests because there was so much work that was needed to be done on the property and the buildings, that Jerry recruited the men and women to assist in this effort, along with times for fun as well. Good work is part of the Catholic way of life; work hard and play hard! Over time, the Family Work Fests became Family Fests because the need for all the work lessened with time.

A typical day in this family vacation site would entail morning Mass in the St. Joseph Auditorium, attended typically by numerous priests, and sometimes Vatican dignitaries, such as Cardinal Arinze. If children had recently received their First Holy Communion, they would be invited and encouraged to dress up in their Communion attire for Mass, and participate in the Eucharistic Procession and Benediction that followed, in order to participate in a special way to honor this wonderful sacrament that they had recently received. Boys of all ages were recruited to participate in all Masses as altar servers.

After Mass and lunch, there are various group activities based upon age. Young children, about 4-12 years old, would go into smaller groups to engage in an activity together, while incorporating some Catechesis. Teens meet in the morning, and in the evenings they meet to have some good, wholesome, healthy fun, with some Catechesis incorporated into the outing. The high point for the teenagers is on one particular night mid-week when they receive letters from their parents and spend hours in adoration with Our Lord. It is quite a touching and emotional time for them. There are even programs for college-age young adults, which include adoration. In addition, young adults volunteer to help run some of the programs. Small children stay with their parents, however, are also able to enjoy the Tiny Tot play area while their parents are in the adult programs. The Family Fest week provides opportunities for the Sacrament of Reconciliation and adoration of the Blessed Sacrament in the chapel, as well as participating in base-ball games, volleyball games, swimming, horseback riding, chess games, and other activities. It's amazing how the activities foster relationships with like-minded families; even parents hanging out with their small children at the swing set are offered opportunities for good conversation among the parents!

Mealtimes are another way for families to meet each other and build relationships. Holy Family Park has an outdoor pavilion with picnic tables to dine with others, or order the Mama C Snack Shack meal option, named after Gwen, who was its first manager. Families can also opt to grill their own food at their campsites. Other activities include musical bonfire family rosaries engaging with age groups participating and then ending with toasting marshmallows and singing songs. Fr. Kevin Barrett use to be seen leading these.

Outside of the Family Fests, at other times of the year, retreats are conducted. These include silent retreats for adults, men or women, youth retreats, Work Fests, Conferences, Totus Tuus (Totally Yours) retreats, Marriage encounters and pilgrimages. Marriage Get Aways and Totus Tuus Conferences were also Gwen's ideas for families.

The Apostolate founded a TV Network called Familyland TV network, hosted on Sky Angel satellite. The network would play very family friendly entertaining shows, offering Catholic and Christian programming for all ages. It contained spiritual programs, talk shows, classic movies, children's shows, all of which were vetted for family friendly material loyal to the teachings of the Church. "Our main goal was to bring about an era of peace that Our Lady promised at Fatima, which I believe will come about when enough families are consecrated to her," said Jerry.

Gwen was always working in the shadows and behind the scenes, but also was very visible to families, whether it was at the retreats or the Family Fests. She would be cleaning the toilets and taking care of other very practical matters. If an umbrella was broken or a chair was broken, she removed it and replaced it. Her attention to detail, again, proved to be an asset for her in making the stay for the families very hospitable. "I would go visit my mom in Ohio on one of the Family Fests," said Laurie, "and see her being pulled in all different ways by people needing her. It was difficult to get away to visit her from Kenosha, due to our own family obligations, and since my husband has only so much vacation time. I just wanted time with my mom, and she would have many people calling her for every little thing. She was also being constantly interrupted by people at the Apostolate. So basically, I had to follow her around the Fest just to be with her. I speak for my other siblings too that we just wanted private time with our mom." Gwen did make it a point to have a private meal with her children while they were in town, instead of being with the crowd.

Gwen and Jerry in front of one of the Cabins at Catholic Familyland.

During a Family Fest at Catholic Familyland.

LIFE IN OHIO, LIFE IN THE APOSTOLATE

First Class Evangelizers

The Apostolate for Family Consecration exists for the primary purpose of renewing the family and the community which comprises the parish and the neighborhood, hence, leading all souls to Christ. In a word, it is the "Social Reign of the Holy Family" in a God-centered Society. **It is an Apostolate for apostolates.** It helps families to live Total Consecration to the Holy Family, while helping families transform parishes and communities into God-centered communities. The Apostolate's strategies and tools include: the St. Joseph Media and Training Centers, "Consecration in the Truth" Multimedia Library; the Lay Ecclesial Team Evangelization System; Membership of generous souls; Family Television Network; Peace of Heart Forums for adult formation; 'Be Not Afraid' Family Hours, and much more.

The Family Apostolate has created and produced the largest **multimedia evangelization and catechetical program library** in the world, which the laity can confidently use as first-class evangelizers and catechists. These videos are theologically sound and in line with the Magisterium of the Church. They comprise **30,000** video programs and TV programs, **with 500 of the top teachers in the Church**. They feature some of the world's greatest teachers, theologians, philosophers, and brilliant Catholic minds in our contemporary world. These programs are 24 ½ minute video segments that are organized into mini teaching programs that the Apostolate would include in their "Peace of Heart Forms" on Papal Documents, Vatican II, scripture, and catechesis. All 24 ½ minute video segments are tied into printed documents that are studied in various formats. For example, Cardinal Arinze would prepare for over 200 hours for each annual visit to the Apostolate Center for videotaping.

Some of these teachers include St. Teresa of Calcutta, St. John Paul II, Francis Cardinal Arinze, Servant of God, Fr. John Hardon, J. Cardinal Francis Stafford, Archbishop John Foley, Scott Hahn, and George Weigel, just to name a few. "Our greatest video series were the 1900 programs we did with Francis Cardinal Arinze, Prefect for Divine Worship and the Discipline of the Sacraments, over a 25-year period of time," said Jerry. "They are about the papal documents of Pope John Paul II, and Cardinal

Ratzinger (Pope Benedict XVI). Cardinal Arinze came to the Apostolate for roughly twenty-five years and was truly a blessing to its mission because of his love for the Church, and his clear and clever way of expressing the faith."

These videos are particularly effective because the teachings are carried out through the vibrant means of video. As families are drawn into deeper union with Our Eucharistic Lord, they can grow in sanctifying grace. This can be a spiritual power that can change the course of history. It can play a major role in bringing about a civilization of love, by unleashing the spiritual power of the Church that is in the Holy Eucharist and the Sacrament of Penance. Cardinal Casaroli, when he was Secretary of State, had this to say: "I am deeply moved by the way the Apostolate for Family Consecration creatively uses the media in controlled conditions to create community, and to draw people to meditative prayer on Scripture and other spiritual books."

The Apostolate's greatest work thus far is the publication of a two-volume set of *The Apostolate's Family Catechism*, written by Fr. Lawrence G. Lovasik, S.V.D. It has been approved and blessed by Pope John Paul II, Cardinal Ratzinger, Cardinal Ciappi, and the Roman Curia. They also have produced many other edifying books and materials. *The Apostolate's Family Catechism* systematically draws the entire family into Scripture, Vatican II documents, *The Catechism of the Catholic Church*, *Veritatis Splendor*, and numerous other church documents. It came out providentially at the same time as *The Catechism of the Catholic Church* and allows the reader to find those references. It includes a complete catechetical program for elementary and high school students, as well as adult faith formation. It is a two-volume set organized by a series of 304 questions and answers format on church teaching. The questions are organized according to the four pillars of the Catechism of the Catholic Church's teachings: The Creed, the Sacraments, Morality, and Prayer. It includes references to Scripture, *The Catechism of the Catholic Church*, Papal documents, and other Church documents. It also includes prayers, discussion questions and more.

Interestingly, *The Apostolate's Family Catechism* has been translated into **Chinese**, Spanish, and Philippino (Takalig). Translations are in progress for: Rwandese, Portuguese, French, Russian, as well as other lesser known languages.

The story of the translation of *The Apostolate's Family Catechism* into Chinese is both interesting and miraculous. Jerry wanted to have it translated and published in Chinese but did not know how to go about doing it. "It is much more difficult to translate in Chinese, more than any other language; one hundred times more difficult," said Jerry.

In the year 2000, Jerry went to the Philippines to meet with Jaime Cardinal Sin. Cardinal Sin was the Cardinal for all of Asia but his diocese was in Manila, Philippines, of which the Family Apostolate had a presence, with numerous buildings there since May of 1994. Fr. Scanlon had mentioned to Jerry that Cardinal Sin invites many to the Philippines, but then never helps them once there. However, it was not so with Jerry and the Family Apostolate. This good Cardinal helped the Apostolate immensely, even sponsoring their 24-7 TV Network.

So while there at this time, Jerry asked Cardinal Sin if he knew of anyone who would be able to translate *The Apostolate's Family Catechism* into Chinese. The Cardinal responded with a resounding, "Yes!" Jerry's face lit up with excitement! This was a huge breakthrough! Cardinal Sin introduced Jerry to Professor Lee and to a Jesuit priest, Fr. John Znang, who led a team and coordinated the translation effort. This monumental effort took two to three years, and in 2006, it was published by Hebei Faith Press. At least 20,000 copies were disseminated in China to a select group of priests and nuns, who are in a teaching capacity and are using the book to teach their students who are thirsty for the Truth. More copies were printed for the public at large.

"In China, a communist country, Catholic priests do not garn the habit in public," said Jerry. "They don't wear their collar. They also do not put the title Father on their published works, so as to not draw attention to the fact that it is a religious (or man of the cloth) who is publishing the work, because their work would be censored and undermined," Jerry continued. "This is miraculous because China is so opposed to Catholicism that they discourage publication of these types of books." Jerry needed permission from the government to print any book, particularly a religious book. So the team of people knew ahead of time that their laborious efforts could come to naught if the government would not give them permission, yet they had to first translate the document so as to present to the government the manuscript. So this was quite a monumental effort ahead of time, with no assurance that it would even pass governmental scrutiny. More astounding was the ability to solicit two to three years of work effort by this team of translators with no guarantee that the book would ever be published.

Other importation publications were the *Preparation for Total Consecration to Jesus through Mary for Families* and the *Drawing Down Divine Mercy* which includes a 40-day Preparation for Families for Divine Mercy Sunday.

The **"Be Not Afraid" Family Holy Hours,** inspired by St. Teresa of Calcutta, are holy hours in front of the Blessed Sacrament. In order to stop abortion and strengthen families, families must have one-hour Eucharistic adoration weekly. The video programs are shown in churches, while confessions are being heard, to educate families in the truth, because that's where the Eucharist is reserved; that's where the power is. The hour contains catechesis, as well as traditional devotions such as praying the rosary.

The **Peace of Heart Forum Series'** purpose is for continuing adult faith formation and to draw adults into spiritual reading. People gather in homes to read a spiritual book; and then view a presentation on it featuring the author or expert on the book, followed by a lively discussion and sharing. Subjects incorporate Sacred Scripture, the lives of the saints, and uncovering the depths of papal documents. They also provide a spiritual support system for the families.

The Video Faculty includes the following:

1,900 programs with Cardinal Arinze	150 with Fr. Hugh Gillespie, S.M.M.	50 with George Weigel
600 with Fr. John Hardon,S.J.	150 with Fr. Gregory Finn,O.S.J.	20 with Bishop Daniel Conlon
500 with Fr. Michael Scanlan,TOR	150 with Fr. Adrian van Kaam, C.S.Sp.	20 with Cardinal Gaudencio Rosales
500 with Dr. Alice von Hildebrand	150 with Dr. Susan Muto	20 with Cardinal BevilaquaAa
400 with Fr. George Kosicki on Div. Mercy	150 with Fr. Frederick Miller	20 with Magr.Josefino Ramirez
300 with Fr. Pablo Straub on on catechetics	150 with Cardinal E Gagnon, R. Curia	10 with Cardinal Adam Maida
300 with Msgr. Peter Elliott, Roman Curia	150 with Bishop Juan Torres	10 with Cardinal Ciappi. Roman Curia
300 with Fr. Randall Paine	150 with Dr. Scott Hahn	10 with Cardinal John O'Connor
300 with Fr. Frank Pavone	150 with Fr. Benedict Groeschel	10 with Cardinal Edmund Szoka, R.C.
200 with Archbishop Arguelles	100 with Cardinal Pio Laghi, R. Curia	10 with Cardinal Alfonso Trijillo, R.C.
200 with Fr. Brian Harrison, S.T.L.	100 with Cardinal Jaime Sin	10 with Cardinal John Foley, Roman C.
200 with Mother Immaculata H.M.I.	100 with J. Francis Stafford, R. Curia	10 with Bishop Thomas V. Daily
150 with Bishop Van Lierde, Roman Curia	100 with Bishop Socrates Villegas	5 with Cardinal Jose Sanchez, R.C.
150 with Bishop Thomas Welsh	100 with John H. Hampsch	5 with Cardinal Schonborn O.P. R.C.
150 with Msgr. John McCarthy, Roman Curia	50 with Blessed Mother Teresa of Calc.	5 with Cardinal Jozef Tomko, R.C.
150 with Fr. Roger Charest, S.M.M.	50 with Fr, Patrick Peyton	5 with Giovanni Cheli, Roman Curia
150 with Fr, Harold Cohen, S.J.	50 with Fr. Albert Krapiec, O.P. Lublin U.	5 with John Haas
150 with Thomas Dubay, S.M.	50 with Fr. S. Michalenko, MIC Lublin U.	
150 with Fr. Bernard Geiger, O.F.M. Conv	50 with Fr. Bruce Nieli, Lublin University	

LIFE IN OHIO, LIFE IN THE APOSTOLATE

Lay ecclesial team members unite families with the parish and the school. It's a world-wide network of committed families and volunteers dedicated to spreading the message of Consecration to the Holy Family. Team members serve their parishes and neighborhoods to help unite families with the school and the parish, using the Family Apostolate's vast library of multi-media resources. Leaders work with their pastors to share these formation resources with parish groups, organizations, and movements.

Jerry and Cardinal Francis Arinze from the Roman Curia
creating a video series and the studios at the Family Apostolate
in Bloomingdale, Ohio.

Then there is the Family Apostolate's Dual Dimension of "Consecrate them in the Truth or Totus Tuus, meaning *Totally Yours* in Latin." Totus Tuus is the motto Pope John Paull II adopted for his Pontificate. It is to inspire and support families, neighborhoods, and parishes throughout the world, in the spirit of St. John Paul II, to live lives nourished by continuous multimedia formation in the truths of the Faith, and given totally to Jesus, through Mary, in union with St. Joseph–the "Dual Dimension of Consecration to the Holy Family." Consecration to the Holy Family must be a commitment to a way of life.

The first dimension consists of giving everything to Jesus through Mary (according to St. Louis de Montfort charism) in union with St. Joseph, or Totus Tuus. The second dimension is taken from Last Supper when Jesus says to His apostles, "Consecrate them in the truth," as depicted in chapter 17 of St. John's gospel. This means a life-long journey of learning our faith, and sharing our faith; in a word, becoming families for others. The root cause of all suffering and unhappiness is sin. Pain, death, disease, poverty and natural disasters all have their roots in original sin or personal sin. Every sin gives the devil more power to tempt souls and work his evil in the world. Reparation for sin takes that power away. So, that is why the Apostolate's mission and outreach strategies are focused on reparation for sin with the goal of reversing the moral decay of our society. Armed with Total Consecration to Jesus through Mary in union with St. Joseph, and the knowledge of the truths of our faith in order to combat the father of lies, families can fight and win the battle against the world, the flesh, and the devil, and inspire others to join them in that fight.

Pope John Paul II knew how important it was for Catholics to enlist in this crusade, and how high are the stakes. In the year 2000, through prayer, he entrusted the world to Mary. He said, "Today as never before, humanity stands at a crossroads. We can turn this world into a garden or reduce it to a pile of rubble." This Apostolate is critical to win this war and draw souls to Christ. Sr. Lucia revealed what Our Lord told her, "The most effective penance is the sacrifice that each one must make to fulfill his or her own religious and worldly duties. One need not live an austere life of painful penances." We can also feel secure in the knowledge that we have a secret weapon, who is Mary, the Mother of God, who intercedes for us to her beloved Son. Because she presents our sacrifices to Jesus as her own, their value is multiplied, called the Marian multiplier. This spiritual reality has been confirmed by theologians and saints throughout the ages, including Mario Luiggi Cardinal Ciappi, papal theologian to five Pontiffs, including St. John Paul II. Cardinal Ciappi also served as the primary theological director for the Family Apostolate from 1979-1996, a move that is unprecedented for a papal theologian, at the same time he was advising Pope John Paul II. In a 1989 letter to the Conikers, Cardinal Ciappi explained how the Marian multiplier worked, which was also first uttered by St. Louis de Montfort, "When we give all our merits to Mary, she multiplies them by her own incalculable merits. This puts into motion positive spiritual forces to repair the damage due to sin. Also, this action significantly changes the course of history, if enough make this commitment. Mary's merits can multiply the effects of one person's holiness and help countless souls."

The Family Apostolate also elucidates the seven responsibilities of our lives, which it refers to as the Supernatural House, to protect and nurture family life and to imitate the Holy Family, who is the perfect reflection of the love of the Holy Trinity, and perfect model of a family, who lives the responsibility of the present moment. This "Supernatural House" consists first and foremost with the foundation of which it is built upon, known as the Sacramental life. Then there are the four outside walls to this spiritual home, which comprise: formation, prayer, family, and community. Finally, the roof consists of work and evangelization. If any of these components are missing from the family, the house will crumble and the family will break down. This is so prevalent today in the turbulent world in which we live.

The motto for the Apostolate for Family Consecration is: "All for the Sacred and Eucharistic Heart of Jesus, all through the Sorrowful and Immaculate Heart of Mary, all in union with St. Joseph," or "All For..." for short. "The genius of the Apostolate for Family Consecration is that it simultaneously renews the Family and the Parish," said J. Francis Cardinal Stafford. The Family Apostolate brings a message of hope to a despairing world. "The renewal of the hierarchical Church must come by renewal of the domestic Church, which is the home and family," says Jerry. "Evangelization begins in the home. But families don't know how or where to begin, as they themselves were poorly catechized."

Many Catholics, even good committed Catholics, have no clear idea what sin is or what acts are really sinful, not to mention the gravity of those sins. They don't know how to properly examine their conscience, what it means to form one's conscience properly in the truth, to follow their conscience, properly understood. A properly formed conscience prepares us to make a good confession. A good confession prepares us to worthily and fervently receive the Holy Eucharist.

The media and the prevailing culture are poisoning the minds of people in a slow and steady manner of junk food. People need to be detoxified through prayer, sacraments, catechesis and doctrinal formation, nature, and being together with other like-minded families to support each other. Catholic Familyland brings all this along with such fun as baseball games, riding horses, swimming, and bonfires.

THE APOSTOLATE FOR FAMILY CONSECRATION HAS THESE AS THEIR FOUNDATIONAL INFLUENCES:

- The St. Louis de Montfort charism of Total Consecration
- St. Maximilian Kolbe Militia Immaculata
- Our Lady of Fatima, with her message of reparation, daily rosary, conversion, attention to daily duty
- Luigi Cardinal Ciappi, Papal theologian with his influence, help, and teachings, especially the Marian Multiplier teaching
- The Gospel of St. John, chapter 17, "…protect them from the evil one…consecrate them in the truth…"
- St. Mother Teresa of Calcutta and her Sacri-State Cooperators, spiritual unions of suffering, family formation in the Eucharistic presence

- St. Pope John Paul II with his writings, teachings, Totus Tuus – Consecrate them in the truth
- The Conikers' own first-hand experience of living in Portugal for a time.

Letter from Mother Teresa of Calcutta

JMJ.   23/3/92

> Dear Jerry and Gwen Coniker,
> Thank you for your kind letter and prayers for me. I am well thank God. It will be a real gift of God if the adoration of the Bl. Sacrament could fully penetrate family life. The holy hour as family prayer in our Society has been the greatest gift of God. "Be Not Afraid" Our Lord will always be with you.
> Bring prayer as much as possible into the family life. Consecration to the Sacred Heart and Rosary family - Very pleasing to the Heart of Jesus. Keep praying for our Society, our Poor & me. God bless you
> c Teresa m

One of many letters of Mother Teresa to
Jerry and Gwen Coniker

Chapter 17

An International Apostolate

OVER TIME, THE FAMILY APOSTOLATE expanded into other countries. Jaime Cardinal Sin invited Jerry to come to his Archdiocese and open a center there. Jerry had a favorable relationship with him, as well as with Archbishop Ramon Arguelles, Cardinal Gaudencio Rosales, and Bishop Jesse Mercado. So in May of 1994, the Family Apostolate established the St. Joseph's training center in Manila. The Women's Catholic Corps would staff it.

There was a sculptor from the Philippines, by the name of Rene Salvacion, who created a magnificent Sculpture of the Holy Family which was complet-

ed in the year 2000, under the leadership of Monsignor Josefino Ramirez who had quite a following in the Philippines. The 30-foot sculpture is located on the island of Guimaras in the Philippines. A smaller statue of the Holy Family is located at the Familyland Center in Bloomingdale, Ohio.

The Center reaches out to all of Asia, including China, for training, education, and multi-media evangelization. Fifty-three of the nation's 80 catholic dioceses in the Philippines have invited the Family Apostolate to come work within their parishes. It's a massive catechetical program which provides the Apostolate's Family Catechism to the poor and those in need, so that they too may be enriched by the knowledge of their faith.

In August of 1999, the Family Apostolate established the St. Joseph's Center in Mexico. This center has a special relationship with the Shrine of Our Lady of Guadalupe, and is located on the side of a mountain within the grounds of a former seminary. Our Lady of Guadalupe is the most frequented Marian Shrine in the world. The Family Apostolate also had permission from the Basilica to set up a large gathering tent outside of the Basilica to promote family hour devotions, spread the movement for families, and the Family Rosary. The Missionaries of Charity, Mother Teresa's order of nuns, is using *The Apostolate's Family Catechism* and the Rosary prayer book in Spanish. Today, this center conducts a Montessori school for children from ages one to twelve. This school gives families training not only to educate, but to bring about family renewal like never before.

Then in 2004, the Family Apostolate opened up a center in Nigeria, Africa. Because of Jerry's close relationship with Cardinal Arinze from the Vatican, and who is from Nigeria, Jerry was able to gain his support and permission from the hierarchy there. So Archbishop Valerian M. Okeke and Bishop Martin Igwe Uzoukwu, with the help of Francis Cardinal Arinze, granted them permission for a center to be opened there in Nigeria. This center provides evangelization and formation training programs featuring Cardinal Arinze. They are using the 1900 video programs produced with Cardinal Arinze to inform, educate, and catechize families.

In the year 2000, a couple from Belgium, Rob and Isabel Alert, helped produce the 40-day Consecration for St. Louis de Montfort video and the 40-day Divine Mercy video. They also produced television programs with Cardinal Arinze to be viewed on the internet. Jerry commented, "It's amazing what we can do in this day and age. The truth can now be communicated in such a forceful way!"

In March, 2007, with permission from the local bishop, Bishop Cyryl Klimowicz, a center was opened in the city of Irkustk, Siberia [Russia] in the St. Joseph Diocese, the physically largest diocese in the world.

Totus Tuus

In Ohio at Catholic Familyland, the Family Apostolate continues its most important work of saving souls, evangelizing, and educating others. They have conducted Totus Tuus retreats periodically throughout the year. Here is one such talk of many that Gwen gave at one of those retreats:

Six Keys to Building Strong
Catholic Families
by Gwen Coniker on February 10, 1996

As we look back in our family life, there were six keys that helped us in building our faith:

1. Consecration of our lives to Jesus through Mary in union with St. Joseph

2. Sacraments of Reconciliation and the Holy Eucharist

3. The Family Rosary

4. First Saturday Devotion (Fatima request)

5. Evangelization (family to family)

6. Catechism of the Catholic Church [and The Apostolate's Family Catechism] (formation).

All of these are keys to strengthening and unifying family life.

FIRST KEY: CONSECRATION OF OUR LIVES TO JESUS THROUGH MARY IN UNION WITH ST. JOSEPH

It was in February 1971 that we were introduced to True Devotion to Mary by the profound writings of St. Louis de Montfort," said Gwen.

What does consecrating your life mean: St. Louis says, "This devotion consists in giving oneself entirely to Mary, in order to belong entirely to Jesus through her. It requires us to give:

1. Our body with its senses and members
2. Our soul with its faculties
3. Our material possessions
4. Our interior and spiritual possessions, merits, virtues and good works

In other words, we give her all that we possess, both in the natural life and in our spiritual life. After 33 days of study and prayer, we wanted to give our lives, our family, and all we possessed to the Blessed Virgin Mary. While we didn't fully understand this, we opened our minds and hearts to learn more and more as we journeyed through life.

SECOND KEY: THE SACRAMENTS OF RECONCILIATION AND THE HOLY EUCHARIST

After making the Act of Consecration, it brought us to a deeper longing to receive Jesus in the Sacrament of the Holy Eucharist. Being sensitive to having a pure heart for Him kept us wanting to be reconciled through the Sacrament of Penance. For our family, this became a way of life. The sacraments are the key foundation in raising a strong Catholic family. The Eucharist is the ultimate, and it shows the extreme humility and mercy of the Lord Jesus Christ present among us, radiating His merciful love to all who come [to Him] in humble and obedient faith.

THIRD KEY: THE FAMILY ROSARY

After studying the Fatima message and living there [for two years] and having consecrated our lives to [Jesus through] the Blessed Virgin Mary, the family rosary became our daily prayer. The rosary calls our attention to the three great mysteries of human existence: joy (faith), sorrow (love), and glory (hope).

Life requires of us faith if we are to grow as a person. Love always introduces us to the wisdom that comes from the school of suffering. We live in hope of that glory which does not pass away. The blessings from God intended to show forth His goodness and love. As such, both marriage and family life call us to holiness.

Prayer is an indispensable aspect of holiness. Parents are to be the educators to their children in the life of prayer. Through family prayer, each family follows the example of the Holy Family of Nazareth. Pope John Paul II tells us, "We now desire…to recommend strongly the recitation of the family rosary. The rosary should be considered as one of the best and most efficacious prayers in common that the Christian family is invited to recite." *(Role of the Christian Family in the Modern World.)*

Praying the rosary reminds each member of the family of the joys, sorrows, and hopes of daily life together. The rosary reminds us of how God's love is at work in all the moments of our day and the many ways we relate to one another. When we gather together with our families in prayer, Jesus is present in our midst.

Mother Teresa says: "The fruit of prayer is a deeper faith and the fruit of faith is love and the fruit of love is service and the fruit of service is peace."

We all long for that peace in our hearts, in our families, in our church and in our nation. May I remind us of what the Holy Father, Pope John Paul ll, said when he visited the United States in October of 1995. "There are two immediate things which the Catholic families can to do strengthen home—life. The first is prayer: both personal and family prayer. One prayer in particular that I recommend to families is the Rosary."

"The second suggestion I make to families is to use the *Catechism of the Catholic Church* [and the Vatican-Approved Apostolate Family Catechism]; to learn about the Faith and to answer questions that come up, especially the moral questions which confront everyone today. I exhort and encourage the Bishops and the whole Church…to help parents fulfill their vocation, to be the first and most important teachers of the Faith to their children."

AN INTERNATIONAL APOSTOLATE

Fourth Key: First Saturday Devotion

Our Lady of Fatima asked for the five First Saturdays—Mass and Communion, Rosary, 15 minutes of meditation on the Scriptural mysteries of the Rosary, and confession [within eight days before or after the First Saturday] in reparation for sins that offend her Immaculate Heart.

Through Divine Providence, four months after we consecrated our lives, our family moved to Fatima, Portugal. As extreme and unusual as it sounds, we sold our home, our business, prepared seven children (expecting our eighth child within thirty days), and flew to a foreign country! Our relatives and friends showed great concern and wondered if we knew what we were doing. Some even thought we were crazy. Jerry's brother, Bill, flew in from New Orleans to check the whole situation out. He learned we were serious and saw that the strong conviction in our hearts were to raise our family in a Catholic environment and live near the place Our Lady had appeared to the three shepherd children: Lucia, Jacinta, and Francisco.

While our family lived in Portugal for two years, we learned more and more what it means to consecrate your life, giving all you are and have to [God through] the Blessed Mother Mary.

Our daily family Rosary, Mass, First Saturday devotion became a way of life for us. We began to build a strong Catholic family (eight children, ages 1 to 12 years old).

While living there, we had many joyful events and family fun-filled times together. We experienced the joy of our new baby, Joseph, and his Baptism, trips to the zoo with elephant rides, fun in the sun at the Atlantic Ocean, touring the castles and the candlelight procession, and Mass on the key days of Our Lady of Fatima, from May to October, at the shrine.

Before we returned to the Fatima Shrine on June 13, 1975, we met with the Bishop of Leiria–Fátima. As we left his office, we met a Jesuit priest who gave us a book, *Sister Lucia's Letters*. In this book was a letter dated December 2, 1940, by Sister Lucia, one of the visionaries, where she talked of the power of consecration of a nation. She said: "Most Holy Father, Our Lady promises a special protection to our country in this war, due to the Consecration of the nation by the Portuguese Prelates to the Immaculate Heart of Mary, as proof of the graces that would have been granted to other nations, had they also consecrated themselves to her."

The Bishop asked us to take this [Fatima] message [of consecration] back to the United States. This marked the beginning and burning desire of my husband Jerry and myself to spread this message of Consecration of [our families] and nation to the [Sacred Heart of Jesus through] the Immaculate Heart of Mary.

What an extraordinary mission for an ordinary family!

We returned to the United States in June of 1973 and our family continued to grow. A few years had passed and while we were expecting our eleventh child, in June of 1975, the Apostolate for Family Consecration was born, on the feast day of the Sacred Heart of Jesus.

We continued to learn about the meaning of consecration as the Family Apostolate developed, which brought us to the Fifth Key to build strong Catholic families, and that is evangelization.

FIFTH KEY: EVANGELIZATION

We experienced overwhelming excitement when Mother Teresa came to our St. Joseph Center of the Apostolate for Family Consecration in Kenosha, Wisconsin, in June of 1981. It was with Mother Teresa's inspiration that we produced video programs on Consecration for families, to be shown in homes and especially parishes, where Jesus is present in the Blessed Sacrament. By praying [and learning our faith together], families are strengthened and unified and powerful reparation is made for the sins of humanity, especially the sin of abortion. Mother Teresa said, "Prayer is essential if we wish the scourge of abortion to be lifted and families to be renewed, [she had stressed family formation and prayer before Jesus in the Tabernacle]."

The video programs are titled "Be Not Afraid Family Hours" and Mother said, "I encourage all families to participate in this powerful devotion which is calling down the Mercy of God upon all of us."

The Be Not Afraid Family Hours feature: a message from the Holy Father,

Pope John Paul II, as well as Mother Teresa, Cardinal Arinze—a Roman Curia Cardinal teaching the catechism and the rosary with meditations, plus short interviews from various Cardinals, Bishops, Priests and Laity.

Pope Paul VI in his encyclical, "Evangelization in the Modern World" states: "The conditions of the society in which we live oblige all of us therefore to revise methods, to seek by every means to study how we can bring the Christian message to modern man. For it is only the Christian message that modern man can find the answer to this question and the energy for his commitment of human solidarity."

So this brings us to the modern means of using technology to spread the Christian message.

SIXTH KEY: THE CATECHISM OF THE CATHOLIC CHURCH

This is the great gift God has given us by our Holy Father, Pope John Paul II, so that we may better know our faith, in order to live our faith in building strong Catholic families.

Also, the *Apostolate's Family Catechism* is a great resource for families because, as Cardinal Ratzinger [who later would become Pope Benedict XVI] said, "It serves the *Catechism of the Catholic Church.*"

SERVANT OF GOD

COMMISSIONE INTERDICASTERIALE
PER IL
CATECHISMO DELLA CHIESA CATTOLICA

Il Presidente

Prot. N. XII/91 C
(Si prega citare il numero nella risposta)

00193 Roma March 4, 1994
Piazza del S. Uffizio, 11

Letter from
Joseph Cardinal Ratzinger
President, Interdicasterial Commission for the
Catechism of the Catholic Church

Dear Mr. Coniker:

Thank you for your courtesy in sending a copy of The Apostolate's Family Catechism published by the Apostolate for Family Consecration. The work's publication in this year of the family could not be more timely. It anticipates many of the themes of His Holiness Pope John Paul's Letter to Families of February 2, 1994. The cross-references provided to the Catechism of the Catholic Church will make it an especially helpful instrument to parents and teachers.

With prayerful best wishes for the success of your vital apostolate, I remain

Sincerely yours in Christ,

Joseph Cardinal Ratzinger

Mr. Jerome F. **CONIKER**
President
Apostolate for Family Consecration
Route 2, Box 700
Bloomingdale, OH 43910
U.S.A

AN INTERNATIONAL APOSTOLATE

*Letter from Pope John Paul II
read by his Ambassador,
Archbishop Cacciavillan, at
the Family Apostolate's annual
Totus Tuus Conference".*

I have learned with pleasure that on October 22-24, the Apostolate for Family Consecration will sponsor a Conference in Pittsburgh on the theme "Consecrate Them in Truth". I would ask you kindly to convey to all associated with this worthy initiative my greetings and the assurance of my closeness in prayer.

Since the Conference aims to support and implement the message of the recent World Youth Day, I renew the invitation which I made in Denver: "I ask you to have the courage to commit yourselves to the truth. Have the courage to believe the Good News about Life which Jesus teaches in the Gospel. Open your minds and hearts to the beauty of all that God has made and to his special, personal love for each one of you" (Vigil, August 14, 1993, No. 4).

It is my hope that the Conference will inspire many Christian families to become ever more authentic "domestic Churches", in which the word of God is received with joy, bears fruit in lives of holiness and love, and shines forth with new brilliance as a beacon of hope for all to see. The faith-filled witness of Christian families is an essential element in the new evangelization to which the Holy Spirit is calling the Church in our time.

I am pleased that the Conference will seek to develop effective means of passing on to families and parishes the rich deposit of the Church's faith as presented in the Catechism of the Catholic Church. Because "family catechesis precedes, accompanies and enriches all other forms of catechesis" (*Catechesi Tradendae*, 68), I encourage the Apostolate for Family Consecration in its efforts to promote an effective catechesis in homes and parishes.

With these sentiments, I commend the work of the Conference to the intercession of Mary, Mother of the Church. To the organizers, speakers and participants I cordially impart my Apostolic Blessing, which I willingly extend to all the members of their families.

From the Vatican, October 10, 1993

Joannes Paulus PP. II

Letter from Pope John Paul II, read by his Ambassador, Archbishop Cacciavillan, at the Apostolate's annual Totus Tuus Conference. Oct. 10, 1993.

SERVANT OF GOD

2000 JUBILEE IN ROME

Over the years, Jerry and Gwen had numerous papal visits with Pope John Paul II. Jerry would be privileged to meet the great pope fourteen times, and Gwen ten times! For the 2000 Jubilee Year of Families, Jerry, Gwen, and their family were invited to Rome by Cardinal Alfonso López Trujillo because of their work for families. Incidentally, on April 29, 1999, Jerry and Gwen were honored by Pope John Paul II by being appointed on the Pontifical Council for the Family for a period of five years. As such, for the Year of the Family, they were chosen among all to be presented as a good example of the family. Jerry was then renewed for another five years as a Consultor of the Pontifical Council for the Family after Gwen's death. There were only 20 couples on the Pontifical Council for the Family in the world.

The date for the Jubilee celebration in Rome was October 14-15, 2000. Close to forty people went to Rome from the Coniker family, including most of their children, their spouses, and roughly twenty grandchildren, nine of which were babies under one year of age! It would be the last time that Gwen would see this great pope.

Both Gwen and Jerry had a few minutes each to speak, and this is what they had to say to the Pope, the Roman Curia, and the hundreds of thousands that were present:

Jerry: "Dear Holy Father, my wife Gwen and I have had the joy of watching our family grow throughout the past years, first with our thirteen children, then their faithful spouses, and now forty-eight grandchildren, through the grace of God all in their faith. We've been married for forty-one years and our love for each other grows every day. We thank God for His blessings upon our family and on the Apostolate for Family Consecration."

Gwen: "In the 1960s, we began to feel a decline in Christian values in our society. Seeing this negative influence affecting our own children moved us to grow closer to God and to trust more in His wisdom. Perhaps because we have dedicated our lives to our family and the Pro-Life movement, we were inspired to found the Apostolate for Family Consecration, an international association focused on your spirituality that promotes parish, lay, ecclesial teams that evangelize and catechize neighborhoods through the creative use of the media in homes, schools, churches, television, and a camp called Catholic Familyland. This camp is 850 acres set apart for families to grow in their faith and deepen their spiritual lives as you, Holy Father, have taught us to consecrate our families to Jesus through Mary in union with St. Joseph, and enter ever more deeply into the profound mystery of the human person."

Jerry: "Holy Father, we want to present to you a spiritual bouquet of over 5 million Masses and 6 million rosaries from our members in the Philippines, Mexico, and the United States. We love you so much. All of our work at the Family Apostolate we offer to the world with enthusiasm and humility. We ask your Holiness for your apostolic blessing on all those who are working with us."

Holy Father: "Only in the life, death, and resurrection of Christ do we come to see that love is the measure of all things in the kingdom of God, because **God is love**. We can fully experience the fullness of God's love in this life only through faith and repentance."

Pope John Paul II had this to say back in October of 1993 to the Conikers about their Apostolate: *"I encourage the Apostolate for Family Consecration in its efforts to promote an effective catechesis in homes and parishes."* *(October 10, 1993)*

Then every single member of the Coniker family present, totaling roughly forty people, were privileged to personally greet the Holy Father one-by-one. What is so extraordinary about this greeting line is when Gwen approached the Holy Father, and after speaking to her in his very weak and frail body suffering from Parkinson's disease, he got up from his chair, painfully and with much difficulty, to say goodbye to Gwen. Normally the Pope does not stand up for anyone, but is sitting, and those who approach him kneel down to kiss his ring as a sign of respect. After their encounter with each other, he then watched Gwen as she departed from him, keeping his eyes fixated upon her. What a special connection that these two holy people had for each other! A member of the Vatican Press Corp told Jerry that he had been covering the Holy Father for the last twelve years and he had never seen the Pope stand for anyone!

"The greatest gift St. John Paul II gave to the Apostolate of Family Consecration," said Jerry, "was his blessing on our new book, *Preparation for Total Consecration to Jesus through Mary for Families.*"

Pope John Paul II standing up for Gwen as she approaches.
This is unprecedented for a Pope to stand for anyone. Jubilee Year Oct. 2000.

Jerry and Gwen speaking with Pope John Paul II.
Jubilee Year Oct. 2000.

Throughout the Years...

The Apostolate for Family Consecration founders, Jerry & Gwen Coniker, have been encouraged by His Holiness Pope John Paul II.

The Coniker Family
13 children and 46 grandchildren

1984

1988

1986

1989

1988

1991

1992

1996

1999

1994

SECRETARIA STATUS

The Supreme Pontiff

POPE JOHN PAUL II

has appointed

Mr. JERRY and Mrs. GWEN CONIKER

to be Members of the Pontifical Council for the Family for a period of five years.

By these Letters the said Mr. and Mrs. Coniker are informed of their

appointment so that they may act accordingly.

From the Vatican, on the 29th day of April, in the year 1999.

+Angelo Card. Sodano

SERVANT OF GOD

AN EXTRAORDINARY VISIT WITH THE FATIMA SEER, SR. LUCIA

Jerry had the opportunity to visit the convent in Coimbra, Portugal, where the Fatima seer, Sr. Lucia, lived. He visited there two times but was not allowed to visit with Sr. Lucia. The only one who could authorize people to see her was Cardinal Ratzinger (later, Pope Benedict XVI), who at the time was Prefect for the Doctrine of the Faith.

Jerry was in Rome again and while there was visiting with Cardinal Ratzinger. He asked him for his permission to see and interview Sr. Lucia. The Cardinal said that he would see what he could do but did not make any promises. Later, Jerry received a letter from Archbishop Tarcisio Bertone, on behalf of Cardinal Ratzinger, giving him permission. Jerry also became acquainted with Carlos, the translator for Sr. Lucia, who knew her well.

On October 13, 1917, the last apparition of Fatima and the miracle of the sun took place in front of seventy thousand people in Portugal. While the people were focused on the miracle of the sun, the three Fatima children had another vision. This vision was of St. Joseph holding the child Jesus in his arms and Our Lady dressed in white with a blue mantle. St. Joseph and the Child seemed to be blessing the world making the sign of the cross.

The Family Apostolate, at some point, had an artist paint an Apostolate of Family Consecration's Holy Family of Fatima picture, according to the description given by Sr. Lucia. The picture depicts Joseph in an authoritarian position holding Jesus next to Mary. This is so relevant since the husband is the head of the household protecting and leading the family.

Jerry flew to Coimbra, Portugal to Sr. Lucia's convent in order to see her and to interview her. It was December 12, 2001 when this wonderful encounter between the two of them took place, along with a videographer, and Carlos, the interpreter. However, Jerry was given strict instructions *not* to have any audio taken. He was only allowed to take video. The visit lasted for thirty minutes.

AN INTERNATIONAL APOSTOLATE

CONGREGATIO
PRO DOCTRINA FIDEI

00120 *Città del Vaticano,*   14 dicembre 2000
Palazzo del S. Uffizio

Prot. N. 1801/33 – 11324
(In responsione fiat mentio huius numeri)

Dear Mr. Coniker:

You requested from this Congregation by letter on October 9, 2000 and via fax on November 22, 2000 authorization to visit **Sister Lucia Dos Santos**, the Fatima seer, so as to film an interview to be included in the program "Fatima and Divine Mercy" due to be transmitted by Familyland Television Network.

This Congregation, after an attentive examination of your request, and aware of the good end that you pursue, grants you a private meeting with Sister Lucia solely to ask her for prayers but not to enter into other issues.

You may therefore contact the Most Rev. João Alves, Bishop of Coimbra (Portugal), so as to arrange the practical details of your visit.

I avail myself of the occasion to offer you my sincere respects and my best wishes for the coming Feast of Christmas,

Yours devotedly in the Lord

Tarcisio Bertone

Mr. Jerry CONIKER
Apostolate for Family consecration
3375 Country Road, 36
Bloomingdale, Ohio 43910-7903, USA

Letter from the Archbishop Tarcisio Bertone on behalf
of Cardinal Ratzinger giving Jerry permission
to visit Sr. Lucia, the Fatima seer.

Jerry showed Sr. Lucia the Apostolate's Holy Family of Fatima picture that the artist painted. He then asked her what she thought about it. Her response was that she felt that the imagery of the painting was the best that a human being could do. She also said that Joseph will come to bless the world.

They discussed Our Lady's request in 1917 for the Consecration of Russian to her. Jerry asked Sr. Lucia when Pope John Paul II consecrated the world to Our Lady on March, 25, 1984 in union with the bishops as to

Jerry Coniker with Sr. Lucia, seer of the Fatima visions. whether Our Lady accepted it, even though the Pope did not specifically mention Russia. Sr. Lucia said, "Yes."

Other things that they discussed were the mysteries of the Mass that were revealed to Sister Lucia when she was a Dorthean nun in Spain. She said that Mary is present at every Mass, and Pope John Paul II confirmed this in his 2003 Encyclical on the Eucharist, *ECCLESIA DE EUCHARISTIA.*

Right after the visit, Jerry and the translator immediately went to a quiet place and recorded what they recollected from the interview. "She is very lively for being in her 90s," said Jerry, "and has a wonderful sense of humor!"

The trip was a success! They returned home to the United States. It is also noteworthy to mention that Pope John Paul II awarded Jerry and Gwen the Pro Ecclesia et Pontifices Award in 2001. Jerry and Gwen went to the Cathedral in Steubenville to receive it. Bishop Gilbert Sheldon, who was the Bishop of Steubenville, presented them with the award on behalf of the pope.

Chapter 18

Third and Final Trial

TOWARD THE END OF 2001, Gwen started to not feel well and went to see the doctor. It was not good news. After conducting a thorough testing, Gwen was diagnosed with cirrhosis of the liver and was told that she had less than a year to live. It was November 2, 2001 when she received this news, the same day as her beloved husband Jerry's birthday. This was apparently contracted by a blood transfusion during one of her caesarean births in the mid 1970s. Hepatitis C was in the blood she received, which caused a liver infection and, years later, led to cirrhosis of the liver. Five years earlier she had liver problems and knew she had a slow killer—liver disease.

As difficult as this news was for Gwen to absorb, she peacefully and willingly accepted her sickness and physical sufferings. To her, God allowed this and it is His will. Of course, that does not mean that the Conikers would not avail themselves of all medical options available in order to seek a cure. In fact, Gwen and Jerry were hoping for a liver transplant, and were pursuing that option which made Gwen hopeful.

The staff and the doctors at the Cleveland Clinic were amazed with Gwen as to how she took the news. One cancer doctor from Puerto Rico said to Gwen, "I've never met a person like you before; someone who took the news and was so gracious about it! I mean everything about you; your spirit, and how you accepted everything!" Then he found out about her work in the Apostolate. He was quite edified by her and went home and told his wife. He rarely tells his wife what is going on at work. He said he was very privileged to have met her. Gwen also made friends with all the nurses. In his opinion and that of her other doctors and nurses, Gwen was a model patient.

"Every day they (the doctors) brought me sad news," said Gwen, "but they broke it to us gently; it's this, then the next day it's that, until finally we knew what it was." It was up and down for Gwen but she did what the doctor told her to do. Gwen later commented, "That's what the doctors noticed in me, that I have a fighting spirit, a good spirit, and I'm positive about things because I told them I've got a lot of life in me yet." And fight she did, not only on the temporal level with her illness but, most especially, Gwen fought on the spiritual level to do the will of God, so that she would draw as close as possible to Him. She would often say, "God is good, He thinks of everything. I know He will be right there for me."

Her children were greatly saddened, to say the least, at this horrendous news. For Thanksgiving, they all went to Ohio with their children to be with their mother and grandmother. Gwen was so very happy! She thanked God for His goodness in being with her family at Thanksgiving. Because of the husbands' jobs and other responsibilities of the families, Gwen's adult children could only stay for a short time before needing to head back the 650 miles to Kenosha, WI. However, Gwen's daughters made frequent trips out to Ohio to be with their mother during this difficult time.

November 2001, Coniker family gathered in Ohio
for Thanksgiving upon hearing the bad news
of Gwen's prognosis.

THIRD AND FINAL TRIAL

For Christmas that year, Gwen and Jerry were able to go to Kenosha and be with the family there. This again, was a tremendous blessing for Gwen who just loved being with them. It would be her last time in Kenosha.

Jerry's sons set up a web cam through the internet so that Gwen could 'see' her family in Kenosha and converse with them since she was in Ohio. This technology elated her because if she could not always be present with them, this was the next best thing!

"It's so important to have faith," Gwen would say. "I don't know how people cope without faith in God. I'm with the Divine Physician now, so we all know that things will work out fine."

Gwen and Jerry went on vacation to North Carolina in April of 2002. Right after the vacation, Gwen went to the Pittsburgh hospital and, then later, to the Cleveland Clinic. Gwen and Jerry were still hoping for a liver transplant, however, while at the Clinic, doctors discovered cancer as well. Things just kept getting worse. This meant that Gwen could no longer receive a liver transplant. Cancer, in addition to the cirrhosis of the liver, was wreaking havoc on her health. Again, she was disappointed but never wavered in accepting God's will for her, despite the difficulty in accepting continual bad news. She left the Cleveland Clinic on May 13, 2002, the Feast of Our Lady of Fatima. Her health declined fast after that, and she spent her last days in pain but peaceful acceptance.

Jerry took Gwen home to spend her final days there in hospice care. She quickly became bed-bound. "So here I am now, right where I wanted to be," remarked Gwen, "out of the hospital and back here at home, at the Fatima House at Catholic Familyland, so God granted me that," she continued. "It's so quiet here, and I have talks with Our Lord all the time and Mother Mary. I just give it all to them. Don't forget me, I ask them! The days get slow and the nights are terrible but I still have more life in me. I have this confidence that God will be right there through everything."

Jerry moved his office to the Fatima house where Gwen was so that he could be there with her and still run the Apostolate. Her daughter, Theresa, would take care of Gwen every day and helped to make the bed, take care of the home, and was very attentive to her mother, taking care of her every need and giving her the medication she needed. One day, Gwen was walking to the restroom with Jerry and walked on his feet since she needed help walking. Suddenly she quipped, "Shall we dance?" It was so apropos since they loved to dance! Gwen never lost her sense of humor!

Gwen's comments to her daughter Theresa: "Your Dad takes such good care of me. He has always been my protector and provider. You see how he brings me fresh water each night, lays out my pills, sleeps on the couch near my bed, and he's doing so much to protect my soul. He brings the Eucharist to me each night and prays with me. He is truly my Knight in Shining Armor." **Dad:** "We pray every night that God will allow Mom, like St. Therese of the Little Flower, to spend her heaven on earth helping her family and the Apostolate." **Gwen:** "So I got a big job ahead of me!"

"She approached death peacefully," remarked MaryAnn Presberg, her sister-in-law. "Her family couldn't get enough of her. People kept coming in droves to see her. She kept outpouring love. For a little sip of water, she was so grateful. 'Thank you, thank you, thank you,' she would say. She certainly had a Marian soul." Laurie, her daughter, commented, "She'd be in bed and she still cared about every little detail. She cared how the light was, or this was, etc. She was so gracious and loving." Laurie continued, "Their uniqueness of the marriage commitment and their love for each other were amazing! Their two hearts were surely united." When Gwen was asked about the love for her husband, children, and grandchildren, she responded with "I love you all but I love your Dad the most."

The last days of Gwen's life were a tremendous blessing for her, her family, and for the Apostolate for Family Consecration. God allowed her, and those around her, to prepare for the temporary earthly separation that was soon upon them. With each passing day, Gwen assured those with her that everything would be all right. "God is in control. He will take care of everything," she would say. The time of her suffering was also a time of joy in what our Faith teaches—eternal life.

THIRD AND FINAL TRIAL

Gwen Sharing Some Thoughts on the Apostolate for Family Consecration with the Catholic Corps

"It's been a long time doing this—seems like 20, almost 27 years, in June. At that time (1975), I had a lot of kids at the table, and in the house. I was able to be a stay-at-home mom, so I was busy. Our older children helped with the cooking, cleaning, retreats, TV programs, and other stuff wherever they could. They remember all those years, but they didn't get the same benefit as the last half of the family, because nothing was in place. It was just all being developed so they didn't have it, but they did appreciate their faith. Now with the notes they give me, the way they live, and what they say to me, I feel like they did anyway (get the formation and benefits from the Family Apostolate), you know. It is so important to have our faith. Anyone who doesn't have faith—I don't know how they cope."

Gwen: "I am confident that this Apostolate will flourish. Mr. C says he's going shortly after me, but that is one thing he has no control over. He can say it all he wants. I said, 'No, God has more work for you. You have to stay here.'"

Jerry: "Providing He'll let you support me like St. Therese of the Little Flower."

Gwen: "I'll be tapping you on your shoulder."

Catholic Corp. Men: "So you just want to do the best you can, starting with each other, because you can't do the work if you are not together as a whole person. We're all working together for the same God, and doing all His work and service as He called us to do."

Catholic Corp. Men: "How can we improve the community and work of the Apostolate?" Gwen encouraged them.

Gwen: "Talk about family and the support you get from family, be it blood family or the Apostolate family. Always act and react in love because love is first. If someone gets hurt, you need to fix it and get it back into the love basket. We have to overcome our stubbornness to reconcile with each other. Pray about it so God gives you the strength to communicate. Then love and reconciliation spreads. Faith, Hope, and Charity, the most important of these is Charity. There's good and evil everywhere. Some families don't have a family support, a love support. There was a man next to me having a colonoscopy who had five children and nobody came to see him. We visited with him at different times. Some of my kids visited with him, too. That sadness and brokenness that begins early in life is there at the end also. He had no wife, and his kids didn't come. There are problems but there are problems everywhere. We can't do the work if you don't work through them."

GWEN WHEN ASKED TO SHARE SOME INSIGHTS ON PARENTING AND MOTHERHOOD

"I'm a plain ol' mom, very ordinary, just doing my duty. As far as experience, and yes, experience is the best, and even with twelve I learned a lot, because they're all different. Each one brings you a certain joy. Like Joe, he likes to call me MAMA. It's like Italian you know, and he calls up, MAMA, and then I'll say Joe Joe. If you have ever been around Italian families, that is how they talk, Joe Joe. Each one brings a certain—brings their own individualism to you, you know. Even though they have the same mom and dad, they all are different. Yes, and each one was special. I remember going all the way down to Mary's (twelfth child) birth, I never got tired of the fact that, you know, we were going to bring another baby home. It's a process they (parents) can't speed up. They've got to learn as they go, and hopefully they're openly willing to be patient enough to learn. Unfortunately, the teens out there aren't just ready to step into all this serious talk. They either have something of interest, something fun, or they are not interested. That's a different generation, I guess. True Devotion to Mary, the only peace that came was from God through Our Blessed Mother."

Gwen was asked what she learned raising twelve children.

Gwen: "One has to have at least five to realize how raising children works! You run your kids to the doctor at the slightest cold thinking they are going to die. They have to be patient to want to learn. You can't stop teaching them. Experience is the best. I could learn a lot more since they are all different and each brings a special joy and individual personality and gifts, even though they have the same parents. Each one has special gifts. I never got tired of bringing a baby home."

Gwen sharing about the joys and support that come from the family: "Family, and the support you get from family is a joy. Jerry was my support 100 percent. I needed a lot of support (in the beginning years) when my kids were really little. It's been a very, very healthy, good life for me—I don't regret anything."

GWEN SPEAKING TO HER GRANDCHILDREN AND CATECHIZING THEM

This is a dream come true for me, in that it's all going be about love and sacrifice and this family experience because all of you, all of the grandchildren, all of my children, and their spouses, drove thousands of miles to come and see me this weekend, because they heard that I was so sick. And before that, you had been saying a lot of prayers with your moms and dads for my life. And it meant an awful lot to me. As I was sitting on the couch the other day, I was just visualizing this very thing that we see here. It's a dream I never thought could happen. I didn't ask for it; everybody just came. So you all touched my heart and it was some of the medicine that made me feel better because today I feel better than I did this whole week and it's because I see you all gathered here. So I want you to have fun, I want you to have a good time. We all have friends, right? Everybody has friends, and I'm going to ask you now, "who is your greatest friend?" One grandchild answers, "Jesus?" Right, and that's who I am relying on right now is Jesus's help and all your prayers that you send to Jesus and Mary for me. So, any time anything goes wrong in your life, and even when nothing is wrong, you should always be able to have Jesus as your friend, right? In the meantime, you can start to think about something that you want to ask me. What does it mean to love someone? What do you do? Patrick, a little boy younger than six answers, "You serve God?" You serve God, righhhhhttt! Wow, yes! And also each other.

When you love your brother you do good things for him, and your mommy and daddy too, right? So you show your love by the good things you do but the number one thing is to teach you about Jesus. Jesus sacrificed for you and has done many things for you so that someday we could be together and have eternal happiness and that's in heaven. And so when a doctor gives you some kind of news like you have a disease and you have an unknown time left that could be weeks, months, a year, whatever timeframe it is. There's no medication to help you, who do I rely on? It all comes back to my friend. I have to rely on Jesus.

Cherished Quotes from Gwen to Some of her Children

"Life is a gift. Try to not take things for granted, and cherish the times you have."

"See how hard my stomach and sides are? I am fortunate to not be in more pain. There are people that are suffering much more than me. What I can do is offer up the suffering I do have for others."

"There have been some very sad times in my life. Times that I lay awake at night and wrote letters, but there have been so many happy times. God has blessed me with a wonderful life with so many wonderful people."

"I just want everyone to know that they are very special. The one that meant the most to me is your Dad and my husband. It has been a real step of faith."

"I am just an ordinary mother doing my duty."

"You see how Dad looks at me; it is so hard to see the sorrow in his eyes."

"I wish I could do more…my heart and mind is often with the Catholic Corps, please tell them I am with them in thought and prayer."

"I am so happy Sheri could make it. Do you see how good God is? He

knew my desire for Sheri to be here, and He allowed me to see her and the new baby. He is so good; I have so much to be thankful for. I didn't think I would make it. I don't want you ever to get upset with God for taking me. He has been so good."

"You have such beautiful children. I really wanted to see them grow up."

"Whenever the nurses leave, you look sad, what do they say to you? Are you doing okay?"

"Please do all you can to remain united. Unity is the key. You are all so different, but each one of you so beautiful."

"Don't be sad. I want you all to do good and be good, so that we can all be together again."

"You have always been there for me in trying times. You have made motherhood a delight."

"I will not leave you the gift of money; you can take care of that. I'll leave you faith and love, two gifts that you cannot buy."

"The ladder to reach that success is Trust in Jesus through Mary."

"Here are a few ABCs of Life's Journey:

Appreciate who you are,

Dodge negativity,

Envision your destination,

Expect the best."

GWEN'S FINAL PROJECT

Gwen lived and ended her life on earth focusing on others, giving to the very end. She started a little project with her son, Michael, who resided in Pittsburgh at the time, on May 26th 2002, to write messages to people and share some of her thoughts at this time in her life. The title that Gwen chose to summarize her life is "**Love is Patient, Love is Kind, Love Never Ends.**" Gwen then worked to establish an objective, rough outline, and a list of people to address.

She completed composing some messages and her opening statement. Gwen also outlined some things she wanted to say and listed whom she wanted to address. God called her home before she was able to finish her little project, but we know her spirit is alive and well and will be touching our lives in her own special way.

FROM A MOTHER'S HEART
by Gwen Coniker, May 2002

May I gratefully acknowledge all those many, many families who have remembered me in their prayers since hearing of my terminal illness last November. I thank you so much for the warm, well wishes, Holy Masses, Holy Hours, and Rosaries that have showered me with comfort and joy.

I am adjusting to my new schedule and healthy diet and feeling the up and down days through the courage and strength that God sends my way. And so I am very thankful to the awesome God who takes care of us all and His love never fails. May His blessings be upon you and your family as we work together in building the Civilization of Love and Life (that Pope John Paul II gave his life for).

As we are approaching the special day set aside for our mothers, I recall a song called "M_O_T_H_E_R_!" We were taught this in elementary school by the good Sisters back in the fifties. I remember singing this tune to my dear mother and this is how it goes.

M is for the Million things she gave me… O is that she is Only growing old… T is for the Tears she shed to save me… H is for her Heart of purest gold… E is for her Eyes ever shining… R is for Right and Right she always be…

THIRD AND FINAL TRIAL

Put them all together, they spell MOTHER, a word that means the world to me.

And as the years went by, these words kept ringing in my ears and all mothers can testify from their experiences, the love and sacrifices that have been made for their families. It is in reaching out to other families that will build a Civilization of Love.

This is my message to all of those that have walked through the journey of life with us. I come from a home life of Irish and Italian descent, my mother, being all Italian and my father being all Irish. My mother and father gave me a good start in life and sacrificed to work extra to provide a Catholic education. I was always surrounded by good people and thank my parents for such a wonderful gift of a good upbringing.

"Mom wasn't sure exactly what she was going to produce," explained Michael, "and when she wanted her messages delivered. With these and other unknowns, Mom didn't know what to tell people if they asked what we were doing. I didn't either so I just requested one-on-one private time. That worked for a couple of weeks. Then my siblings started getting a little restless and curious about all the one-on-one time I was getting and started pushing for some answers. Mom was getting a lot weaker and was starting to have very few periods of being awake. We had made some good progress, documenting her ideas and completing the drafts of three messages, so I sat down with several of my family members and explained to them what we were doing."

Michael continued, "I really feel that Mom's life has been a bed of roses. A beautiful bed of roses offered up to God. Within the beauty, there were thorns, wounds, struggles, confusions, pains, sorrows, joys, and glories."

Gwen was always offering up her sufferings to the Lord. Within the last month of her life, she offered her suffering for Sheri's new baby about to be born, her granddaughter. Sheri, in turn, offered her labor pains for her mother. "You're going to be happy with your little girl, your little baby daughter," she said to Sheri confidently. Sheri responded to her mother, "You'll be okay, Mom. I'm going to come there as soon as I can so I can see you." Gwen then gave her daughter some advice, "Just relax for your birth; don't press on the gas. I want you to have a simple, good birth, and I can find out tomorrow how it went." Sheri indeed gave birth to a beautiful blonde-haired baby girl!

On June 8, Michael's wife, Marie, printed three of Gwen's messages on nice stationary. Michael read them to her, who was very weak in bed and could barely talk or move. However, she gathered the strength to sign them and said she wanted to write a message to her children. Michael then asked her, "Mom, do you want the messages to be delivered while you are still living?" She said, "I think not." She was very weak but very determined to compose the message to her children. Two thirds through dictating the message, Gwen paused and Michael cried. Michael told her it was a very beautiful message and that it would be cherished. Michael said, "I told her it was hard for me to speak and asked if I could have Marie help read the message back to her."

She whispered, "No, let's finish it."

Michael continued, "Upon uttering the final words of her message, Mom went to sleep and didn't tell me how to have it signed."

On June 10th, Michael, who was in Pittsburgh, was contacted by his brothers, Robert and Joseph, to tell him that their mother was very weak and had been sleeping virtually all the time for the last couple of days. Michael recounts that conversation: "Robert asked me to give my final farewell, because it seemed like Mom was to slip into a coma or die very soon. I arrived at about 5:15 p.m. Mom was sleeping the whole day and had an IV because she didn't have the strength to eat or drink and did not have the strength to talk to anyone for the past couple of days. I requested private time again, and was graciously granted it by several of my siblings present at the house."

"In sitting at my mother's bedside, I was very confused on how to handle her project at this time. Did she have anything else to say in her message to her children? Did she want to sign it? Did she want to write her message to Dad? As my mother lay asleep, I read her messages out loud a couple times then started talking to her about my questions and confusion. I let her know what was on my mind and in my heart and began to cry. 'I could write a small message to the remaining people we listed and find a nice way to deliver your thoughts,' I remarked to her. She was unable to respond then. I continued, 'But I can't write Dad's message for you. I don't know what to say to him. Only you know what to say. You asked us to take care of him. What do you want us to do? I can have dinner with him every week or so and get together with him as he would like. Is that what you would like? Is there anything else you want in your letter to your kids? Do you want to sign it?'"

Gwen then gathered her motherly strength to help her crying little boy and opened her eyes and nodded 'yes.' She was awake! Michael then asked her, "Would you like some water?" Another yes nod. She drank some water. Michael then said, "How about some of this shake, Mom? It will help give you some energy." She gave him a slight smile. Michael then exclaimed, "I think she was thinking, 'you silly boy!' After she sipped some shake, I held up the paper for her to sign. She was struggling just to move her arm. I asked her if she really wanted to sign it. She said, 'Yes.'"

At that time, there was some stirring at the door. Gwen whispered, "Tell them this is very important." The family members were very eager to share some special moments with their mother but sacrificed to support Michael's efforts.

"With a couple practice tries, Mom signed the letter to her children," Michael recounted. "I then asked her if she wanted to write a message to Dad. She said, 'I gave him my message in person.'" Gwen then composed short messages to Fr. Bernard Geiger and Fr. Kevin, at Michael's prompting, and signed them.

As mentioned previously, it was Fr. Bernard Geiger who had invited Jerry Coniker to return to the United States from Portugal to work as his Executive Director for St. Maximilian Kolbe's "Knights of the Immaculata" in Kenosha, Wisconsin. At that time, Fr. Bernard was the superior of the Franciscan Marytown community and editor and director of the "Knights of the Immaculata." Jerry worked with Fr. Bernard from 1973-1975, until the founding of the Apostolate for Family Consecration. In 1998, through the permission of his superiors, Fr. Bernard has been on the staff ever since for the Family Apostolate, and gave

Gwen the last rites.

Here are the final messages to her children, the Catholic Corps, and others:

LETTER TO GWEN'S CHILDREN

My Dear children,

I have been thinking about writing you for the last couple of days. It was a bit difficult to write this letter because I was feeling very sick, unlike my days on earth with you. However, they are coming to an end. Not that I didn't want to write, but I couldn't think and hold my thoughts as good as I wanted to. But here they are now:

I hope my words come through better now than before. It is easy to say, "I love you," over and over. It is not enough, but you have been the most wonderful, helpful, loving family I could ever want. There is so much. It was Jesus that brought us and kept us together. I have a strong husband. I can't forget he has been everything to me. I love him very much.

My prayerful wish is that each one of my children will raise their family close to God and find God's will for their life. All my children and grandchildren, I love you.

Mom

LETTER TO THE CATHOLIC CORPS

To My beloved Catholic Corps, I find it a great joy to have shared so many experiences with you in sharing a life together serving the Church through the work of the Apostolate for Family Consecration.

You perform a vital role in serving the mission of the Family Apostolate, encouraging and preserving family life. Your sacrifice and desire to know, love and serve God within your vocation is a beautiful witness of your Faith.

THIRD AND FINAL TRIAL

Your heroic efforts are sure to bring many souls to heaven and share in everlasting happiness.

I really appreciate all your love, prayers, and warm wishes over the years. Thank you for everything you have done and continue to do.

May God bless you and your loved ones,

I love you,
Mama C.

LETTER TO GWEN'S SISTER, GEORGIA

To My Dear Sister Georgia,

Through the years we have had lots of fun and with the help of our mom and dad, two special people, we have learned a lot. They gave us a great family life and instilled in us family love. Thank you for being at my side as a loving sister, in joyful and difficult times. We were a large group, between your children and our children. Our children always enjoyed visiting with you, Uncle Don and your children. We had great times together. I just want to thank you so much for always being there for me.

Love your "Sis" Gwen

FINAL DAYS

It was June 10, 2002, when Gwen asked to see all her children. Within thirty minutes of her request, all twelve of her living children were at her bedside, along with her sister. They happened to all be in town then at the same time to be near her. She was very weak and could barely speak a few words. She looked intently and gazed at each and every one of her children going from one to the next with a look of love in her eyes. She even held Kara, her new granddaughter (Sheri's daughter) in her arms as best she could.

Mom then requested to have the messages she composed read to all present. That was a special time where tears were shed and Gwen's love for her family shined. Then at 8:00 p.m. on June 10, she asked all of her children to come close and composed her message for Dad, entrusting him to our physical care, saying: "I just want everyone to know that they are very special. The one that meant the most to me is your dad and my husband." Gwen paused to gather strength then said, "It has been a real step of faith. However, I have no regrets…none."

On June 11th, Gwen had a surge of energy and sat up for the first time in days! She talked with those around and requested pizza and Coke. It seemed like she was going to bounce back and regained some strength. She was thoroughly enjoying her meal! After she drank half of her Coke, her daughter tried to put the rest in a smaller glass. Gwen refused to let the glass go, probably fearing that Jerry might put her back on her health food diet! Theresa called Michael at his house and told him that he should come and talk with Mom because she had a burst of energy. The family said to their mother that it looked like she was cured and she immediately said that she would give it up for the lives of Kay Kocisko, a life member of the Family Apostolate, and Roseanna Tamayo, a Catholic Corp life member, who were both terminally ill.

Gwen said, "There are times of hardship, people out of work and various struggles." She recalled that her mom and dad's commitment was always there as a model and example for her. She said, "I remember a home life of many good things but had some hardships as well. I had a strong attraction to the Sacrament of Marriage because I loved children. I was blessed with thirteen children and raised twelve. I was married on the feast day of Our Lady of the Assumption. I consecrated my life to Jesus through Our Blessed Mother and made a lifelong commitment to my husband, Jerry. I, Gwen, take you, Jerome, to be my husband. I promise to be true to you, in good times and in bad, in sickness and in health. I will love you and honor you all the days of my life…What a deal!"

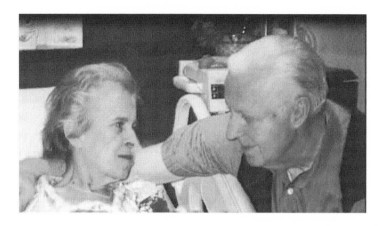

Jerry and Gwen shortly before her death on June 16, 2002

Gwen and some of her daughters and newborn
granddaughter by her bedside!

Chapter 19

Our Loss, Heaven's Gain

ON JUNE 14, 2002, Michael was contacted by his sibling to come quickly to Mom as she was not doing well. "I couldn't get there until early evening," recalled Michael, "and Mom was sleeping then. She was very weak and tired her remaining days." Gwen was talking to people down to the end. One could say that she had a "living" wake.

In the early hours of June 15, 2002, Fr. Bernard Geiger, OFM Conv. was called by Jerry to Gwen's bedside. Jerry had been sleeping next to Gwen in the living room on a futon folding sofa bed next to her ever since she became bed ridden. Sheri, their fifth daughter and fifth born, was staying with them upstairs. She, too, was called to come down immediately as well as Gwen's sister, Georgia. Jerry said to come quickly as he felt that the time was near; so the four of them surrounded Gwen's bed.

Gwen was sixty-two years old. Fr. Geiger has been the Conikers' spiritual director since 1973. He anointed her with the Anointing of the Sick. Sheri leaned over to her mother and put her ear next to Gwen's mouth. At that very moment, Sheri heard Gwen take her final breath. At that very moment, at 5:30 a.m., Gwen Coniker breathed her final earthly breath. "I'll never forget that moment," said Sheri. "I was so close as to hear my mother's final breath on earth. It was so surreal and moving, yet very sad at the same time." It was a bittersweet moment indeed.

OUR LOSS, HEAVEN'S GAIN

Sad at the loss of such a great soul, but happy that her eternal reward will be great in heaven and she is at peace; our loss and Heaven's gain. Gwen's life passed to Our Lord the day before Father's Day.

In terms of Gwen's final project that was in progress with her son, Michael, this is what he had to say about it:

> *I know Mom wanted to write many more messages to so many other people and even more individualized ones. Mom very much wanted to write a message to the Presberg and Kocisko families and all those who have come to be a part of and have helped the Apostolate for Family Consecration. I am very sorry that we ran out of time. She kept giving and thanking through her very final words. On a table next to her deathbed were two unfinished cards: One for a daughter-in law's birthday (probably Aleli) and the other for Jennifer Hall's graduation. Donna, Jennifer, Ricky and Brian Hall: Please know that God loves you and so do I.*
>
> *Mom had several notes that she made and intended to expand upon. She wanted to recall some of the times in her life. She wanted to talk about the joyful, sorrowful, and glorious times. She wanted to recall times growing up with two sisters, the significance of Baptism and growing in her faith.*

Gwen was laid in state for a week in the St. John Vianney Chapel of Catholic Familyland in Bloomingdale, Ohio. Many came to pay their respects. Flowers adorned the casket and chapel. The funeral was held in the same chapel on June, 22, and then Gwen was laid to rest that same day in a crypt in the St. John Vianney Chapel. There is a kneeler in front of the casket and vault that houses her remains, where people can come to pray.

The Funeral Mass was long yet beautiful. Jerry went all out. He, along with his sons, put together a beautiful musical video of family pictures with Gwen throughout of the years. Jerry could be found consoling everyone else.

Present at the Funeral Mass were many clergy, roughly five bishops, including newly ordained Most Rev. Roger Joseph Foys, Bishop of Covington, Kentucky. Bishop Foys was previously the Vicar General for the Diocese of Steubenville and instrumental in the purchasing of the closed diocesan seminary by the Apostolate for Family Consecration. Others present were Camaldolese Monks, neighbors of the Apostolate, family members, Catholic Corps Communities, Apostolate members, and personal and Apostolate friends.

The celebrant was the Most Reverend Gilbert I. Sheldon, Bishop of the Diocese of Steubenville, where the Apostolate for Family Consecration center is located. Rev. Fr. Bernard Geiger, longtime spiritual director of Gwen and Jerry, was the homilist. Rev. Mr. Randy Redington, the AFC staff Deacon was MC and deacon for the wake and funeral. Gwen's son, Joseph, gave the main eulogy.

Gwen is survived by her beloved husband, Jerry, twelve children and 66 grandchildren, the oldest grandchild who was sixteen years old at the time.

FUNERAL HOMILY
given by Fr. Bernard Geiger, OFM Conv.

Your Excellency Bishop Sheldon and Bishop Foys, Reverend Monsignors, Fathers, Deacon Randy, venerable brothers, sisters, members of the Catholic Corps and beloved family and friends of Gwen Coniker.

"The souls of the just are in the hand of God and no torment shall touch them." These are the opening words of today's funeral Mass that we just heard. How actually they express the faith that sustains all of you Conikers on this bittersweet day. You yourselves chose this reading from the book of Wisdom for this Mass. For you rightly perceive Gwen as the just and valiant woman who was your spouse, your mother, your sister, and your grandmother.

We can see exactly how just and valiant Gwen was in the words she herself wrote some ten years ago for Challenge and Change, Fr. Peter Lappin's book on the early history of the Apostolate for Family Consecration back in 1975. Gwen's life was in grave danger. Her doctor had warned her not to have any more children for he was convinced she would not survive another birth. But here was Gwen, pregnant again, this time with Theresa Marie. For Challenge and Change, Gwen wrote these words, 'The doctor insisted that he was very concerned for my life. He felt that I was being foolish not to consider the children that I already had and that it was dangerous to think of another pregnancy. So when the eleventh pregnancy came, I went to see the doctor. He almost did not take me in as a patient. He was just too afraid. Let's not worry, I said. Let's take it a day at a time, and I'm sure everything will work out. I just knew that no one knew better than God Himself. He allowed this pregnancy, and I had to remain firm in my beliefs. So this birth was frightening since the doctor had made it so. But I couldn't consider an abortion.'

It was at the time of this pregnancy in 1975 that Gwen had written her famous Christmas letter to her family. She went on to explain why she did so with the words, "I write this little message to the family thinking that if I was not with them at Christmas time, they would have a little thought of mine they could share with one another, and in case I did, they wouldn't hold it against the baby."

As I pondered what to say today, I turned to Gwen and the Holy Spirit and said, "Gwen, this is your Mass, you always wanted me to keep my homilies short, so now you have to tell me what you want me to say." What came to me was a concise Christian vision of life. I think Gwen wants to leave you as her special heritage, her last words to you, the family; that Michael recorded for you before she died. Gwen said, "Everyone is special. The one who is most special is your dad, my husband. It's been a real step of faith."

These words are the key to Gwen's vision of life. A vision she wants each of you to have too. Gwen saw the precious goodness of God in each of you, her family. This vision was God's gift to her through the Holy Spirit's gifts of knowledge, understanding, and piety. These gifts and all the gifts are given to all of us in the Sacrament of Baptism. They are in us as channels, as capacities for receiving and using divine Light and the light they bring us does not come to us automatically, however, at least in the amount we need to receive all that we need. We must ask for it in prayer. Gwen obviously did ask for it in prayers, and God gave it to her in abundance. And so she came to see how precious each one of you is in God's eyes. But, it's not enough to receive that Light, we must respond to it in faith. And that is why Gwen said, "It's been a real step of faith."

She believed in you. She believed in your goodness, and she wants you to believe in your goodness, too, your own and each other. When you believe in someone's goodness, you treat that person with respect, with reverence. And as we come to understand one another in God's plan for us better, the more we become willing to commit ourselves to fulfilling God's plans for us, both for ourselves and for each other. That commitment is the core of Christian hope. For Christian hope is reaching out to God and to what he is calling us to. Trusting that He will enable us to fulfill His plans for us.

This, to me, explains that exquisite respect and trusting regard Gwen had for each of us, which always made us feel important and treasured. We knew that she wanted what was best for us and was always ready to help us in every way she could. The Catholic Corps men and women tell me they could always call on Gwen for help. She would tell them 'come on over, we'll talk.' She was and is the real mother of everyone here at Catholic Familyland.

Gwen also had that vision of piety that sees everyone, especially her family and children, as someone bonded to her in close relationship. If you weren't in her immediate family, you felt that you were a spiritual brother or sister or son or daughter in her extended family. You felt accepted, treasured, and loved.

OUR LOSS, HEAVEN'S GAIN

Brothers and sisters in Jesus, Mary and Joseph, this is, I believe, what Gwen wants to leave to you as her special heritage, that you ask the Holy Spirit daily, and even several times a day, for the Light of his gifts, so that you can have God's vision of Him and of yourselves and of one another, and to ask for the power of the infused virtues, so that you can believe strongly in God's goodness, so that you can believe that His goodness is in you, and that it is in each of us. She wants you to have the humble, down-to-earth self-respect that she had and the exquisite respect for each other that she has had for each of you. A respect and reverence that translated into an unfailing daily personal commitment, a warm, generous love and self-giving and practical service that marked her whole life.

Gwen, we will never forget you, we'll always love you. We ask you never to forget us, to help us with our prayers, to do all that God is calling us to do. In these past days, weeks, months, a deep mystery has been unfolding. I wish I had the knowledge, the understanding, and the time to do it justice.

And Gwen, I hope this homily isn't too long, I tried to make it shorter, I really did.

EULOGY AT GWEN'S FUNERAL BY JOSEPH CONIKER

My name is Joseph Coniker. I'm the eighth child of my mother, Gwen, and the third son. And a little statement about my mom: She's always been very joyful, very welcoming, and very compassionate in so many ways. She's also been very spontaneous…those who have known her. So in that spirit, yesterday, when I was here for the rehearsal, I put an object underneath one of the seats here in the audience. So if you could reach down and check underneath your seat and check for a blue marker and raise your hand, the individual who has that blue marker underneath their seat. It's taped underneath the seat. I'll give a hint, it's toward my right, that front of the aisle, the woman in the pink. We're not going to be introducing everybody here, obviously, but I would like for you to introduce yourself and where you're from and how you knew my mother. Could you stand up and just introduce yourself?

"My name is Catherine Zbeigen and I'm from Euclid, Ohio. I knew your mom as the holy woman she was."

Great, thank you, Catherine. Thanks for being here.

There's a lot of thanks and a lot of joy and a lot of praise that I have for the opportunity to say hello and good-bye to my mother. It's an opportunity not all get, and I realize that. But I did. My mother died in the state of grace. She died receiving the sacraments at the most opportune time, from talking to Fr. Bernard Geiger.

My mom, I remember…we talked about example, about her last night. I remember growing up with my mom, and she always said she never liked public speaking. She never liked getting in front of a podium and talking to others. And I remember her telling me that in conversation as a child. Then I would see, growing up, she would always be talking; she would always be in front of people. And although it was uncomfortable, she was very personal, very real. She was able to inspire, to identify, to communicate, one-on-one and also through a podium. And I remember, in high school, I used to be scared to death of speaking in front of class, drama, large groups. But since then, in the last ten years of my professional life, because of the inspiration from my mother and her example, I've attended various Dale Carnegie/Franklin Covey programs, spoken at several international business conferences. And even with this, it's hard for me to speak to you today about the few things I have to share about my mother. So out of respect for my mom, if I cannot make it through the points that I want to share with you, I will gracefully leave and I hope you understand.

OUR LOSS, HEAVEN'S GAIN

My mom died on June 15, 2002. Ten years prior to that, I remember walking the streets of Rome with my mother. We had a cappuccino on the side streets. She was with me; she counseled me; she talked to me; she advised me the day before I got married in St. Peter's Basilica, Vatican City, Rome. My mom died one day prior to our tenth anniversary of my wife, Aleli, and I. It's a very bittersweet moment for me. Standing here today is bittersweet for many reasons as well. I remember all of the love and all of the agony and also the joy when my sister, Mary, had her wedding here. And all of the effort that my mom and dad and friends and relatives put up for a beautiful wedding. And it's so ironic for me to be here now sharing a few moments with you, a few words with you, with my mother in front of me. Out of respect for my mother, I hope I can get through this. It'll be less than five minutes.

Yesterday we talked about my mom's ability and her centrifugal force of love—to be able to share her love with each individual, but also create a centrifugal force of love where people could feel it and others would draw from love. Today I want to talk about faith and love. Mom's "circle of influence" and faithfulness and success. Yes, faithfulness AND success, because in my opinion they are dependent on each other, they are not mutually exclusive. Success by my mother was faith and family, not the riches and the comforts of the world. Because of my mom's profound faithfulness to God, to her spouse, to her children, God enables her to success in many areas. God enabled her to expand her circle of influence because she was so, in my opinion, perfect, as a mother. She was able to be a mother more than just to our family, but to those of you and to those who are watching television and to those who are not here. She had the ability to touch your soul. She had an ability to touch other families' souls, to touch the heart. Her circle of influence was expanded. So many of you developed such a deep relationship with my mom. My mother exemplified the ability of how to live out a commitment. And because of that, I'm so proud. Mom's circle of influence: faith and love.

One of my last words with my mother… She had a conversation with me. And she told me, "I will not leave you the gifts of money, Joe. You can take care of that yourself. I'll leave you faith and love, two gifts that you cannot buy."

My mother lived a life of example. Like I said last night, she never had to lecture or demand action. By her example and behavior she was able to inspire me, inspire others. She represented the pro-life movement by her ultimate example, by her conscious decisions to accept life even if it meant sacrificing her own. By her example, she represents everything the pro-life stands for, because the pro-life movement is more that Roe vs. Wade and the laws that passed in Congress. I have met my senator in Pennsylvania, Senator Santorum. I have a friend in Congress. They do not have the power to affect the abortion issue. The power lies in the hearts of the mothers, of my mother. And at that time and the decision in her life, to be confronted with a life and death decision, she chose life. That's the heart of pro-life. Mothers have that power.

I have a rose of life in my car. When I look at that rose, it reminds me of my mother in so many ways. She is always with me. I will never forget and will always remember the legacy she created that being pro-life is about making a decision for life. I am so proud of my mother. I have four children and a fifth on the way. I cannot imagine a time during birth if Aleli and I had to go through this type of decision process, if it's the baby or the mother, the baby or Aleli.

My mother made it clear and so did my father that their ultimate goal as parents was to help us, as family members, you as Apostolate members, get to Heaven. Mom asked that we continue to pray for her. She asked me, "Joe, continue to pray for me when I die. Do not assume that I'm in heaven." Mom, you know I always listen to you, most of the time. I pray for you and I did pray for you. I feel that you are in Heaven today. I will pray for you. I will pray to you.

OUR LOSS, HEAVEN'S GAIN

My mom created an atmosphere where the family helps each other, the family helps each other get to Heaven. Mom provided us that foundation. Our family has committed to praying for my mother, so that when she is raised to the gates of Heaven, that she will help, in turn, all of us, in our lives, in our families, to help her children get to Heaven, to help you, your children—you knew Gwen, you knew my mom—to help you get to Heaven.

I'll leave you with a last point. It's a question and an answer that I asked my mother, a person who died with such grace and dignity, just the way she lived her life. I asked my mom, "A hundred years from now, Mom, how do you want people to remember you?" My mom said, "I'm not sure what you're looking for, but what sticks out is that motherhood WAS my career, which evolved into grand-motherhood." Mom, it is finished. You taught us how to fly, and then you flew away. We'll love you forever.

This beautiful song was written and composed by the Catholic Corps Women's Community in honor of their beloved "Mama C." It is so apropos as to how Gwen felt and lived:

WHEN I SAID I DO

When I said I do, I had no clue, what I'd be doing,
The mystery, how it would be, or what the future would bring.
Now looking back through all the years,
Smiling still after so many tears,
I know the prize was worth the price,
The joy is greater than the sacrifice.
God's love would give, time and again,
new life for us to welcome in,
The babies laughed, the children played,
they grew up strong and good just like I'd prayed.
Now my life has proved, my words were true,

my commitment kept no matter what we went through, Some have re-
grets for their own choice,
but as for me, I only rejoice!

Now looking back through all the years,
Smiling still after so many tears,
I know the prize was worth the price,
The joy is greater than the sacrifice.

What I have now is a family,
something that will last for eternity.

O what has become of me?
In giving all I am set free.

I said "I do" to you. If I could do it again,
it's the only thing I'd do.

HEARTS TOUCHED

The life of Gwen Coniker seems to have had such a positive impact on so many: Her children, spiritual children, those she met throughout the years, and those who have come to know her through the work of The Apostolate for Family Consecration. Letters started pouring in from those who knew her, and were nurtured by Gwen's love, and who were inspired by her virtuous life, including many from the Roman Curia giving their reflections and condolences.

The following are but a sampling of reflections and condolences by family members and the Roman Curia. For more, please see Appendix B:

Our family is a circle of strength and love. With every birth and every union, the circle grows. Every joy shared adds more love. Every crisis shared together makes the circle stronger.

—Joe Coniker, eight child and third son

OUR LOSS, HEAVEN'S GAIN

We will forever cherish the precious moments we've had with you, Mother. Your spirit will live on within us. Our lives will be forever blessed because they were touched by you, our precious rose. You are the miracle of our lives and we thank God for giving you to us. Thank you for teaching us the meaning of love. Go in peace our sweet mother. Rest in Our Lady's gentle arms and watch over us from above. Mom, your children are raised. Your job is finished. You taught us how to fly and then you flew away. We'll love you forever.

—Robert Coniker, seventh child and second son

Mother, with this card I send my deepest love and my sincere prayers for all that you do. What did I do to deserve that God above would give me a wonderful Mother like you. Love you always and forever,

—Maureen, first child and first daughter

There is nothing like the feeling of a mother's love. She gives warmth in her smile, her hugs, her cooking, her cleaning, her advice and her love. Even when God takes her to the land up above, you will always feel your mother's love. My last words to my mother were: "I love you, thank you for all you have taught me. I will learn from all you did. Until we meet again!" Love,

—Kathy, second child and second daughter

Dear Dad and our beloved Mother gone before us, Thank you so much for all of your sacrifices for our family and other families, your faithfulness to the Catholic Church as well as each other. You and Mom have been a great example for many people as well as to your twelve children. You and Mom have fulfilled your commitment to the fullest. And because of that I truly believe that the Good Lord has blessed us all abundantly. God bless you always,

—Peggy, fourth child and fourth daughter

SERVANT OF GOD

Dearest Nana,

Hail Mary, full of grace, the Lord is with you! The angel said those exact words to Mary. Nana was so much like Mother Mary, because she was so kind, soft, caring, gentle, loving, and understanding! She was a great Nana! All of Nana's creative ideas and activities will be passed on for many more years to come!

All of Nana's high spirited and Christ-like characteristics will always live on in many other people's hearts and mine! You will never be forgotten and you will always live on in my heart! I look forward to meeting you again in heaven. You are now in a beautiful place and will stay happy for all eternity!

God sent you here to earth for a reason. And we all know what that reason is…to be the best model, mother, and reach out to everyone and even anyone in the world and touch their hearts! You've changed so many peoples' lives because you gave up everything you had, and made a devotion to Christ. And now, it's our turn to reach out and change many more lives for generations to come.

You were the perfect person sent to us and you've had the choices like anyone else does! Your choice was to give it all to God, and suffer for the sins of the world. It's almost as if you were a reflection of Christ Himself or a martyr by dying for the sake of Jesus, our Lord.

What can we say…we were very blessed to have such a special person like you as our Nana. Your generosity and your kindness proves to me (and I'm almost positive many more other people out there in this world) that you truly are (deep down in our hearts) a saint and my Guardian Angel to watch over me and help me to live a happy, holy life, just as you did.

I love you very much…and your spirit will live within mine forever and ever until the end of time! I love you!

Love, Your Granddaughter,
—Elizabeth Marie Clark (10 yrs. old), granddaughter

OUR LOSS, HEAVEN'S GAIN

My Dear Jerry,

The transition from this life to the next by Gwen last Saturday is an event of immense magnitude for you, for your children, for the entire Apostolate for Family Consecration, and for friends like me.

I have known Gwen for almost twenty years as your dedicated consort, who is a good mother to her children, and who is on fire for the spread of the kingdom of Christ through the Apostolate for Family Consecration.

On the one hand, I offer you my heartfelt condolences on your irreparable loss.

On the other hand, I congratulate you for having had a wife who was so convinced of our Catholic Faith, who loved it and who lived it.

In spirit I shall be with you at Holy Mass at her burial next Saturday. I look forward to mid-July when I shall be able to pray over her grave and celebrate Mass for her at Catholic Familyland.

Wishing you and all your children our Blessed Mother's comforting presence, I remain,

Sincerely Yours in Christ,

—Francis Cardinal Arinze,
Prefect, Congregation for Divine Worship
and the Discipline of the Sacraments

…I join in praying for Gwen so that the luminous example of her life, lived with total dedication to God and neighbor, may give light to many families in their journey towards God. I am sure that Gwen from heaven will intercede for many graces for her dear ones and for the Work she founded.

—Chiara Lubich (Foundress of Focolare)

SERVANT OF GOD

It is understandable that after 48 good years together, her departure to the Eternal Father has created a vacuum in your heart; however, be consoled that your "Sweet Pie" still lives and intercedes for you day and night from her place of rest. Her charism of unconditional selfless love and service to the Apostolate for Family Consecration, will forever be remembered and cherished and serve as a model for others to imitate her spirit of dedication and service to this noble apostolate.

—Archbishop Robert Sarah, Congregation for Evangelization

…rest assured, Jerome, that from heaven Gwen will be helping you more than ever with all your needs. Pray to her for my intentions, for the apostolates of the Prelature throughout the world.

—Javier Echevarria, Prelate of Opus Dei

…It will be our joy to pray with you and others that Gwen's holiness will be officially recognized by the Church–raising her to the honors of the altar in order that all families may be encouraged by her example and helped by her prayerful intercession–especially as the family has been and still is, under such strong attack in various ways…

—Sr. Helen Therese, Monastery of the Holy Cross

OUR LOSS, HEAVEN'S GAIN

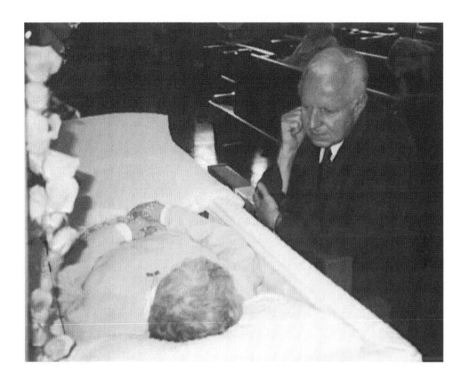

Jerry praying by Gwen's coffin. June, 2002

Chapter 20

Final Thoughts

IN A DAY WHEN ONE WHOSE DOGMA is that there is no dogma, and 50+ percent of marriages are ending, Gwen and Jerry's marriage stood little chance of surviving. For one thing, they married very young; 19 and 20 years of age respectively. They had twelve living children, which would be enough stress on any marriage and could cause lots of troubles. They also incurred countless financial difficulties. Still, their marriage not only survived but thrived. This is truly amazing, but their secret is their total reliance on God and His will to see them through the tough times. They received many graces through prayer and the sacraments, as well as through the great work that they did for the Church.

In St. Paul's letter to the Ephesians, St. Paul exhorts married couples to a strong mutual love, referring even to Genesis 2:24 that marriage is a divine institution. *"Wives should be subordinate to their husbands as to the Lord. For the husband is head of his wife just as Christ is head of the church, He Himself the savior of the body. As the church is subordinate to Christ, so wives should be subordinate to their husbands in everything. So also, husbands should love their wives as their own bodies. He who loves his wife loves himself. For no one hates his own flesh but rather nourishes and cherishes it, even as Christ does the church, because we are members of His body"* (Eph. 5:22-24; 28-30). So according to St. Paul, Christian marriage takes on a new meaning which reflects the intimate love of Christ to His Bride, the Church. It is this Christ-like loyalty and devotion in Christian marriage that reflects clearly the union of Christ and the Church.

This is better understood as a reciprocal relationship between husband and wife, the submission being the experiencing of love, rather than our modern negative concept of submission. In fact, the two spouses are subject to each other "out of reverence for Christ." They model their reciprocal relationship on the relationship of Christ to the Church. It is not one spouse dominating the other. Just as Christ, the Bridegroom, gave Himself up entirely for His Bride, the Church, out of love for her, to sanctify her, and continually builds her up; so too, the husband gives himself totally to his wife out of love for her, protecting her, building her up, and leading her toward sanctity. The wife, in turn, nurtures her husband, guides him toward sanctity, and allows him to lead and protect her out of love for him, since he is the head. It is this spousal form of the analogy of head-body which becomes an analogy of groom-bride, or rather of husband-wife, which clearly illustrates the nature of the union between Christ and the Church. As a head and a body make up one union, so too, the husband, as head, unites with the body, his wife, and the two become "one flesh." This can find its basis in the text of Genesis which speaks of one flesh (Gn 2:24),

Gwen lived her marriage in this way, the way that St. Paul describes, to a remarkable degree, allowing Jerry to lead. This is clearly evident when she subordinated her will to her husband's, during her toughest trial of having to leave roughly half of her children behind to follow Jerry to Ohio; something which caused her great suffering. They loved each other mutually and tremendously. They never doubted their love for each other. They fully always trusted that each one loved the other. Their hearts were united as one. Gwen was the heart of the home and Jerry was the head of the home. She was a shining example of faith and trust.

Gwen also greatly loved her children, but as she said, "I love you very much [to her children] but I love my husband more." In a sense, Gwen was also saying that she loved God more for she was following the exhortation by St. Paul for wives to obey their husbands, which in turn, points to God's will for marriage, since the Scriptures are divinely inspired text. Gwen loved God with her whole heart, her whole mind, and her whole strength. Today, in the culture that we live in, many wives would have left their husbands, especially when it came to moving to Ohio. But Gwen had great confidence in Jerry.

Gwen had a Marian soul. She was spiritual, peaceful, loving, humble, and regularly passed on spiritual truths she felt she should impart to other people. She didn't complain and thanked God often, a reflection and example of love, and God Himself. She took care of things behind the scenes and out of the spotlight. She was also someone very normal and natural, and not someone who boasted of having founded an apostolate. She was fun to be around and could make the saddest situation happy! She didn't show others the suffering inside her, and was still able to function cheerfully. She was sanctified by her daily duty. Gwen never neglected her primary duty of wife and mother. She became holy by doing her daily duty, just like St. Thérèse of Lisieux.

Gwen's life and the way she lived it can teach us many essential things on how to be a good wife and mother, and how to attain holiness in the ordinary circumstances of our lives. If we could only abandon ourselves to God as she did, we would all become the persons we are actually called to be.

GWEN INTERCEDES

The following is a story about Gwen's intercession in helping a woman with her marriage. Mary Ann Presberg, Jerry's sister, was giving a talk in Ohio at the Family Apostolate, and afterward, a woman came up to her crying, "I can't go home," she cried.

"Why," responded Mary Ann?

"This has been such a beautiful experience, and I don't want to go home because I hate my husband, and he's dying of cancer," she responded. "He's so mean to all of us. My children are beginning to hate him," she continued.

Mary Ann responded, "Go and pray by Gwen's crypt." So the woman did as Mary Ann suggested. When she came back two hours later, she was absolutely radiant!

FINAL THOUGHTS

She was transformed and said, "I love him [my husband]! I will never leave him! I'm going home to take care of him. He's a wonderful man." Mary Ann, who was incredulous, asked, "Really? This is what you came away with in prayer?"

The woman answered, "I can't even explain to you what happened at that crypt. All my animosity and hatred for my husband left me, and now I see what a wonderful soul he is! I can't explain exactly, but when I started to pray to her, she helped me to stop and to ponder how selfish I was, and helped me to learn how to take that away." The woman left very happy and Mary Ann was edified.

It is interesting to note that the Apostolate for Family Consecration was founded on the Feast of the Sacred Heart, which is a movable feast. The Apostolate celebrates this Feast in a special way because in addition to the Sacred Heart of Jesus and its importance, it is also a time for celebration by the Apostolate on their founding. So in 2007, the movable Feast of the Sacred Heart of Jesus fell on June 15th, the day Gwen died. That year was also the 5th anniversary of her passing and the year that her Cause for Beatification and Canonization was opened. It was also on that date in 2007 that the Apostolate for Family Consecration received Pontifical Status from the Pontifical Council of the Laity from Rome. It is no coincidence that she died on June 15th because the last time the Solemnity of the Sacred Heart fell on June 15th was in 1917, the same year that Our Lady appeared to the three shepherd children at Fatima, Portugal!

How truly Providential that it was this holy location of Fatima, Portugal that Jerry and Gwen Coniker took their family to live, in order to protect their family, and to learn God's will for their family, and to finally discover the true message of Fatima from Our Blessed Mother: It was not only for their family, but for the Family Apostolate and the Family of Holy Mother Church to help **'Save the Family' throughout the world.**

MORE HAPPENINGS WITH THE APOSTOLATE POST GWEN'S PASSING

On August 6, 2004, Jerry Coniker was appointed by then Pope John Paul II as Consultor to the Pontifical Council for the Family for a period of an additional five years.

SERVANT OF GOD

SECRETARIA STATUS

The Supreme Pontiff

POPE JOHN PAUL II

has appointed

Mr. JERRY CONIKER

to be Consultor of the Pontifical Council for the Family for a period of five years.

By these Letters the said Mr. Coniker is informed of his appointment so that he may act accordingly.

From the Vatican, on the 6th day of August, in the year 2004.

+Angelo Card. Sodano

Jerry Coniker was appointed by then Pope John Paul II
as Consultor to the Pontifical Council for the Family
for an additional five years, 2004

On September 3, 1999, the "Daily Catholic" conducted a survey of 23,455 prominent Catholics, who nominated 728 candidates for the "Top 100 Catholics of the 20th Century." Voters chose as the 70th selection the team of Jerome and Gwen Coniker.

On Sunday October 7th, 2000, Bishop Gilbert Sheldon, representing Pope John Paul II, awarded Jerry and Gwen Coniker the Pamela Dunlap Benemerenti Medal for their work and Fidelity to the Papacy.

On December 15, 2000, Jerry and Gwen were received into the Pontifical Portuguese Order of the Knights of St. Michael of the Wing. Thus, Gwen was named "Lady Guenevere."

FINAL THOUGHTS

By the end of November, 2004, Jerry presents the draft version of his book, *Preparation for Total Consecration to Jesus through Mary for Families,* to the Pope himself personally.

After the fifth anniversary of Gwen's death, June 15, 2002, the Most Rev. R. Daniel Conlon, Bishop of Steubenville, opened the Cause for the Beatification and Canonization of Gwen Cecilia Coniker. She became Servant of God on September 9, 2007.

On March 29th, 2008, Jerry and Gwen (posthumously) Coniker were given the annual Pro Fidelitate et Virtute award by the Institute on Religious Life, for their faithful teachings to enrich the spiritual life of families.

Today, all the Coniker children are grown with families of their own. Jerry and Gwen have seventy-five grandchildren! Moreover, all the Coniker children are in the faith and are practicing Catholics!

All For the Sacred Heart of Jesus, all through the Sorrowful and Immaculate Heart of Mary, all in union with St. Joseph.

Appendix A

Prayer for the Servant of God, Gwen Cecilia Coniker, & Family Unity

All For the Sacred and Eucharistic Heart of Jesus, all through the sorrowful and Immaculate Heart of Mary, all in union with St. Joseph.

HEAVENLY FATHER, Gwen Coniker was a model for family fidelity. She taught parents and grandparents how to sacrifice everything to fulfill God's will and become persons and families for others. Thank you for her work in the spirit of Pope John Paul II for the renewal of the Church and society through family consecration.

Gwen was a person for others who joyfully lived Your will by fulfilling the responsibilities of each present moment. She faithfully and lovingly carried out the duties and commitments of her state in life. She showed us how to be always grateful in the deepest of trials, and how to discern and do God's will moment by moment. Gwen also showed us how to gracefully die a prolonged and painful death without complaint or self-pity.

Heavenly Father, we ask you to glorify Gwen. May the Church raise her to the honor of the altars for the encouragement of *"family and parish consecration in the truth"* to the Holy Family, and for the protection of our families from the evil one (cf. John 17:15-17).

We make our prayer and petition for the work of the Apostolate for Fam-

APPENDIX A

ily Consecration and our special requests (mention your intention) through Christ our Lord. Amen.

Our Father. Hail Mary. Glory Be.

Nihil Obstat:	Rev. James M. Dunfee
	Censor Librorum
Imprimatur:	+ Most Rev. R. Daniel Conlon
	Bishop of Steubenville
	October 21, 2002

Condolences by Coniker Children, Roman Curia, Clergy, Religious, Others

A Daughter's Personal Meditation on Her Mother's (Gwen) Passing

As I pondered my mother's passing, I felt God gave me this understanding.

In my mind, I saw her take her final breath, and her soul leave her body. I saw her surrounded by a silent darkness. In the distance, I saw a bright light moving towards her. As the light approached her, I could see it was her Guardian Angel. He took her by the hand and led her into the light. I imagined what it must've been like for her to cross the threshold into Heaven; there before her in all their splendor and glory, the Angels and Saints rejoicing!

Mother Mary and St. Joseph were there to greet her and led her to Jesus. Her daughter, Angelica, who died prematurely when Gwen fell down the stairs, embraced her and introduced her to the grandchildren she had never met. All in Heaven were singing songs of joy!

Amidst all this rejoicing, I saw her turn around to look back at the place she had just come from. She saw her husband and children surrounding her bed, weeping and calling out to her. She saw their tears and heard their cries. And for a moment it seemed the heavens were silent, as she watched over her loving family, grieving and mourning their loss.

—Mary, twelfth child and seventh daughter

When I think of my mother, my heart is filled with loving thoughts, this is what I believe describes my mother.

- *Simple and deep love for God and others*
- *Hardworking*
- *Full of Love*
- *Loved Life*
- *Enjoyed Life*
- *Gave Life*
- *Loved music*
- *Loved her husband*
- *Loved her children*
- *Never judged anyone*
- *Always forgave and forgot*
- *Generous Heart*
- *Pure Soul*
- *Love music, laughter, and joy!*
- *Mom was simple but true, and the most beautiful person I ever knew.*

Love,
—Lauri, third child and third daughter

SERVANT OF GOD

Precious Mother,

Thank you for teaching me the meaning of love. I always loved being in your presence all my years growing up and still to your last day. My heart aches to be with you.

You always came in to take care of my family for each new baby and how you couldn't wait to hold the new baby grandchild. How the kids loved when Nana came to sleepover and for my fifth child we came to you, how I thought I wouldn't see you again. I will never forget our last days together. You held on 'til I could see you and hold you in my arms one last time. I still hoped and prayed for your healing, you held on to see your newborn grandchild Kara Marie.

You were so concerned about leaving all of us, what we would feel. Mom your love is never-ending, oh how we miss you. Dad, thank you for being there for all of us and for your kind loving words.

Mom, you have such great love for each one of your children, people say how can every child feel loved, oh if they only knew you, Mom. Your great love and example has touched so many families. Your love will live on forever, I will pass every ounce of love and joy you showed, on to my family.

Thank you Mom and Dad for my faith and your loving faithfulness you had for each other. Dad, your love and care you gave Mom was a sign of true love and such a great witness to us all, we love you Dad.

Mom, I will never forget your loving smile, you even made us smile at your bedside, and how we miss you beyond words can say. I keep saying I love you and I miss you and hope to be with you again. You had your wish to have Dad and all your children around you again like before the move to Ohio, all of us together on your last days forming a big hug around you.

Thank you Mom for a wonderful life and for all the love you have given to us all.

APPENDIX B

I will always love you.

Your daughter,

—Sheri, fifth child and fifth daughter

Dear Mom,

I know you can hear me and that your loving spirit will always be with us. As I am starting to write you this message, it is about 5:15 p.m. on June 15, 2002, so it is only about twelve hours since your soul left your body. I remember Dad telling us kids many years ago that we have no idea what it is like to lose a close loved one. I think I am starting to understand what he meant. As Jesus wept at the tomb of Lazarus, I find myself weeping at the thought of the physical loss of you in my life. You are so loving, caring, and special. It is truly in the total giving of yourself that you have received so much.

Mom, I am so heartbroken to see you go. You are so wonderful. You have touched so many lives for the better. Thank you so much for your joyful, fun-loving spirit, selfless sacrificing, and countless acts of charity. Thank you for being a great listener, advisor and at appropriate times, a director.

Thank you for teaching me that life on earth is a gift from God and our pathway to eternity. God gives each of us life and calls us home at a unique time. I wish you could physically be with us longer, but we are at peace submitting to God's will.

Mom, we know you had struggles in life, but you showed us how to press on in hard times, seeking and accepting God's will, while remaining true to your values and commitments. I know your marriage was tested to its core, when Dad decided to move the AFC and the younger half of our family to Ohio, in 1990, leaving behind your closest friends—your five married daughters and their families. During the tough times your true qualities showed through, and we repeatedly witnessed your desire to be a good faithful servant of Our Lord.

As we all are imperfect people, living in an imperfect world, thank you for showing me how to turn to Our Lord to receive His Unconditional Love and Forgiveness. Thank you for showing me how God asks us to share the same Unconditional Love and Forgiveness with all people.

I know you have done your best with the gifts God has given you. Through your weaknesses, God has made you strong, and through your sacrifices, He has made you eternally happy.

You shared the truths of our Faith by living them and by enjoying the present moment, while preparing for eternity. You made many moments special like festive Holiday celebrations. You made us feel special on our Birthdays by letting us pick our favorite meal and providing a couple nice gifts. I remember your classic St. Patrick's Day parties, with green clothes, food and drinks. You always made Christmas mornings a wonderful experience with special presents, for each of your twelve children, around the tree. You created a wonderful atmosphere with cheerful decorations and joyful Christmas music.

The last couple of months with you have been very special to me. Thank you for sharing your thoughts and love, all the way through your last words. You will always have a special place in my heart.

Love, your son,

—Michael, sixth child and first son

Dear Mom,

God granted you and us the gift of final preparation for you to meet Him in His Glory. We know your love will always be with us and that you will intercede in your own unique special ways. You showed us how to celebrate the gift of life, in the present moment, while balancing the sacrifices that prepare us for our final hour and doorway to eternity.

You answered the question I asked you (if dying would be difficult for you) in your own profound way, by showing me, rather than telling me. Even though someone gives his or her life completely to our Lord, dying is difficult because we were made to love.

By your example, you showed us how to live, how to value life, how to trust in God and how to leave this world in His Peace. We know that due to the effects of Original Sin, we must all experience death. We also know that at the end of the world, our bodies will be reunited with our souls. Please continue to pray and intercede so that we can all join you in our Heavenly Father's celebration. Thank you for the gift of your life to us.

Mom, you lived and ended your life on earth focusing on others, giving to the very end and graciously receiving the love offered to you. Love is Patient; Love is Kind, Love Never Ends. Your love will always be with us and you will always have a special place in our hearts.

Love,

—Michael and your children, sixth child and first son

Dear Mom,

Happy Mother's Day! This is truly the most special Mother's Day ever. I need to express to you how much I love you and how much you mean to me. It is hard for me to come to grips with the fact that God may call you home soon. I have never experienced losing a loved one and I am afraid that I don't know how to act or feel.

I do have a tremendous feeling of love for you and of gratitude for my life and for everything that you have done for me. My life and everything that I am has been a blessing from you. You are a model of God's infinite love, because the love that you have so abundantly given to me; you have also given to your twelve other children. Your love has never been partitioned but given in whole to each of us.

You also lend proof to the saying that "a mother is only as happy as her un-happiest child." You have always brought unity, peace and love into every situation. Your unconditional love and mercy for every child leaves an impression on our hearts and an example for us to follow.

Although, I feel sad at the thought of losing you, I take comfort in our faith, which you have also blessed me with. By faith we believe in what we cannot know with our senses. We believe that you will be with God in paradise. Go in peace knowing that it is God calling you home to be with Him. I pray that we can all make the journey to our Lord as beautifully as you. I know that I will grow in grace and strength with you watching over me.

With Love Forever!

—Robert, seventh child and second son

My mother knew how to make everyone feel special. No matter what the situation, she made you feel like you were the most important person in the world! When there was a birthday, sacrament, or holiday, Mom found a way to make it extra, extra, special. She made each year better than the one before.

Mom always told me, "Love is patient, and Love is kind, Love bears all things, believes all things, hopes all things, and endures all things." My mother truly lived this to the fullest. She also told me that if I lived this to the fullest, it would be followed by an equally important practice… SMILE…always remember to smile.

I am very blessed to have such a wonderful mother whom I will always cherish in my heart.

Love you always,

—Maria, tenth child and sixth daughter

APPENDIX B

Where do I begin? How can I put into so few words the feelings that engulf every inch of my heart? This woman, this precious child of God, this amazing servant of Christ, this humble beautiful mother of mine! My heart, my life, my inspiration, my rose! The truest example of Christ's love and mercy that I have ever known! How is it that I was blessed to have this beautiful mother touch my life in so many ways, too many to count. My heart aches for her every moment of everyday, the sun doesn't shine as bright without the rays of her smile; music will never sound as beautiful without the beautiful sounds of her laughter.

I have meditated long and hard on what to write. I have so much to write about, if I had to choose one thing to write about in this book for my dear father, it would be this memory that will penetrate my heart for as long as I live.

June 15, 2002, 5:30 a.m. I walked into the room where my precious mother had been lying for thirty days. As I entered the room and saw her lying in her bed, it all looked the same as it had for the past thirty days. It looked the same but there was a feeling of deep sorrow that filled the room, this room that once emulated one feeling and that was love. I ran to her bedside to hold her, not believing the news that she had died. As I approached her bedside, I looked into her wide-open eyes and I saw that she was gone. My mother was gone, her body was there but her soul was gone.

I looked into her eyes that once were filled with so much grace, life, and love, and I saw there was nothing there anymore; she was gone. I held her hand and kissed her cheek and pressed her hand to my face as I wept on her chest, knowing that was the last time I will ever hold and kiss my mother. Everything was in slow motion. There are no words to describe the feelings in that room on that morning.

We had our last Mass with our mother in that room where we had been blessed with so many Masses with her. Then we prayed the Rosary around her bedside just as we had done so many times before. Then we all took our final moments with our mother.

The men from the funeral home arrived to take our mother. We all stood around her and formed the circle of life, embracing one another crying out, "Goodbye, Mama. Goodbye, Mama. Mama, Mama." We turned on the song, "FLY"—we listened to the precious words of that song as the men lifted our mother from her bed and placed her on the gurney. They began to wrap her in a white sheet; we cried out as they were covering her precious face. They started to wheel her out of the room. We all followed holding each other and weeping. My father was weeping so sorrowfully. I went to him and we held each other. He began chanting over and over, "Thank you, God, for mother. Thank you, God, for mother. Thank you, God, for mother." We watched as they put her in the hearse and drove away. "Fly, fly little wing, Fly where only angels sing, Fly away, the time is right Go now, find the light."

Goodbye my mother, goodbye, thank you for blessing my life with your amazing Faith, Hope, Charity, & LOVE, always LOVE.

My heart will be forever filled with my love for you and the memory of your love for me!

With all that I am, your baby Daughter,
—Mary Beth, thirteenth child and ninth daughter

A Note from a Granddaughter to a Grandmother Gone Before Us

September 27, 2003 (Gwen's birthday)

Dearest Nana,

Today is one of the most special days of the year because it is your birthday, the day that you were born, September 27, 1939.

I thank you and Papa for bringing my mom into this world and I also thank you for bringing the whole Coniker family into the world. Family is the most precious thing that anybody could ever have. It is also something that you can cherish and treasure for the rest of time.

I also thank you for having a big family and keeping this family close together, because without family you'll have nothing, because family is the only thing that can help during good times and in bad.

Families are the people that support and love you. You cannot run or hide from your family. You have to learn to face things in life and to know that you can't turn your back from it. I was told this by my mother, one that I love so much. Thank you for instilling this in your family, which will be passed on, as it has been to me, my family and all families.

So I am thanking you, Nana, for bringing this family into the world. I love you so very much. Happy Birthday. I miss you.

Love—Your Granddaughter,
—Christina Marie Skurski (16 years old), granddaughter

STATE OF OHIO
HOUSE OF REPRESENTATIVES

IN MEMORY OF GWEN C. CONIKER

1940 - 2002

On behalf of the members of the House of Representatives of the 124th General Assembly of Ohio, I offer heartfelt condolences to the family and friends of Gwen C. Coniker at the death of this outstanding human being.

Her personal sacrifices of time and energy to family, friends, and community will certainly live on in the memories of all those who knew and loved her.

Her life and love gave joy to everyone who knew her. The warmth and understanding which she extended to others will stand as a tribute to a truly fine person.

Gwen C. Coniker was born on 1940. In her numerous roles as daughter, wife, mother and grandmother; co-founder of Apostolate for Family Consecration Catholic Familyland and Familyland Television Network, she led an exemplary life manifesting those virtues which we all seek to emulate.

Thus, I offer this token of profound sympathy to her family and friends.

K. EILEEN KRUPINSKI
State Representative
98th House District

C512

APPENDIX B

Heartfelt condolences to you and your entire family for the loss of your beloved wife, mother, and grandmother, Gwen. Assurance of my prayers and those of the Pontifical Council for the Family for the eternal repose of her soul

—Alfonso Cardinal Lopez Trujillo President,
Pontifical Council for the Family

Dear Jerry,

Please accept my sincere sympathy and the promise of my prayers on the death of your dear wife, Gwen. I promise to offer Mass for the repose of her soul and for the spiritual comfort of your entire family.

Gwen was a wonderful woman, wife, and mother, and your lives brought faith, consolation, and inspiration to many.

You have the consolation that Gwen is interceding for you and your wonderful family before the Lord.

May God give you all the strength to bear the burden of grief you now feel.

Sincerely in Christ,

—Archbishop John P. Foley President,
Pontifical Council for Social Communications

Dear Jerry,

I wish to extend to you and to the other members of your family, my deepest sympathies on the death of your beloved wife. I join you, your children and grandchildren, and all the members of your family in thanking God for the gift of Gwen's life and in praying for her eternal happiness in the Kingdom of Heaven.

I know that Gwen shared in the Lord's suffering especially in her final days here on earth. My you find consolation and strength in the Lord's promise that we who share in His suffering will share fully in His glory and that we who die with Him will live with Him forever.

As a faithful wife, devoted mother and grandmother, and loving family member and friend, Gwen was an instrument of God's love and goodness. She reflected a deep love of Our Lord and His Church. May the spirit and example of her life continue to live on in the lives of all those she loved.

With sentiments of sympathy, I remain,

> *Sincerely yours in Christ,*
> —Anthony Cardinal Bevilacqua Archbishop of Philadelphia

Dear Jerry,

I want to extend to you and to your family my deepest sympathy in the death of Gwen. I'd like to share with you and your family my favorite thought of death. I like to think of death as a rose God gives to a family, but one he doesn't divide evenly. Gwen receives just the bloom, thornless, fragrant and beautiful. You who are left behind receive just the thorn of loss that hurts like the dickens.

But remember, God could not give Gwen her rose, without asking you to hold the thorn. He could not take her to Himself without taking her from us. May the thought of her rose be your consolation as you lovingly and courageously hold your thorn for Gwen.

Be assured of my prayers for her and for all of you.

> *Sincerely Yours in the Sacred Heart*
> —Most Reverend Roger L. Kaffer Auxiliary Bishop of Joliet

Dear Jerry and Family,
I was deeply saddened to learn of the death of your dear wife and mother, Gwen. Gwen was a beautiful example of commitment to the Lord and of

surrendering to His will. While she continued to fight the good fight, she was ready to receive her everlasting reward in the presence of the Lord.

While Gwen will be missed greatly, we now have her to help us continue our earthly fights. I will remember her and your family in my prayers.

I am sincerely yours in the Lord,
—Most Reverend Elden Francis Curtiss Archbishop of Omaha

Dear Jerry,

I was so sorry to hear about the death of your wife, Gwen. Her many years of service and dedication to you, your family, and the Church have been an inspiration for all of us. Please be assured of my prayers for you and your family during this time.

Sincerely yours in Christ
—Most Reverend Samuel J. Aquila Bishop of Fargo

Dear Jerry and Family,

I am sorry about Gwen's death, but I am not sorry that her life has ended up as a triumph of grace. What Gwen did for her family and for all families all over the world will not be forgotten, either in heaven, where the new is most important, or here on earth. God bless Gwen Coniker.

With profound condolences and in solidarity with her and your Family Apostolate, I remain,

Yours sincerely in Christ,
—Monsignor John F. McCarthy

… Thinking of her, we can only thank God for her life, for what she has been for your wonderful family and for the Church…

—Augustin Cardinal Mayer

SERVANT OF GOD

As I read through all the lovely things concerning Gwen, the tears started coming to my eyes, which is really saying to me that my heart was being touched in a most beautiful and peaceful way. Thank you for sharing all of this love which knows no ending...

—Fr. Michael Maher, S.M.

...While Gwen may physically no longer be at your side, I have no doubt that you often feel her presence and her help in going forward with your life and mission. Together you accomplished a great deal in founding and realizing the growth and success of the Apostolate for Family Consecration...

—Archbishop Renato Martino

Note from a woman that watched a video on Gwen

...Many emotions struck me as I watched the tape. One thing that carried throughout was Gwen's incredibly contagious smile. How interesting it was to see from early pictures of her young life to late pictures as she was about to be born into eternal life, how gorgeous and stable was that smile...another miracle that was so obvious was the passing on of that incredible smile.

Appendix C

Timeline of Jerry and Gwen Coniker's Lives

Jerry Coniker:

- **1938 November 2** – Birth of Jerome Francis Coniker at Ravenswood Hospital in Chicago, IL, the youngest of three children of John Coniker and Margaret Cecilia Coniker (née Cummings).
- **1950 July 23** – Death of Jerry Coniker's father.
- **1958 June** – Stroke of Jerry Coniker's mother.
- **1958 About August 19** – Death of Jerry Coniker's mother, Margaret. She suffered a severe stroke and went into a coma. One evening while Jerry was spending the evening watching over her, she came out of her coma, sat up in bed and said to Jerry, "Gwen is a good girl. She will be good for you. You marry her." Soon after, she died. Gwen had visited Jerry's mother while she was in the hospital.
- **1959 February 14** – Jerry, age twenty proposes to Gwen, age nineteen.
- **1959 August 15** – Marriage of Jerry Coniker to Gwen Billings.
- **1961 May 13** – Jerry founded Coniker Enterprises (23 years old), an organized, retainable communication system to bring order from chaos. He created a Control Master time-management system, service manuals, policy manuals and the like. Later, his company's name would change to Coniker Systems, Inc.

SERVANT OF GOD

Gwen Coniker:

- **1939 September 27** – Birth of Guenevere (Gwen) Cecilia Billings at Edgewater Hospital in Chicago, IL, the youngest of three daughters of George Henry Billings, who was Irish, and Rose Katherine Billings (née Polito), who was Italian.

- **1953 November 28** – Death of Gwen's sister, Geraldine (24 years old). Gwen was 13 years old.

- **Jerry and Gwen Coniker:**

- **1955** – Gwen at 15 years old met Jerry in a high school class at St. Gregory's on the north side of Chicago. For Jerry, it was love at first sight. For Gwen, she at first found him a nuisance. However, she finally gave into his persistence to go on a date with him.

- **1955 September 27** – Gwen's sixteenth birthday. Jerry was either invited or invited himself to Gwen's Sweet Sixteen Birthday Party. They loved to go dancing at Chevy Chase on the near north side of Chicago and the Aragon Ballroom, a very elegant upscale ballroom in Chicago. They liked to take walks in the gardens by the ballroom.

- **1957 June 6 – Graduation from St. Gregory's High School** – Jerry and Gwen broke up for about seventeen months due to pressure from Sr. Anna Marie and the priest who was a counselor at the High School.

- **1958** – Gwen visits Jerry's mother while she was in the hospital.

- **1958 November 2** – Jerry calls Gwen for a date after their year+ break-up.

- **1959 February 14** – Jerry, age twenty proposes to Gwen, age nineteen.

- **1959 August 15** – Marriage of Jerry Coniker to Gwen Billings on the Feast of the Assumption at St. Matthias Church in Chicago, IL. They honeymooned at Lake Delevan and the Wisconsin Dells. They then lived in a two-bedroom apartment on top floor of the Billings' house.

- **1960 June 22** – Birth of their first child, a daughter, Maureen Therese.

- **1962 January 16** – Birth of their second child, a daughter, Kathy Lynne.

- **1963 March** – Conikers moved to a three-bedroom apartment in Niles, IL.

- **1963 July 8** – Birth of their third child, a daughter, Laurie Ann.

APPENDIX C

- Moved to Highland Park, Illinois to a rented three-bedroom ranch house.
- **1964 September 24** – Birth of their fourth child, a daughter, Margaret Rose.
- **1966 February 18** – Death of Gwen's father of a brain tumor.
- **1966 February 26** – Birth of their fifth child, a daughter, Sharon Marie.
- **1968 February 19** – Birth of their sixth child, a son, Michael John.
- Moved to a four bedroom house in Deerfield, Illinois which they purchased.
- **1970 August 3** – Birth of their seventh child, a son, Robert Anthony.
- Moved to a five-bedroom colonial-style house in Deerfield, Illinois which they purchased.
- **1971 February 4** – Gwen and her four oldest children were in a car accident with another car with one person in the car, a mother of three children. That woman died a few days later. Gwen and her children were not injured.
- **1971 February 20** – Jerry and Gwen start the 33-day prayer and preparation for the Total Act of Consecration via the St. Louis Grignion de Montfort charism.
- **1971 April 28** – Feast of St. Louis de Montfort, Jerry and Gwen make their Act of Total Consecration to Jesus through Mary.
- **1971 September 7** – After much prayer and discernment, the Conikers decided to move the family to Portugal with two other families who were their friends because to them, the United States was becoming more and more immoral with atheism gaining strength. They did not want to raise their children in such an atmosphere devoid of God. They sold their home. They found a wonderful, competent, and enthusiastic young man to take over the organization of over four hundred people fighting against improper sex education and abortion. Lastly, Jerry sold his company, Coniker Systems, to Flick-Reedy Corporation. For the **summer months of 1971**, they rented a summer cottage along Powers Lake in Wisconsin because their house was sold, while preparing their move to Portugal. Upon their leaving the United States on September, 7, 1971, Gwen was eight months pregnant with their eighth child. During their two-year hiatus in Portugal, Jerry and Gwen returned to the United States a few times; August 25, 1972 and December 18, 1972, and Jerry on April 24, 1973.

- **1971 September 7 – 1973 June 13** – The Conikers lived in Portugal in a three-story duplex house in São Pedro, Portugal (twenty miles east of Lisbon). Life there was like a two-year retreat. It was a time for slowing down, enjoying family, praying, and visiting Fatima monthly. While in Portugal, The Apostolate of Family Consecration was conceived, but born in America.
- **1971 October 28** – Birth of their eighth child, a son, Joseph Vincent.
- **1973 June 13** – The Conikers move back to the United States with Gwen eight-months pregnant with baby number nine. They settled in Kenosha, Wisconsin, overlooking Lake Michigan in a three-story red brick house at 6126 Third Ave. Jerry became executive director of the Knights of the Immaculata, founded by St. Maximilian Kolbe who promoted Consecration to Our Lady and died a martyr of love in a Nazi concentration camp.
- **1973 July 22** – Birth of ninth child, a son, James (Jimmy) Francis and Gwen's first C-Section. Gwen had a blood transfusion and contracted hepatitis C later.
- **1974 September 4** – Birth of their tenth child, a daughter, Maria Ann.
- **1975 March** – Jerry left Marytown and his position as executive director of the Knights of the Immaculata.
- **1975 June 18** – Founding of the Apostolate for Family Consecration which at first resided in the master bedroom of the Conker home on Third Avenue in Kenosha. Gwen helped type up the bylaws and constitutions.
- **1975 October 3** – Approval of bylaws and constitutions by Archbishop William Cousins of Milwaukee, Wisconsin.
- **1975** – Purchased the House of St. Joseph at 6305 Third Avenue, Kenosha, WI, the first center of the Family Apostolate. Gwen was the bookkeeper for a number of years for the Apostolate.
- First goal – Build Peace of Heart Forums which are weekly gatherings in family homes, parishes, and schools utilizing the media, videotapes, and books created by the apostolate on various truths of the faith. Parish Peace of Heart Forums would last for nine weeks, the length of a novena.
- **Kenosha's Five Buildings** on Third Ave: The St. Joseph House was first building purchased and was used as the main Apostolate Center. The Immaculate Heart

Center was next to St. Joseph House and was used for retreats, dining, and housing of retreatants. On the other side were the Coniker's home and the Kateri house, named after the St. Kateri Tekakwitha, who was a Mohawk woman who lived in the 17th century. This is where the Women's Catholic Corp stayed. The fifth house, located on the same street, was where the Men's Catholic Corp lived.

- **1975 Christmas morning** – Gwen's Goodbye and Christmas message to each of her family members from a loving mother in anticipation of not surviving the birth of her eleventh child according to doctors' predictions.

- **1975 December 27** – Birth of their eleventh child, a daughter, Therese Marie. Gwen refused to abort her when her own life was in danger.

- **1976 May 1** – Jerry and Gwen meet Mother Teresa for the first time at Felician Sisters' Motherhouse in Chicago, Illinois..

- **1976** – Coniker children first meet Mother Teresa in St. Louis, MO at one of her convents.

- **1976 April** – Miscarriage of their daughter, Angelica.

- **1976 August** – Jerry recruits his Sacri-State member to offer her sufferings for the mission. This person was Sr. John Vianney in Elm Grove, Wisconsin. Sr. John Vianney would later tape programs from her bedside with the assistance of the Apostolate members on a children's version of *The Apostolate's Family Catechism*.

- **1977** – Coldest day of the year, first meeting of the Advisory Council held at House of St. Joseph.

- **1977 June** – Jerry meets again with Mother Teresa in the Bronx of New York where she shared her Constitutions from her own order with Jerry.

- **1977 October 23** - Birth of their thirteenth child, a daughter, Mary Elizabeth.

- **1978 April 22** – Jerry and Gwen meet Mother Teresa again in St. Louis at a meeting organized by the Institution on Religious Life.

- **1978 October 5** – First formal meeting of the Advisory Council held at Divine Word Seminary in Techny, IL. Jerry laid out nineteen phases for the Apostolate of Family Consecration.

- **1980 June** – First Peace of Heart Forum video programs at Eternal Word

Television Network (EWTN) in Alabama, founded by Mother Angelica who allowed Jerry and Gwen use of her studio facilities for one week. Fifty programs were produced in that week! Topics included consecration according to St. Teresa, the rosary, one series each on St. Matthew's gospel and St. John's gospel, and two series on St. Paul's letters. While these tapings were being made, Gwen took some of the children to Brooksville, Florida to visit her mother, Rose Billings.

- **1980** – Jerry met Fr. Rodrigo Molina, S.J., a Jesuit priest from Spain and founder of *Lumen Dei*, an apostolate for consecrated laity and priests when Fr. Molina visited the St. Joseph Center. He told Jerry, "For the Family Apostolate to be successful, it was essential to have one spirituality which inner core members could focus on. The priests, imbued with the Apostolate's spirituality must guide its leaders in the spirit of the founder so that the unity of spirit remains intact." Jerry would do this on March 26, 1986. Later, Jerry and Fr. Molina would make a spiritual pact in Spain and the *Lumen Dei* Apostolate whereby they both spiritually united each other and their respective apostolates.

- **1980 Dec. 21** – Archbishop Weakland of the Milwaukee Archdiocese met with Gwen and Jerry. Prior to this meeting, they flew to New York city to visit Cardinal O'Connor of the New York Archdiocese.

- **1981 Summer** – First TV production in the Family Apostolate's own studio at their St. Joseph Center in Kenosha, Wisconsin. Mother Teresa was present at that production. Soon after both Jerry and Gwen became ill with the flu and a violent headache respectively; part of the cross in order to bear fruit.

- **1981 Nov. 27** – First marriage of Gwen and Jerry's children; Maureen Coniker married Mat Skurski. Many other Coniker children's marriages followed soon after!

- **1982 February** – The first of many overnight retreats begin at the St. Joseph Center in Kenosha, Wisconsin. They averaged about two per month. They also started to organize neighborhood Chapters or Lay Ecclesial Teams. These are where people would gather in homes using the Peace of Heart

Forums as their key resource to reflect, read together, and learn together and then to do apostolic work outside the Chapter. Lay Ecclesial Teams would use the media in churches, schools, homes to transform people and neighborhoods toward God-centered communities.

- **1982 August 30** – Birth of first Coniker grandchild, a daughter named Cheryl Skurski by Maureen and Mat Skurski. Many grandchildren soon followed!

- **1983 November** – Jerry and Gwen and son Robert's first Pilgrimage to Vatican City for the Extraordinary Holy Year of Redemption (1983-84) to meet with Cardinal Ciappi, the Pope's theologian, and other cardinals of the Roman Curia. Cardinal Ciappi introduces the Family Apostolate to Pope John Paul II and the Roman Curia. Cardinal Ciappi's endorsement played a key role in opening doors for Jerry and Gwen at the Vatican. While there, they met personally with Pope John Paul II for the first time for about ten minutes, and a second surprise meeting by Gwen that same day with the pope briefly at the General Audience where she was greeted personally again by him. Jerry was in a meeting at that time.

- **1984 March 25** – Feast of the Annunciation. Pope John Paul II re-consecrates the world to Mary.

- **1985 June** – Jerry, Gwen and Coniker boys go to New York to meet with Mother Teresa at her Missionary of Charity home in the Bronx, videotaping an interview of her and a "Right to Life" talk of hers. While in New York, they stayed with Dr. Charles Wahlig, O.D. an optometrist and a widower, which set off a series of interesting events related to Our Lady of Guadalupe. Dr. Wahlig was a prominent author and eye doctor known for discovering the images in the eyes of the image of Our Lady of Guadalupe. Moreover, he knew well the history of that Shrine, telling Jerry and Gwen that this Patroness of the United States should really be honored under the title of "The Immaculate Conception," and the image as "The Image of the Immaculate Conception," for this is how she declared herself to Juan Diego in 1531. Dr. Wahlig's story and research was videotaped as a Peace of Heart Forum series and later shown in hundreds of churches through the Apostolate's "Be Not

Afraid Family Hours" during the Marian Year of June 1987 – August 1988.

- **1986** – Catholic Corps created by Jerry and Gwen Coniker; both the women's and men's.

- **1986** – The Apostolate begins to annually record Cardinal Arinze teaching on Pope John Paul II and catechetics.

- **1986 March 26** – Jerry chose Pope John Paul II's Marian and family-orientated spirituality to be the single spirituality of the Family Apostolate; to consecrate as many as possible in the Truth.

- **1986 Summer** – The Apostolate created seventy-three programs on the philosophy of John Paul II with the help of Dr. Richard E. Dumont and another professor of philosophy at Xavier University in Cincinnati. Another forty video programs on Philosophy and Pope John Paul II's teachings especially pertaining to Mary's role in the economy of salvation, the laity, and family life were created and was greatly facilitated with the help of two key persons who knew John Paul II personally while they were all at Lublin University in Poland, a university which greatly formed the now St. Pope John Paul II. These two persons were Fr. Meiczyslaw Albert Krapiec, O.P. and Fr. Andrej Szostek.

- **1986 June** – Jerry and Gwen go to Rome again to interview and videotape various members of the Roman Curia.

- **1986 Early September** – Jerry decides to launch a national campaign and Novena for the re-consecration of the United States to the Immaculate Conception, tying it into the idea of the image of Our Lady of Guadalupe, upon hearing the news that Pope John Paul II will be visiting the United States. To reach as many people as possible this campaign encompassed using the apostolate's videotaped resources, their television ministry, mailings, newspaper ads and enlisting the Chapters to host Novenas throughout the Marian Year, the first of which began on June 17, 1987. One hundred and forty out of one hundred and eighty-six bishops signed the re-consecration forms which were bound together in a thick binder which Jerry and Gwen would later personally give to the Holy Father, Pope John Paul II in Rome on August 15, 1988.

- **1987** – Apostolate launched first Be Not Afraid Family Hour.

- **1987 January** – Gwen's mother, Rose Billings, moved in to live with the Conikers since she had terminal cancer.

- **1987 June 7 – 1988 August 15** – The Marian Year declared by Pope John Paul II.

- **1987 June 17** – First Novena held for the Marian Year.

- **1988** – Conikers move to 6130 Third Ave. Kenosha, Wisconsin. The home at 6126 Third Ave. was then used by the Apostolate for the Catholic Corp men's residence.

- **1988 June** – Jerry and Gwen meet again with Mother Teresa and interviewed her in the New York Bronx at her Missionary of Charity Motherhouse.

- **1988 July 2** – Death of Rose Billings, Gwen's mother. It was the First Saturday.

- **1988 August 15** – Jerry and Gwen again at the Vatican with their entire family, now eighteen members to present the binder which held the re-consecration forms signed by one hundred and forty bishops after the General Audience. To have the Pope re-consecrate the United States to the Immaculate Conception was one of the most important events in the history of the United States and the Family Apostolate.

- **1989** – First Holy Family Fest held at Franciscan University of Steubenville.

- **1989 November 5-17** – Jerry and Gwen in Rome with daughters Mary and Theresa in order to document the Marian spirituality of Pope John Paul II, the backbone of the Family Apostolate's Marian Era of Evangelization Campaign. While there, he again interviewed members of the Roman Curia. The apostolate created one hundred thirty video segments while there. They briefly met the pope again at the General Audience and he blessed them.

- **1989 November 18** – Jerry and Gwen receive a formal apostolic blessing through the Secretary of State's Office in the form of a letter.

- **1990** – The Apostolate for Family Consecration moved to Bloomingdale, Ohio, where it acquired the old Steubenville diocesan seminary complex, 850 acres. It is now known as the John Paul II Holy Family Center or Catholic Familyland. There, they conduct family fests, retreats, conferences, television products, Lay Ecclesial Team evangelization programs, and tri-media catechetical resources.

- **1990** – Gwen's farewell address to family in Wisconsin.
- **1993** – First Totus Tuus conference held in Pittsburgh, PA with Francis Cardinal Arinze.
- **1993** – Launched USA Family Catechism.
- **1994** – Cardinal Ratzinger endorses Apostolate's Family Catechism.
- **1994 May 10** - The Apostolate goes international by opening a St. Joseph Center in the Philippines.
- **1995** – Holy Family Fests sell out.
- **1996** – Catholic Familyland expands to hold more families and builds state of the art television/conference center.
- **1996** – First Totus Tuus conference at Catholic Familyland.
- **1998** – First Marriage Get Away at Catholic Familyland.
- **1999** – Familyland Television Network is launched.
- **1999 April 29** – Pope John Paul II appointed Jerry and Gwen to be members of his Pontifical Council for the Family.
- **1999 August** - The Apostolate opens a St. Joseph Center in Mexico.
- **2000** – Completed Family Catechism in Spanish.
- **2000** – Large 30-foot statue of Holy Family completed by artist, Rene Salvacion, which is displayed on Guimaras Island in the Philippines.
- **2000 October 14-15 Jubilee year of Families**. - The entire Coniker family goes to Rome again for the Jubilee year. Coniker family selected to represent the theme for the Jubilee of Families in Rome. The entire Coniker family goes up to greet the pope.
- **2001** – Lay Ecclesial Teams & AFC initiative opens in Europe.
- **2001** – Jerry interviews Sr. Lucia of Fatima who approved & blessed the Holy Family of Fatima portrait.
- **2001 October 7** – Jerry and Gwen received the Pro Ecclesia et Pontifice Award from Pope John Paul II in recognition for their service to the Church. The award was presented to them at the Cathedral in Steubenville by the Most Reverend Gilbert Sheldon, Bishop of Steubenville.

APPENDIX C

- **2001 November 2** – Gwen diagnosed with cirrhosis of the liver due to a blood transfusion from a C-Section and given a year to live. This also is Jerry's birthday.

- **2001 December 15** – Jerry and Gwen were received into the Pontifical Portuguese Order of the Knights of St. Michael of the Wing. Thus, Gwen was named "Lady Guenevere", Jerry was named Sir Jerry, and Michael (because he was the first son), was named Squire.

- **2002 April** – Jerry and Gwen vacation in North Carolina at the home of Tracy and Amy McManamon to discuss them taking over and being directors of the Apostolate and to finalize details.

- **2002 April 28** (Feast of St. Louis de Montfort) Gwen was admitted to the Cleveland Clinic.

- **2002 May 13** – Gwen returned home under hospice care.

- ✝**2002 June 15** – After being anointed, Guenevere (Gwen) Cecilia Coniker dies at her home in Bloomingdale, Ohio at the John Paul II Holy Family Center in the arms of her loving husband Jerry. There was a week-long wake then the Funeral Mass. Gwen is laid to rest in crypt at St. John Vianney Chapel on the grounds of the Apostolate for Family Consecration in Bloomingdale, Ohio.

- **2003** – Center takes root in Nigeria, Cardinal Arinze's home diocese.

- **2004 August 6** – Jerry re-appointed Consultor to the Pontifical Council for the Family again for another period of five years by Pope John Paul II.

- **2004 End of November** – Jerry presents draft version of his book, *Preparation for Total Consecration to Jesus through Mary for Families.*

- **2005** – Pope John Paul II passes on to eternity. Apostolate carries on with an ever more vigorous commitment to spreading his spirituality and legacy.

- **2005** – Cardinal Ratzinger, who in 1994 endorsed the Apostolate's Family Catechism, elected Pope Benedict XVI.

- **2006 November** – Translation of *The Apostolate's Family Catechism* into Chinese is completed.

- **2007 July 10** – Cause for Beatification of Gwen opened by Most Reverend

SERVANT OF GOD

R. Daniel Conlon, Bishop of Steubenville.

- **2007 September 9** – Gwen was made Servant of God by Most Reverend R. Daniel Conlon, Bishop of Steubenville after the fifth anniversary of her death of June 15, 2002.
- **2008 March 29** – Jerry and Gwen (posthumously) received the Pro Fidelitate et Virtute Award from the Institute on Religious Life.

Appendix D

Church Documents

IN ORDER TO BETTER understand the Church's teachings as it pertains to the dignity of human life and procreation, and warnings about the many ill effects of contraception, please refer to the following Church documents which can be found on the Vatican Website: http://w2.vatican.va/content/vatican/en.html

1. *Humanae Vitae* – Of Human Life, Encyclical letter of Pope Paul VI on the regulation of birth (July 25, 1968 – the Feast of St. James the Apostle)

2. *Donum Vitae* – The Gift of Life, On the Respect of Life Rising and Dignity of Procreation, Instruction by the Congregation for the Doctrine of Faith, (February 22, 1987, the Feast of the Chair of St. Peter the Apostle)

3. *Familiaris Consortio* – On the Role of the Christian Family in the Modern World, Apostolic Exhortation of Pope John Paul II (November 2, 1981, Solemnity of our Lord Jesus Christ, Universal King)

4. *Christifideles Laici* – On the Vocation and Mission of the Lay Faithful in the Church and the Modern World, Post-Synodal Apostolic

SERVANT OF GOD

Exhortation of Pope John Paul II (December 30, 1988, Feast of the Holy Family of Jesus, Mary and Joseph)

5. *Evangelium Vitae* – The Gospel of Life, Encyclical letter of Pope John Paul II (March 25, 1995, Solemnity of the Annunciation of the Lord

Bibliography

- Lappin, Fr. Peter. Challenge and Change, Volume One: The Foundation. Bloomingdale, OH: Apostolate for Family Consecration, 1999.
- Luncheon Video Tribute by the AFC at Jerry's Funeral. n.d. July 12, 2018.
- Pronenchen, Joseph. "National Catholic Register." National Catholic Registe. July 20, 2018. http://www.ncregister.com/daily-news/remembering-the-co-founder-of-the-apostolate-for-family-consecration (accessed 07 21, 2018).
- Wells, Lee. "The Miracle of Loreto." n.d. http://www.catholictradition.org/Mary/loreto1.htm (accessed August 24, 2017).

Acknowledgments

Mary Ann Hall (edits)

Michael Wick (guidance, advice)

Dcn. Randy and Mary Ellen Redington (key information on the lives of Gwen & Jerry and edits)

Those Coniker Children and relatives whom I interviewed who shared their experiences of their parents/relative

Jerry Coniker – advice, edits, guidance, information, assistance

Dcn. Tom Gaida – book cover

Made in the USA
Middletown, DE
14 September 2019